# MAVERICK GUIDE TO
# BERMUDA

**mav-er-ick (mav'er-ik),** *n.* 1. an unbranded steer. Hence [colloq.] 2. a person not labeled as belonging to any one faction, group, etc. who acts independently. 3. one who moves in a different direction than the rest of the herd—often a nonconformist. 4. a person using individual judgment, even when it runs against majority opinion.

### The Maverick Guide Series

The Maverick Guide to Australia
The Maverick Guide to Bali
The Maverick Guide to Barcelona
The Maverick Guide to Berlin
The Maverick Guide to Bermuda
The Maverick Guide to the Great Barrier Reef
The Maverick Guide to Hawaii
The Maverick Guide to Hong Kong, Macau, and South China
The Maverick Guide to Malaysia and Singapore
The Maverick Guide to Morocco
The Maverick Guide to New Zealand
The Maverick Guide to Oman
The Maverick Guide to Prague
The Maverick Guide to Scotland
The Maverick Guide to Thailand
The Maverick Guide to Vietnam, Laos, and Cambodia

# MAVERICK GUIDE TO
# BERMUDA

## 2nd Edition

### By Catherine Harriott

PELICAN PUBLISHING COMPANY
Gretna 2004

*To Den and Lilly in loving memory*
*and to my wonderful family, Tony, Kim, and Sam*

*The word "Pelican" and the depiction of a pelican are trademarks
of Pelican Publishing Company, Inc., and are registered
in the U.S. Patent and Trademark Office.*

ISBN: 1-58980-087-7

*If dialling from North America, place a (1-441) before the phone numbers. If
calling from the United Kingdom, (001) precedes the number.*

*Information in this guidebook is based on authoritative data available at the time
of printing. Prices and hours of operation of businesses listed are subject to change
without notice. Readers are asked to take this into account when consulting this
guide.*

Printed in Canada
Published by Pelican Publishing Company, Inc.
1000 Burmaster Street, Gretna, Louisiana, 70053

# Contents

# Introduction

When I'm away from Bermuda, I miss the colours. Every white-roofed cottage is painted, but never with greys or beiges. They are gumdrop coloured or pastel pink. The crystal-clear sea is azure blue and green—even on a cloudy day—and the sunsets are always amazing, throwing a warm, pink glow onto the beaches and houses.

When I'm away from Bermuda, I miss the fragrances. The Easter lilies in April, the frangipani tree in June, and the salty air in September—it seems with each season, Bermuda releases a perfumed gift.

And Bermuda *is* a gift to the world. There, in the middle of the Atlantic Ocean—yet less than a two-hour flight from New York—and surrounded by a coral-reef necklace, sits this subtropical paradise, neat and trim and bursting with 400 years of history, forts, caves, and shipwrecks.

## The Inside Scoop

I have given nine years of my life to Bermuda, and this Maverick Guide is the second edition. The first contained everything I had ever learned about this jewel of an island while living here, and this book reflects the changes that have taken place since then.

I've been east, west, central, to every village, to every parish. I've tried almost every restaurant, visited every hotel, and experienced numerous tours on your behalf. I know what it's like to go undersea helmet diving on the reef, to enjoy a leisurely afternoon tea, to walk the alleyways of St. George's and discover its rich, diverse history. I've been to every National Trust property, every nature trail, every beach, and all the festivals. I've travelled by bus, ferry, and scooter. Although as a visitor you can't rent a car, take this opportunity to let someone else do the driving for a change and hop on the pretty pink and blue buses, or ride the ferry from tiny harbour to miniature quayside. The ferries have names such as *Patience* and *Serenity* and are a lovely, stress-free way to view the island.

9

This guidebook includes all the budget information from my first book, *Bermuda on a Budget,* which was the first guidebook to Bermuda with a budget slant. You will be pleasantly surprised to find affordable places to stay, eat, and visit. In the index, I even have a list of free attractions for when you run out of cash—so you see, you can afford Bermuda. As in all the other Maverick series of guidebooks, it also includes the midpriced and luxury hotels as well as upscale restaurants.

I try not to miss Bermuda for too long, but shortly after you have left her shores, she will haunt you to return.

*Have a Bermudaful day.*

# 1

# How to Use This Book

## Quick Guide

**BARGAIN HUNTERS**—go to the "Budget-Priced Eateries" and "Budget-Priced Accommodations" sections in chapters 7 through 12. Also go to the "Private House and Apartment Rentals" section in chapter 2.

**HISTORY LOVERS**—go to chapter 5: "Culture and Heritage." Also go to the "Sightseeing" section of chapter 11: "The East End."

**SHOPPERS**—go to chapter 8: "The City of Hamilton." Also go to the "Shopping" sections of chapters 8 through 12.

**WATER-SPORTS LOVERS**—go to chapter 6: "The Sports Scene," in the "Introduction to Water Sports" section. Also go to the "Water Sports" sections in the area chapters 8 through 12.

**THOSE WITH CHILDREN**—go to chapter 2: "Before You Leave Home," in the "Bringing Children to Bermuda" section.

**ENGAGED COUPLES**—go to chapter 2: "Before You Leave Home," in the "Getting Married in Bermuda" section.

**BEACH LOVERS**—go to chapter 9: "The South Shore."

**BUSINESS PEOPLE**—go to chapter 7: "The Business Traveller."

**ART AND THEATRE LOVERS**—go to chapter 5: "Culture and Heritage," in the "The Art Scene" section, and chapter 8: "The City of Hamilton," in the "Theatres and Concerts" section.

## Book Outline

As outlined in the table of contents, chapters 2 to 5 of this book acquaint you with Bermuda including tips on getting married, bringing children along, airlines, transportation (buses, ferries, scooter rentals, and horse and buggy rides) as well as lots of history and background to the island.

A chapter devoted to sports is next, including an introduction to great water sports. Water-sports companies are covered in each of the different area chapters, 8 to 12.

As well as a great tourist destination, Bermuda is also a major international offshore (tax-friendly) jurisdiction, with thousands of business visitors each year. "The Business Traveller" chapter outlines the background to Bermudian business companies and practices, where the business-friendly accommodations are, and where to find all the services the business visitor will need.

Bermuda is divided into nine parishes, but the parish boundaries are confusing and sometimes even locals aren't sure what parish they are in; so for ease of use, I have separated the book into five different areas, which I think you will find a lot easier to follow.

These areas are detailed in chapters 8 to 12, subdivided into the following sections:

**1. Transport, 2. Accommodations, 3. Restaurants, 4. Sightseeing, 5. Guided Tours and Cruises, 6. Water Sports, 7. Shopping, 8. Nightlife, 9. Handy Phone Numbers.** The South Shore chapter has an extra section dedicated to beaches.

The first area covered is Hamilton, the capital city of Bermuda, which is great for shops and restaurants. The second is the South Shore, where all the top beaches are. Then comes the West End of the island, where you will find the Royal Naval Dockyard, a favourite visitors' attraction. Next is a chapter on the East End, where you'll discover the historical town of St. George's. The last chapter is devoted to the rest of Bermuda, mainly the middle parishes Paget, Pembroke, and Devonshire.

To help make this book easy to navigate, find at the back a fully comprehensive index with accommodations and eateries listed separately. There's also a list of things to do on Sundays, and another list of free attractions.

## Bermuda's Hotels

Bermuda has every type of accommodation, from large 400-room hotels to small guest apartments and guesthouses. In between, there is that Bermuda invention, the cottage colony. A cottage colony comprises a nest of small cottages alongside a main clubhouse that, among other things, houses a restaurant. These luxury accommodations often have their own private beach; if not, they have a pool, and some have both.

Bermuda's hotels often top the list of readers' favourites in *Travel and Leisure* magazine. The Fairmont Southampton Princess, The Reefs, and Ariel Sands Beach Club have all made the top-10 list.

---

**The Code to Bermuda's Hotel Meal Plans**
AP (American Plan)—room, breakfast, lunch, and dinner
MAP (Modified American Plan)—room, breakfast, and dinner
BP (Bermuda Plan)—room and full breakfast
CP (Continental Plan)—room and light breakfast
EP (European Plan)—room only

---

For your convenience, every accommodation listed in this book includes the name, address, and telephone, fax, and toll-free numbers, as well as any e-mail addresses and Web sites.

The double-occupancy rate for accommodation in Bermuda starts at about $90 per room per night, through to $700 per room per night. It depends on what your needs are. Take your pick from ultramodern to a more traditional Bermudian cottage setting.

---

**Additional Hotel Room Charges**
To assist in calculating the cost of your vacation, please note that most places add to the room rate the Government Occupancy Tax of 7.25 percent (per person) plus 10 percent for maid service. Hopefully this enables you, the traveller, to properly budget your vacation without any surprises.

---

You may wish to save money by staying in a cottage, apartment, or efficiency unit. Bermuda has a wide variety of small accommodations, with facilities ranging from basic to those with more substantial services and on-site facilities such as laundromats, grocery deliveries, pools, and barbe-cue patios. There is no such thing as "roughing it" in Bermuda, so "budget" in this book represents great value for money. I have visited them all at least twice. Some small properties are situated in quiet residential areas with pleasant garden settings, others are very near to the city, con-venient for shopping and restaurants, and there are even some close to Bermuda's world-class pink-tinged beaches.

One of the advantages of staying in an informal, fully equipped apart-ment or cottage is greater flexibility and freedom compared to the more structured atmosphere of a large hotel. This is especially convenient for families not wanting to stick to rigid timetables. Also, one of the main budget benefits of staying in an efficiency unit is the saving made by not having to dine out for every meal.

If you are an active senior, you may be interested in staying at the Bermuda Biological Station for Research with the Elderhostel Programme. For details on these adventure vacations, go to chapter 2, "Before You Leave Home."

## Bermuda's Restaurants

The variety and diversity of cultures in Bermuda contribute to its cui-sine. Portuguese pastries, Indian curries, Italian pastas, Jamaican patties, and English cream teas are just some of the victuals available.

In each section on restaurants you will find high-priced, medium-priced, and budget categories, which include fine-dining restaurants, pubs and taverns, cafés, diners, tea rooms, coffee shops, bakeries, delis, and snack bars. And there are a number of excellent restaurants in the hotels, either for guests or nonguests (reservations are usually recommended).

**Tipping:** Restaurants often add an automatic 15 percent on the bill for gra-tuities, although some of the smaller establishments do not. It is wise to check your bill to see if gratuities have been included or not, especially as the stan-dard credit-card bill often leaves a space for you to fill in a tip and you could inadvertently tip twice. Some hotel and restaurant owners have reported that the automatic 15 percent gratuity on meals has gone a long way towards ruin-ing the service provided by wait staff and, human nature being what it is, this may be true. In other words, why work for a tip if it is a foregone conclusion?

## Bermuda's Sights

You can discover numerous interesting sights and forms of entertainment around the island. This book promotes cultural, historic, and ecotourism.

Bermuda is very much a place for nature lovers, hikers, or anyone interested in history or culture. The nature trails, small national parks, museums and National Trust properties, and many forts dotting the island, not to mention the sightseeing excursions and cruises provided by private business enterprises, are all ways to enjoy Bermuda to its fullest.

Bermuda delights in its pomp and circumstance, with colourful ceremonies and annual festivals. Street fests, culture fests, the arts, and musical ceremonies with the Bermuda Regiment Band—you'll find them all in this book.

# 2

# Before You Leave Home

## About Bermuda

The first impression of Bermuda is one of delightfully painted cottages with bright white-stepped roofs and manicured gardens surrounded by limestone walls laden with hibiscus and oleander. The white roofs are specially designed to catch rain, as this is the main supply of fresh water (no acid rain here) and it is perfectly safe to drink. Bermudians call a good downpour "tank rain." When it's raining at night, I love to lie in bed and listen to the water-tank filling up with free water.

Bermuda is a subtropical, self-governing, British Overseas Territory. In May 2000, Bermudians gained full British citizenship, whereby they automatically attained the right to live and work in the U.K. and the European Union.

Located 600 miles off the coast of South Carolina, in the Atlantic Ocean, the island has a total of 21 square miles and a population of approximately 63,000. The best way to upset the locals is to say Bermuda is in the Caribbean—it is about a thousand miles north of there. However, it is not surprising that people think Bermuda is in the Caribbean, as travel agents and Web sites often lump it with those islands.

Bermuda's seven main islands are connected by bridges and causeways and separated into nine parishes: Sandys (pronounced "Sands"), Southampton, Warwick (pronounced "Warrick"), Paget, Devonshire, Pembroke, Smith's, Hamilton (not to be confused with the city), and St. George's.

Bermuda has one of the richest economies in the world, with a highly developed infrastructure of international business, a world-leading offshore insurance market, banking, and telecommunications, along with numerous lawyers and accountants. For Bermudians, the cost of living is high, with properties sold and rented at inflated prices. The average price for a house is $1 million.

During the 400-year history of Bermuda, only the Spanish attempted (unsuccessfully) to invade the island. The massive ring of fortifications built for coastal protection were the keystone to the British defence of the West. In all, about 55 forts were built, creating an impregnable island, and today many of these have been restored and landscaped in an effort to preserve a very important part of Bermuda's historical heritage. Visitors can enjoy spectacular views from the ramparts, explore cavernous tunnels, examine dozens of original powerful cannons, walk the drawbridges over dry moats, and generally soak up the nautical atmosphere.

Although Bermuda has a definite British flavour, there are Bermudian people originating from the West Indies, North America (Algonquian Native Americans), West Africa, and the Portuguese islands of Madeira and Azores. A remarkable aspect about the island is that it was uninhabited before 1609 and, therefore, there are no indigenous people of Bermuda, like the Aborigines of Australia or the Native Americans of North America. Slaves existed here between 1616 and 1834, working as farmers, sailors, domestic servants, and craftsmen. After the abolition of slavery, the hardworking people of the Portuguese islands were initially brought over to work in the farming and landscaping community. All of these cultures influence life as we know it today in Bermuda.

## Airline Information and Tips

With 10 Eastern Seaboard gateway cities in close proximity, including New York, Baltimore, Boston, Atlanta, and Halifax, Canada, Bermuda is quick and easy to get to.

New York City—2-hour flight
Toronto, Canada—2¾-hour flight

London, England—7-hour flight

The following airlines have regularly scheduled flights into Bermuda, but flight frequency may change during low season (November to March). For an up-to-date comprehensive schedule of incoming and outbound flights, go to www.bermudairport.com.

**Air Canada** (www.aircanada.ca). Departs every morning from Toronto. Also from Halifax, Nova Scotia on Saturdays (Tel. U.S. 1-888-247-2262 or from London 08705-247226).

**American Airlines** (www.AA.com). Departs twice a day from New York. Also daily from Boston and Raleigh/Durham (Tel. 1-800-433-7300).

**British Airways** (www.britishairways.com). Departs London four times a week (Tuesday/Thursday/Saturday/Sunday) from Gatwick (Tel. 1-800-AIR-WAYS).

**Continental Airlines** (www.continental.com). Departs twice a day from Newark (Tel. U.S. 1-800-525-0280 or Canada 1-800-231-0856).

**Delta Airlines** (www.delta.com). Departs every day from Boston and Atlanta (Tel. 1-800-241-4141).

**USAirways** (www.usairways.com). Departs every day from Philadelphia, Boston, Charlotte, Washington, D.C., and La Guardia. Also has a weekly flight from Fort Lauderdale (Tel. 1-800-622-1015).

## AIRLINE DISCOUNTS

American Airlines (www.AA.com) offers the following advice on obtaining low fares:

1. Plan in advance. The lowest fares often require a purchase seven, 14, or 21 days prior to departure. The further in advance, the greater the likelihood that low-fare seats will be available on preferred flights.

2. Most low fares are for round-trip travel or travel in which you return to your originating city.

3. Some low fares are offered based on the day of the week. The lowest fares often require a Saturday-night stay at the destination.

4. Fares vary by season. Travelling during the low season is less expensive than travelling during high season.

5. Be aware that the lowest fares are often non-refundable. By paying a $100 fee, you can apply the cost of the trip towards a future non-refundable trip (check when booking, as this provision may not be available for your ticket).

Note: You can check-in at www.AA.com and print out your boarding pass between 12 hours and 1 hour before departure. You can then take your pass and head straight to your gate. Use "curbside check-in" to speedily check your bags in.

## OTHER HINTS ON LOWERING FARES

Airlines are not obligated to give you the lowest fare, unless requested to do so by you. Always ask the airline for the lowest available fare in your week of travel, as the rates for different days and times of departure can vary significantly. The early bird catches the worm—the best time to get discounted airline tickets is between 1 A.M. and daybreak. The next day these cheap seats are bagged quickly.

**Consolidators:** Subject to availability, consolidators offer tickets up to 50 percent lower than regular flights. Some restrictions apply. Consolidators advertise in the Sunday travel section of many U.S. and U.K. newspapers.

APEX flights usually need 21 days advance booking. Cancellation is not permitted. Ask your travel agent to quote available APEX flights to Bermuda.

**Web sites:** The Internet is a popular medium to search for discount travel. Flights can be booked directly on-line by using a safety log-on password to protect your credit card. The travel Web sites listed below will take you through some easy steps. For instance, the Travelocity site first asks you to key in your departure and destination cities and dates. It then downloads different flight and airline options for you to choose from, starting at the cheapest flight available.

Here is a list of travel Web sites where you can book flights and/or hotels directly and search for cheapest fares (note: some sites charge a nominal booking fee):

www.travelocity.com
www.cheaptickets.com
www.expedia.msn.com
www.americanexpress.com/travel
www.discountairfares.com
www.travelzoo.com
www.travelweb.com (search on Hamilton, Bermuda for hotels)

At the end of the day, though, it is extremely difficult to obtain low airfares to Bermuda. Why? Well, because the airlines have a monopoly, as Bermuda does not have its own airline as other island destinations sometimes do, plus there is no competition on existing routes. Another factor causing the high airfares is hardly any charter flights or low-cost airline carriers coming into Bermuda (although there have been some discussions with JetBlue Airlines). The success of business travel into Bermuda has also helped swell the average fare. Airfares to destinations in the Caribbean are cheaper because they have a much larger market. However, airlines have pulled out of some of these destinations due to a low profitability margin, so it is important that Bermuda doesn't alienate the airlines with too much competition. The government is constantly trying to turn this around, and some progress has been made, especially with British Airways' specials. It should be noted that whenever there is a reduced price to Bermuda, tickets are quickly gobbled up, so try to be quick off the mark.

### HANDY FLYING AND TRAVEL TIPS
### (COURTESY OF BOB CARTER
### WWW.HOMESTEAD.COM/TRAVELBITS)

1. Try getting to the airport at least three hours before your flight time. Take along a book to read or find something fun to do (like watching the passing parade of interesting travellers). The time passes quickly and you'll depart in a more relaxed frame of mind.

2. Take a sweater in your tote to wear on the plane in case it gets cold, as it often does on planes. Ask the flight attendant for a blanket and pillow as soon as you are seated. If you want to sleep on the plane, wear your seat belt over your blanket so the flight attendant won't disturb you.

3. When packing, put small items such as spare glasses inside your shoes. Shoes are usually rigid and can protect items that might otherwise be broken. Put all liquids in plastic bottles or containers. It's always wise to place the bottle into a well-sealed plastic bag as well. Don't depend on protecting breakable items with clothing.

4. Pack some of your travelling companion's clothes in your bag, and vice versa. Both of you will then have a change of clothing if one bag is lost. It's a good idea to take a change of clothes in your on-flight bag.

5. It's helpful to take along several plastic bags to hold such things as soiled laundry, damp items, and muddy shoes. Small bags are excellent for storing toilet articles, stationery items, and medicine.

6. Get plenty of small bills and change for tipping purposes as soon as you enter a country. This way you won't waste money overtipping because you don't have change.

7. It's a good idea to carry the name, address, and telephone number of the hotel where you are staying. Simply ask for a business card when you check in. It comes in handy should you get lost and need to find your way or for taxi drivers.

8. When figuring your travel budget, take into account transportation, lodging, and meals first. Then figure in expenses such as shopping, entertainment, tips, laundry, and foreign exchange fees. Usually it's the spur-of-the-moment expenses that wreak havoc with travel budgets.

9. Remember this advice for sightseers: Never stand when you can sit, never sit when you can lie down, and never pass up a chance to use the bathroom.

Important Note: Since the events of September 9, 2001, to ensure the safety of your flight the airline rules have changed dramatically. There are more stringent suitcase size restrictions (as well as extra charges for bags over 70 lb., or for a third bag brought onboard). And there are stricter safety regulations for carry-on luggage. Don't pack knives, nail clippers, scissors, lighter fluid, or matches in your carry-on bags. Don't wrap any gifts or lock your luggage, as airport screeners may need to inspect them. Check with your airline prior to departure for any other restrictions.

## Cruise Ships

Do you know that the word "posh" comes from the early days of taking a cruise, when only the rich could afford to go? It stood for "**P**ort side **O**ut, **S**tarboard **H**ome"—which was the best and most expensive way to travel.

The first ships that carried tourists to Bermuda were the old steamships from the United States. Visitors were definitely posh. They came to avoid the harsh winters, and after the Second World War they came more frequently. Today, there are approximately 200,000 cruise-ship visitors per year.

A cruise is an excellent introduction to Bermuda and a great money-saver, as it is all inclusive: You don't have to worry about accommodations, meals, entertainment, flights, or transport. However, cruise-ship passengers don't really have a lot of time to explore Bermuda to its fullest, especially as visitors can't rent cars. But many cruise-ship passengers enjoy their taste of Bermuda so much, they return to stay in a hotel. The cruise lines also report that Bermuda is the one destination that people choose for the location and not just the cruise.

Bermuda has a very strict policy as to how many cruise ships are allowed at any given time. That way, the island doesn't get overcrowded and you can still find a seat at a restaurant when you get here. Cruise lines dock in the city of Hamilton, St. George's historical town, or the Royal Naval Dockyard in the western tip.

Seven-day cruises to Bermuda from New York or Boston are operated by **Royal Caribbean Cruises** (www.royalcaribbean.com), **Celebrity Cruises** (www.celebritycruises.com), **Norwegian Cruise Line** (www.ncl.com), and **Carnival Cruises** (www.carnival.com). The **Radisson Seven Seas** (www.rssc.com) cruise line is slated for a series of regular summer visits—check with your travel agent for further details.

## Package Deals

**The Harmony Club** (Tel.1-888-HARMONI, www.harmonyclub.com) is Bermuda's only all-inclusive hotel and that may account for why it is so successful. Package deals do not include airfares. They do include, however, deluxe room, unlimited open bar, meals, afternoon tea, live music, tennis, pool, sauna and Jacuzzi, and admission to two night clubs in Hamilton. This is for adults over 18 only, double occupancy only. The Harmony Club is not situated on the beach; however, it does have a shuttle service to Stonington Beach, nearby, and it is set in beautiful gardens and next to nature trails.

During November, Bermuda hosts the **Culinary Arts Festival** and offers packages inclusive of hotel, air travel, and festival participation. The festival features cooking demonstrations, wine and gourmet food tasting, and seminars by celebrity chefs, both local and international (concierge@bermudaescapes.com, Tel. 441-294-4910, or call Bermuda Tourism at 1-800-BERMUDA).

Here is a list of Web sites that offer deals on accommodations:
www.cheaptickets.com
www.expedia.msn.com
www.travelweb.com (search on Hamilton)

Here is a list of wholesale vacation companies with packages to Bermuda (note: Bermuda is listed in the Caribbean region in many of the following Web sites):

**TNT Vacations** (www.tntvacations.com, Tel. 617-262-9200)

**Continental Airline Vacations** (www.coolvacations.com, Tel. 1-800-301-3800)

**Liberty Travel** (www.libertytravel.com, Tel. 1-888-271-1584)

**Delta Vacations** (www.deltavacations.com, Tel. 1-800-654-6559)

**Magic Carpet Vacations** (www.gomcv.com, Tel. 1-800-225-4570)

**Travel Impressions** (www.travelimpressions.com, Tel. 1-800-284-0044)

**Apple Vacations** (www.applevacations.com, Tel. 1-800-365-APPLE)

**American Airlines Vacations** (www.aavacations.com, Tel. 1-800-321-2121)

**Holiday House** (www.holiday-house.com)—book through your travel agent only

**Air Canada Vacations** (www.aircanadavacations.com)—Canadian vacations to Bermuda

**Red Seal Tours** (www.redsealvacations.com, Tel. 1-800-668-4224)—golf-package vacations out of Canada

## Private House and Apartment Rentals

**Bermuda Rentals:** For a list of over 40 separate private properties in which to stay, including cottages, apartments, and villas located island-wide, check out *Bermuda Rentals* (Tel. 416-232-2243, info@bermudarentals.com, www.bermudarentals.com). Airfares are not included. Bermuda Rentals offer personal service and customise your vacation to suit individual tastes.

**Bermuda Getaway:** For another fantastic list of houses and apartments—complete with photos and room rates—go to www.bermudagetaway.com. This comprehensive site is linked to the owners of the properties, who can then assist you with their availability.

## Passports and Customs for U.S., Canada, and U.K.

**Passports and Visas:** To speed up the process coming through Customs, have ready your passport, return ticket, and accommodation address. If you are staying with a family on the island, make sure you have their street address with you. All visitors who are not residents of Bermuda require a round-trip ticket or onward-bound air- or sea-passage ticket. A full passport is the preferred mode of entry. (By the way, in case of loss, it is a good idea to leave a photocopy of the identification page of your passport at home, as well as bring a copy with you, separate from your passport.)

Passengers who fail to provide the following will politely be refused admittance on arrival by Immigration and Customs:

**U.S.A.:** Preferably U.S. passport. Alternatively, original birth certificate with raised seal or certified copy, or either a U.S. re-entry permit, U.S. Naturalization Certificate, or U.S. Alien Registration card.

**Canada:** Preferably Canadian passport. Alternatively, birth certificate or certified copy. Either one, along with photo ID. For people born outside Canada, a Canadian Certificate of Citizenship or proof of Landed Immigrant Status is required.

**United Kingdom:** Full valid passport or British Visitor's passport.

By the way, a driver's licence is not acceptable as proof of citizenship. Married women whose identification documents are retained in their maiden name but who are travelling under their married name should also carry their marriage certificate or certified copy.

**Duty-Free Clearance:** You can bring in 200 cigarettes, a quart of wine, a quart of liquor, and $30 of gifts. Anything else is usually taxed at 22.25 percent. No fruits, vegetables, or plants are allowed. For duty-free allowances on departure, check chapter 3, "Once You're Here."

**Departure Tax:** Here's some good news—the old ann(
Tax of $20 per person is no longer required on airport de
been incorporated into air and cruise fares.

**Extended Visits:** Visitors with a return ticket can stay up to 21 days.
Longer vacations are allowed with permission from the Department of Immigration. According to the Department of Immigration blue form "Application for Permission to Extend Visit":

> Persons seeking an extension of stay MUST make application prior
> to the expiration of the existing permission as stamped in passport and
> immigration arrival card. Applicants MUST appear, in person, with
> their host/sponsor, and by appointment at the Department of Immi-
> gration, Government Administration Building, 30 Parliament Street,
> Hamilton (Tel. 295-5151, Extensions: 1455 or 1385).

**Drugs and Guns:** The gun law in Bermuda is simple—*no guns allowed*.
Neither are drugs or any other kind of weapons admitted (including spear
guns). Penalties are very harsh, and ignorance of the law is no excuse. Customs police often search luggage as well as cruise-ship cabins.

Prescription drugs must be declared at Customs.

Crime was once practically unheard of; however, this is now on the
rise—especially drug related. Visitors are reminded to be careful with belongings and not to leave their common sense at home. Make sure that
bags and belongings are secured to the basket of motor scooters to prevent
snatching (better yet, don't leave wallets in them), and don't leave valuables in hotel rooms or out of sight on the beach (do you really think that
wallet hidden in your shoe is safe?). Secure sliding windows before retiring
to bed. Keep to well-lit areas after dinner and don't accept rides from
strange men. Women should not walk alone on the walking trails, or at
night. And tourists should steer clear of the area known as "Back of Town"
in Hamilton.

**Pets:** All animals and pets who do not arrive in Bermuda with proper
documentation will be turned away. There are no quarantine kennels available. For further information contact the Department of Agriculture &
Fisheries, P.O. Box HM 834, Hamilton, HM CX, Bermuda (Tel. 236-4201).

## Medical Coverage

Set in the tropical grounds of the Botanical Gardens, King Edward VII
Memorial Hospital, 7 Point Finger Road, Paget (Tel. 236-2345), offers
modern facilities and medical care that is the envy of other island countries. No one is excluded for emergency care; however, it is a good idea to

.ave insurance coverage before leaving your country. Major insurance company policies are honoured—keep receipts for future claims.

Local doctors and surgeons are listed in the Bermuda Yellow Pages under "Physicians and Surgeons." Drugstores ("chemists") are listed under "Pharmacies," which gives details of late-night and Sunday openings.

No vaccinations are required to enter Bermuda.

## Currency

The multicoloured Bermuda dollar is on par with the U.S. dollar. Every place accepts either. Many restaurants and stores accept traveller's checks and credit cards (not Discover Card, though). If you are relying on using your credit card for payment, check first, as not every hotel and restaurant accepts credit cards, especially the smaller ones. Banks will change other currencies and traveller's checks (bring passport for ID). The most convenient traveller's checks to bring are U.S. dollars. Bermudian dollars can be obtained from ATMs (see "Banks and ATMs" in chapter 3, "Once You're Here").

Americans wishing to cash a cheque may go to **Bermuda Financial Network,** 133 Front Street, Hamilton (Tel. 292-1799, support@easypay.bm). It is also a representative for American Express and will help with any queries cardholders may have.

## Voltage

Power outlets are 110V, the same as in the U.S. and Canada. Visitors from the U.K. need an adapter for their shavers, hairdryers, and other small electrical appliances. Plugs are flat-pin, two-prong American style.

## Weather

One of the best things about Bermuda is the climate. The Gulf Stream, which flows between Bermuda and the North American continent, keeps the climate warm. Temperatures don't usually reach higher than the mid-80s, and even in the cooler winter months of January, February, and March the days are about 65 degrees (although some days drop below that). Humidity is on average about 77 percent, though the months of July and August can be very sticky. Flora and fauna survive all year, and due to year-round rainfall, Bermuda is consistently green and lush. There is *never* any snow or frost, and this may account for the fact that 64 percent of all Canadian visitors arrive in the low season of November to March.

## AVERAGE TEMPERATURES AND RAINFALL
### (Taken Over a 10-Year Period)

|     | Minimum | Maximum | Rainfall (inches) | Sea Temperature |
|-----|---------|---------|-------------------|-----------------|
| Jan | 58.8    | 66.3    | 5.85              | 62.6            |
| Feb | 58.0    | 67.4    | 5.50              | 60.8            |
| Mar | 59.2    | 68.3    | 4.55              | 62.6            |
| Apr | 60.2    | 69.8    | 3.82              | 64.4            |
| May | 65.9    | 74.7    | 3.19              | 69.8            |
| Jun | 71.6    | 79.2    | 5.15              | 73.4            |
| Jul | 74.7    | 83.9    | 4.75              | 78.8            |
| Aug | 75.8    | 85.0    | 5.12              | 82.4            |
| Sep | 74.0    | 83.1    | 5.76              | 80.6            |
| Oct | 70.8    | 79.2    | 5.91              | 75.2            |
| Nov | 66.3    | 74.1    | 4.23              | 69.8            |
| Dec | 61.5    | 70.0    | 4.98              | 62.6            |

**Hurricanes:** Hurricane season runs from June 1 to November 30. Compared to other storm locations, Bermuda is a comparatively safe place to be, as the buildings are made of solid stone with eight-inch-thick walls and special hurricane-proof roofs. However, Hurricane Fabian—the first Category 3 hurricane Bermuda has seen since 1953—hit the island on September 5, 2003, unleashing 150-mph winds and causing widespread minor structural damage and four deaths. Lashing winds snapped trees, tore off several roof tiles, and caused 26,000 homes to lose power. Guests at some South Shore hotels had to be evacuated, and the airport was closed for two days due to impassable roads. Bermudians were praised, though, for pulling together and quickly getting the island back on its feet and open for business. Two hotels, the Fairmont Southampton and the Sonesta Beach Resort, both located on the South Shore, were closed for the remainder of the year for repairs. They were scheduled to reopen in the spring of 2004.

Other direct hits were Hurricane Emily in 1987 and Dean in 1989; neither caused major destruction. Hurricane Felix in 1995 only closed down the island for a day. It was a very important day—the country's Independence Referendum was delayed. (Some saw this as an omen, as Bermuda's English dependence was started due to a hurricane—see "Bermuda's Fascinating History" in chapter 5, "Culture and Heritage.")

## Public Holidays

Most stores, all the banks and government offices, and many restaurants (hotel restaurants being the exception) and attractions are closed on public holidays. The buses run on Sunday timetables.

* New Year's Day—January 1
* Good Friday—Friday before Easter
* Bermuda Day—May 24
* Queen's Birthday—Last Monday in June
* Cup Match and Somers Day—Thursday and Friday before first Monday in August
* Labour Day—First Monday in September
* Remembrance Day—November 11
* Christmas Day—December 25
* Boxing Day—December 26

## Getting Married in Bermuda

Many couples who wish to tie the knot are turning to more unusual locations, such as Bermuda. They are looking for romance, sunshine, and enchantment. Bermuda is host to approximately 500 overseas couples every year who take advantage of spectacular scenery, romantic pink beaches, balmy summer weather, and, once all the guests have gone home, a great honeymoon!

Bermuda has certain quaint traditions to make your wedding a little more interesting, such as the Bermuda cedar-tree sapling on top of the wedding cake that the couple are supposed to plant at their new home—very environmentally friendly. Walking hand in hand through a Bermuda Moon Gate signifies eternal love and happiness for the couple, and no Bermuda wedding would be complete without one. The Bermuda wedding cake is three tiered. One tier, for the bride, is made of fruit, preserved in rum, and saved for the christening of the couple's first child; one is for the groom, which is a plain pound cake and gold plated to signify wealth; and the third is served to guests.

There's a tremendous amount of work associated with organising a wedding. It gives you a headache just thinking about all the necessary arrangements, even for a small wedding. Booking the church or location, flowers, cake, reception, entertainment, buying the rings, choosing a honeymoon spot—the mind boggles. Add to all that doing it overseas and bringing your guests with you, and you have a major job on your hands. To save time and worry, let your guests book their own hotel accommodations (after perhaps suggesting a few possible places from this guide). Think very seriously about hiring a wedding consultant/planner, who will save you a lot of legwork and time.

If you are planning a wedding and honeymoon in Bermuda, good luck and God bless.

## WEDDING CONSULTANTS AND LOCATIONS

To save a lot of planning headaches, it's a good idea for the bride and groom to use an experienced wedding planner such as **The Wedding Salon Limited** (Tel. 292-5677), **The Bridal Suite** (Tel. 292-2025), **Bermuda Wedding Associates** (Tel 293-4033), **Bermuda Bride** (Tel. 232-2344), or a company based in Florida: **A Wedding For You Inc.** (Tel. 954-472-0320 or 1-800-929-4198).

All these wedding consultants can arrange everything for the big day, from a traditional Bermudian horse and carriage to the idyllic setting for the ceremony: church, cliff top, lush tropical garden, onboard a yacht, or on a tropical beach. Churches in Bermuda (and there seems to be one on every corner) are a good choice for the conventional wedding, and many are historic and have lovely sea views.

## GIFT REGISTRIES

You can book your bridal registry at classy Front Street stores such as **Trimingham's** (Tel. 295-1183), **H. A. & E. Smith's** (now owned by Trimingham's, Tel. 295-2288), and **A. S. Coopers** (Tel. 295-3961). These stores have catered to brides for many years and sell superior gifts.

Smaller stores include **Bluck's** (Tel. 295-5367), which specialises in fine crystal and china, and **Vera P. Card** (Tel. 295-1729), another store with a fine reputation for quality gifts.

**Gibbon's** (Tel. 295-0022) is a department store with a bridal registry that may cost a little less than the others.

**International Imports** (Tel. 292-1661) on Par-La-Ville Road in Hamilton is popular for professional kitchenware, and **Masters Ltd.** (Tel. 295-4321) is a store with more practical wares for the house.

All these stores frequently cater to brides to be, as Bermuda weddings are big business.

For a donation of money towards the couple's honeymoon, **Meyer Travel** (Tel. 295-4176) has a honeymoon gift-registry programme.

Wish to donate a gift to a registered charity in your name? For a directory of registered charities in Bermuda, call the **Centre on Philanthropy** (Tel. 292-5320).

## LEGAL REQUIREMENTS

Booking early is extremely important, as weddings are very popular and vendors, caterers, and photographers soon get booked up during the April to October season. There are also certain legal regulations that you need to adhere to. However, if you are utilising the services of a wedding consultant, they will usually see to all the licensing documentation for you.

1. Notice of Intended Marriage: You will need at least two weeks' notice. Forms can be obtained from the Government Administration Building, 30 Parliament Street, Hamilton, HM 12 (Tel. 297-7709), or from the Department of Tourism offices in Boston, New York, Atlanta, Chicago, Toronto, or London. Send the completed form to: Registrar General, 30 Parliament Street, Hamilton, HM 12, Bermuda (Tel. 297-7709).

2. Request for Marriage Certificates are available at the Registrar General's office also. Copies of final divorce decrees must be included, and divorced couples cannot be married in a Roman Catholic church. Also, Catholics not residing in Bermuda or who do not have close family ties in Bermuda cannot be married in a Catholic church. (Enquiries may be addressed to The Bishop of Hamilton, P.O. Box HM 1191, Hamilton, HM EX, Bermuda.) Anyone under 21 (unless widowed) must receive parental permission, and this must be included in the application. You cannot be married at all under 16.

3. Notices are placed in the local paper twice during a two-week period (called the "Banns"). Only British subjects residing in England, Scotland, or Northern Ireland marrying a British subject residing in Bermuda can have their Banns called in church. Once issued, the license is then valid for a period of three months.

4. Non-religious ceremonies are carried out at the Registrar General's Marriage Room on Parliament Street, open 10 A.M. to 4 P.M. Monday to Friday, and 10 A.M. to noon Saturday. The wedding offices hold about 25 people, but in any case you must have two witnesses to sign the wedding documents.

5. Individual churches all vary on whether they offer pre-marital counselling. Some ministers will not marry without some sort of counselling, and this usually costs about $200 for two sessions. A donation to the church's building fund is sometimes requested and most welcome.

## BOOKING THE WORKS

**Reception:** One of Bermuda's favourite outdoor wedding spots is **Astwood Park**—a picturesque cliff with a South Shore backdrop. Astwood Park is also a popular site for wedding photos. Looking for a garden setting? The **Botanical Gardens** in Paget (Tel. 236-4201) has 36 acres of lush tropical gardens. If you are planning a wedding in a park or on a boat, sensible shoes are a must. And always have an alternative location ready in case it rains.

A candlelit wedding at a historical property is another option. **Verdmont,** a 17th-century museum, allows weddings, as does **Waterville** in Paget, and they make great photo spots. For details, call **The National Trust** (Tel. 236-6483).

For the ultimate in different wedding locations, you could try **Gibbs Hill Lighthouse,** although with its 180 steps, I don't think the bride will be carrying her white train up there. The old lighthouse keeper's residence is now the **Lighthouse Tea Rooms** (Tel. 238-8679) and would make a fine place for a small reception.

Hotels, of course, are popular venues for the reception, and Honeymoon Point at **Sonesta Beach Resort** (Tel. 238-8122) is magnificent. Sonesta is located on a spectacular peninsula with dramatic views of the South Shore coastline. **Ascots** at Royal Palms Hotel (Tel. 295-9644) has an English garden setting and **Ariel Sands Beach Club** (Tel. 236-1010 or 1-800-468-6610) offers a beachfront location where you just may bump into Catherine Zeta Jones and Michael Douglas. They frequent this hotel because their family owns it and they own a house nearby.

**The Clocktower Centre,** Royal Naval Dockyard (Tel. 234-1709), holds up to 400 people in a cedar-floored converted warehouse.

If money is no object, **Fourways Inn** (Tel. 236-6517) caters to weddings in an Old-World, 18th-century cottage colony.

**Transport:** A traditional bride and groom in Bermuda get to the church on time via a horse and carriage. **Shilo Ranch** (Tel. 236-6678), **Tucker's Carriages & Stables** (Tel. 236-7059), and **Terceira's Stables** (Tel. 236-3014) are just three of the stables that offer this service. For a change from a horse-and-carriage ride, maybe a white London taxicab is more your style. Call **The London Taxi** (Tel. 234-7729, Fax 238-2800, londontaxi@logic.bm). Or for small limousines, **Simon's Limousine Services** (Tel. 234-7427) provide personal touches, such as pick-up at the airport and taking the bride to the hairdressers, etc.

**Rental Equipment:** If you need to rent equipment for the reception, then **Rent-It-All** (Tel. 296-4505) has all sizes of tents, tables and chairs, tablecloths and skirts, drink fountains, Moon Gates, trellises, and peacock wedding chairs. **Bermuda Rentals Limited** (Tel. 292-7172) is another party and catering supplier (chairs, tables, linens, skirting, china, etc.).

**Photographers:** An excellent photography studio is **Visual Impact Photography** (Tel. 295-4755, Fax 295-9072). **Photographic Associates** (Tel. 295-5619), **Photography by Stan** (Tel. 293-0081), **Graham Mocklow** (Tel. 236-4348), and **Affordable Photography** (Tel. 234-5013) are four others.

**Bakeries:** Here's a novel idea—a cake decorated with a photograph of the lucky couple from **New Delhi Bakery** on North Street, Hamilton (Tel. 292-0276). Another baker, **Crow Lane Bakery** (Tel. 292-2220), offers free consultation and samples as well as photo cakes. Be warned, though—the traditional Bermuda cake costs a minimum of $600.

**Invitations:** Need invitations, place cards, etc., printed? **Print Express** (Tel. 295-3950), **Engravers Limited** (Tel. 295-7118), and **Pulp and Circumstance** (Tel. 292-3224) are three businesses to choose from.

**The Dress/Tuxedo:** You will probably bring your wedding dress with you, but if you decide to buy it here, **The Bridal Salon** (Tel. 295-6771) sells dresses and accessories. Ladies, need some sexy lingerie? **Eve's Garden** (Tel. 296-2671) on Front Street in Hamilton has lots of saucy fashions. For tuxedo rentals or purchases, try **The English Sports Shop** (Tel. 295-2672) or **Anthony's** (Tel. 292-3889).

**Hair:** Popular hair and makeup salons include **Headway Hair Centre** (Tel. 292-8983), **Strands Hair Salon and Spa** (Tel. 295-0935), **Tangles** (Tel. 292-8294), and **Tangles Mobile Beauty** for at-home care (Tel. 236-1727). For spa treatments, **Bersalon Spas** (Tel. 292-8570) offer special bride's services.

**The Ring:** Bermuda is a wise place to purchase the wedding and engagement rings and even the bridesmaids' gifts. Bargains abound due to the fact that Bermuda has no sales tax and a low import duty. **Crissons** (Tel. 295-2351), **Solomon's** (Tel. 292-7933), **E. R. Aubrey** (Tel. 295-2110), and **Astwood Dickinson** (Tel. 292-5805) are just a few of the fine jewellery stores in Bermuda.

**Flowers:** Every bride needs flowers, and what could be better than a bouquet made with exotic tropical flowers? Flowers are also very expensive; so you may want to save money by having the church flowers moved to the reception, or better yet, marry in a garden in full bloom. **Designer Flowers** (Tel. 295-4380), **Just Roses** (Tel. 236-3238), **Demco Florist** (Tel. 292-7777), **Petals Bermuda** (Tel. 236-2343), and **The Bermuda Florist** (Tel. 236-2333) are just a few florists to choose from.

**Caterers:** Bermuda has a wide variety of caterers, to fit every size of pocket. **The Little Venice Group Catering Service** (Tel. 295-8279) offers a choice of four restaurants and one night club and can cater to up to 500 guests on site or up to 1,000 off site. **M. R. Onions Restaurant** (Tel. 292-5012) offers in-house and on-site catering, specialising in cold party platters. **The Flying Chef** catering service (Tel. 295-1595) is experienced in all manner of weddings and parties. Another caterer is **Magic Moments** (Tel. 236-4086).

**Decorators:** For that extra touch in creating the right atmosphere at the reception, you could use the services of a professional decorator. Bermuda has several, including **Balloons n' Things** (Tel. 238-4500), **By Hand** (Tel. 238-5106), and **Celebrations** (Tel. 295-4785).

**Entertainment:** For music for receptions and parties, consider **Tempo** (Tel. 238-0474), **Michael Fox,** pianist (Tel. 295-4319), **Island Steel Band** (Tel. 293-0959), **Tropicana Steel Pan** (call Robert Symons, Tel. 293-5350), **The Bermuda Strollers Calypso Group** (Tel. 238-0088), **The Sharx Band** (Tel. 295-6657), **The Kennel Boys** (Tel. 293-8846), and **Tropical Heat Band** (island music, Tel. 232-2917).

**Cruises: Longtail Boat** (Tel. 296-5263, Fax 296-9908, mvlongtail@hotmail.com) offers buffet-style parties and water-shuttle service to photo spots. **Jessie James Cruises** (Tel. 296-5801, Fax 296-7088, www.jessiejames.bm) has a 57-foot motor yacht available for wedding parties. Its maximum capacity is 40 people. **Coral Sea Cruises** (Tel. 235-2425, bevans@northrock.bm, www.charterbermuda.com) offers lunch, dinner, and wedding-reception cruises in a 60-foot glass-bottom boat.

**Luxury Cruises:** Try *Lady Tamara* and *Lady Erica* (Tel. 236-0127).

# Bringing Children to Bermuda

So is Bermuda a good place to bring the kids? Well, the answer is yes, especially if you bring them during the warm months so they can play on the beach and in the ocean. Children in Bermuda are very friendly, often seen hopping around the island on buses and ferries, fishing off the bridges, or just hanging out. Bermuda is a young child's paradise, but for today's teenagers there is not much happening, unless they are very interested in water sports. Many of the larger hotels such as **Elbow Beach, Sonesta Beach Resort,** and the **Fairmont Southampton** have children's programmes.

**Flying Tips:** Airlines sometimes offer a special kid's menu—order at the time of booking or at least 24 hours before your flight. In any case, bring along a snack and drink in case of meal delays (or no meals on board at all). Request bulkhead seats at the front of the plane, as they allow more legroom for fidgety little ones. If you have a baby who weighs less than 20 pounds, request a sky-cot in advance. Little ones under two fly free, on an adult's lap (ask for a special lap restraint), or you can reserve a separate seat for a 50 to 90 percent fare reduction. Also, there are discounts for children under the age of 12. British Airways has special child seats for children up to two years.

**Hotel Booking:** When booking your hotel, try to anticipate any facilities you may require. It's a good idea to let Reservations know of special needs before arriving. In addition, find out the exact rate for having children in your room, plus how close the nearest beaches and bus stops are.

**Getting Around:** The hardest challenge in bringing little ones to Bermuda is the present transport system. Because tourists are unable to hire cars, they have to rely on buses, ferries, walking, taxis, or renting scooters. I would not recommend the latter, as accidents are frequent. On average, there are eight motor accidents a day, and that is just the reported ones—far too many for a small country.

Money will run very low quickly if you travel everywhere by cab, although you should allow for some cab money, especially for emergencies and after 5 P.M., when the buses are not as frequent. The key is to be prepared. Have tickets or tokens with you at all times. Try to plan your return journey times with the help of the bus and ferry schedules, and carry necessities with you (water, snack, sun block, favourite toys, wipes, and sun hats—anything you can think of to make your trips run smoothly).

## CHILDREN—THE THINGS THEY LOVE TO DO IN BERMUDA

- Play on the pink soft beaches, ramble over historic forts with great guns, and let off steam in the parks.
- Ride the popular government ferry.
- Ride the red Dockyard or Hamilton nontrack train.
- At the eastern end of the island, in St. George's, you can find the *Deliverance,* a replica 17th-century sailing ship. It's fun for children to use their imaginations on (see "The East End," chapter 11).
- Children get very excited when they see the Gombeys, musical groups of spectacularly dressed dancers from a tradition with African, West Indian, and American Indian roots. They wear masks, brightly coloured flowing cloaks, and tall headdresses adorned with peacock feathers. Gombeys carry tomahawks and bows and arrows and make music with drums, whistles, and whips. You can catch them occasionally playing around Bermuda, especially on Boxing Day (December 26), at displays during November to March, or at Harbour Nights during cruise-ship season on Wednesdays in Hamilton.
- Kid-friendly eateries include Coconut Rock, Reid Street, Hamilton (underground café with MTV and children's three-course meals) and Rosa's Cantina, Front Street, Hamilton (children's meal specials). Other eateries located in Hamilton and ideal for young appetites are: Four Star Pizza for takeout, The Double-Dip Ice Cream Parlor, The Ice Queen, La Trattoria Italian Restaurant, Kathy's Kaffee, KFC, and M.R. Onions. For more details, check chapter 8, "The City of Hamilton."

## FAMILY-FRIENDLY ACTIVITIES

**Aquariums:** First on the list is a visit to the **Bermuda Aquarium, Museum & Zoo,** Flatts Village, Smith's Parish (Tel. 293-2727, www.bamz.org). There's a lot to do and see for all ages, with animals, tropical fishes, and a giant eel, to name a few. Kids love the touch pool full of live sea creatures such as starfish and cucumber fish, where they can get their hands in and pick them up. There's also the Local Tails Room: a discovery centre for the little ones.

Another fishy place for children is the **Devil's Hole Aquarium,** Harrington Sound, Smith's Parish (Tel. 293-2072). For a small charge you get to feed giant turtles and fishes.

**Parks:** There's a growing number of playgrounds and adventure parks around Bermuda. **Warwick Long Bay Children's Playground** on the South Shore has fun play equipment—pretend train, climbing equipment, slides, etc. A trail leads down to beaches alongside the playground. Be careful, though, as the surf can be rough at this bay, with a strong undertow. There's no refreshment stand at Warwick Long Bay, so bring a picnic. Another adventure beach park with play equipment is **Shelly Bay Park** on North Shore Road, Hamilton Parish. The bay here is calm and shallow— ideal for wading. For traditional swings, slides, and playground equipment for the young, try **Mullet Bay Park,** Mullet Bay Road, St. George's.

**The Royal Naval Dockyard** has a playground with climbing equipment shaped like a ship (adjacent to the Maritime Museum entrance). This park has timed fountains that kids love to run through and cool down in.

**Caves:** Another great place for families is **Crystal Caves,** Harrington Sound Road, Bailey's Bay, Hamilton Parish (Tel. 293-0640). These caves were the inspiration for the children's television show "Fraggle Rock," by the late Jim Henson. It seems only fitting that two small boys discovered Crystal Caves, because the caves have been amazing children ever since.

**Minigolf:** The only miniature golf park in Bermuda is at the Bermuda Golf Academy & Driving Range Ltd., **Mini Golf Adventure,** Industrial Park Road, off Middle Road, Southampton (Tel. 238-8800). Open 9 A.M. to 10 P.M. daily, this is a fabulous, family, 18-hole miniature golf game set in landscaped grounds with waterfalls and green slopes. Or maybe let the little ones romp on the jungle gym before you practice on the driving range. Meals are available at the reasonably priced clubhouse/restaurant and bar, **Alegria Restaurant** (Tel. 238-1831, closed Monday).

**Bowling:** Bermuda has two bowling alleys. **Warwick Lanes,** Middle Road, Warwick (Tel. 236-5290), is open 2 P.M. to midnight. There are special "bumper" lanes for children and all sizes of shoes for rent, and prices are reasonable (adults: $4 a game, children: $2.75 a game, shoe rental: $1.50).

The other bowling alley is at Southside, **Southside Family Bowl,** on the former U.S. Navy Base in St. David's (Tel. 293-5906).

**Glass-Bottom Boat Tours:** What could be more interesting for a suburban child than to peer through a glass-bottom boat and check out the multicoloured reef fish through crystal-clear water? For a detailed description of water tours, go to the "Guided Tours and Cruises" sections in chapters 8 through 12.

**Dolphins:** To make your vacation really memorable, you may think about taking a trip to **Dolphin Quest** (www.dolphinquest.org), hosted by the Fairmont Southampton Hotel and now situated at the Royal Naval Dockyard (Tel. 234-4464). (This attraction was previously on the South Shore at the hotel but was closed due to hurricane damage.) You can book directly from the U.S. at Tel. 540-687-8102, or in Bermuda at the Dockyard number above.

Dolphin Quest, Bermuda, is one of four in the world, and it has been successful in nurturing and breeding dolphins. Here is an outline of the Dolphin Quest Programmes (source Dolphin Quest):

> Ultimate Adventure (ages five and over). Duration: 1 hour, $275 per person. Opportunity to interact with the animals in small intimate groups and get to know the trainers who work closely with these remarkable animals. They will guide you through a 40-minute in-water adventure that is catered to your desires. You also get to ride a water scooter alongside a dolphin (price includes admission to the Bermuda Maritime Museum, a Dolphin Quest beach towel, and a photo).
>
> Dolphin Discovery (ages five-nine—two adults may accompany each child). Duration: 1 hour 20 minutes, $150.00 per person. This program will introduce your child to the world of marine mammals through a hands-on dolphin experience in Dolphin Quest's lagoon followed by a free activity camp for the children. Designed for individual children or families with younger children.
>
> The Encounter (ages 10 and over). Duration: 1 hour, $195.00 per person. Join the trainers in the lagoon for a chance to touch, play with, and learn about dolphins. Explore the sights and sounds of the dolphin world. How do they investigate, learn, and feel? What do we share with these wonderful creatures and how do they enhance our lives?
>
> Dolphin Dip (ages 10 and over). Duration: 30 minutes, $135.00 per person. Fun-filled dolphin experience. From shallow-water platforms to swimming alongside dolphins in the deep Bermuda waters, you will truly enjoy this amazing opportunity. Chance to interact with the dolphins while learning about the environment.
>
> Fins and Flippers (ages three and over). Duration: 30 minutes, $87.50 per person. During this entertaining dockside program, participants will discover the joy of getting to know the dolphins. Meet the

dolphins from the floating dock, and learn how you can contribute to marine-mammal conservation. Bring a swimsuit and get a closer view of these magnificent creatures from the submerged platforms during a five-minute encounter (optional).

## Adventure Holidays for Seniors

Are you fit and active and looking for some adventure in your life? Then you may be interested in the Elderhostel Programme at the Bermuda Biological Station (or Bio Station, as it is locally known) in St. George's (Tel. 297-1880). Elderhostel is an educational, nonprofit organisation specialising in adventure vacations for senior adults looking for something different. People 55 years and older are eligible to participate, but participants' spouses can be any age. Companions can be 40 and upwards. Some of the courses in Bermuda allow grown children and grandchildren ages 13-15.

Basic and clean accommodations are provided, though central heating or air conditioning is not. Both the academic portion and the accommodations of the Bermuda Elderhostel Programme are based within the 15 acres of the Bermuda Biological Station for Research. Participants are expected to share rooms, and hearty meals are enjoyed at the facility's dining hall.

Courses include "Bermuda Houses and Gardens," "Family Program: Coral Island Adventure," "Atlantic Coral Reefs—Anatomy of an Oceanic Island," "Bermuda's History and Cultural Heritage," "Bermuda: A Walking Classroom" (designed for the energetic hosteller who is used to walking three to six miles per day on a regular basis), and "Snorkelling the Coral Island" (which is intergenerational). One-week and 10-day courses run from September to May. Rates are $1,310 to $1,382 depending on course and time of year (airfare not included).

If you are interested in adventure holidays for seniors and would like further information, write to: Elderhostel Inc., 11 Avenue de Lafayette, Boston, Massachusetts 02110-1746 (Tel. 617-426-8056, www.elderhostel.org), or check out the Bermuda Biological Station Web site: www.bbsr.edu.

# 3

# Once You're Here

## Top 10 Tips for a Great Vacation in Bermuda

1. Don't be surprised if perfect strangers greet you. It's all part of the Bermudian friendliness. It is considered rude to start a conversation in Bermuda without beginning with the traditional greeting of "Good morning," "Good afternoon," or "Good evening."

2. There is no actual rainy season, but it is wise always to carry a fold-away plastic rain jacket (or rain poncho). You never know when you are going to get caught in a shower.

3. Many stores and attractions close by 5 P.M. and on Sunday and public holidays. It is a good idea to phone first for opening (and closing) hours of restaurants and attractions to avoid wasted journeys (especially in the low season).

4. During November to March, Bermuda Tourism arranges free winter weekly activities, such as guided tours and lectures, afternoon teas, and ballroom dancing. February is Golden Rendezvous Month for senior citizens, offering weekly events, cultural open houses, bus tours, and dine-around menus at participating restaurants. Check local newspapers for details during November through March, or call the Department of

Tourism (Tel. 292-0023). A November to March Activity Package is available at the Visitors' Service Bureau, Hamilton.

5. Bus-stop poles are pink or blue-striped—pink at the top for buses going in the Hamilton direction and blue-striped at the top for out of Hamilton direction. Also, it is more economical and convenient to purchase multiday bus and ferry passes.

6. Read the *Royal Gazette* newspaper every day, *Bermuda Sun* on Wednesdays and Fridays, and *Mid-Ocean News* every Friday for a list of events and store sales in Bermuda.

7. Sunscreen is a must for everyone, even on cloudy days. Don't forget sun block on feet, ears, eyelids, and backs of legs. It's hats on for babies and small children. Drink plenty of (non-alcoholic) fluids in the heat.

8. The best time for a hiking holiday is before or after the hot humid summer months of July and August.

9. Bring a copy of *The Maverick Guide to Bermuda* with you (couldn't resist that one).

10. Relax, slow down—you're on vacation.

## What to Wear

Dress is conservative in Bermuda, and walking around improperly dressed is frowned upon. You'll feel uncomfortable anyway. There is no topless or nude bathing; in fact, it is an offence for men to go shirtless in the street and on a scooter, and swimsuits should be worn on the beach only. Oh, and don't catch the bus in your swimsuit either, even if you're wearing a beach wrap over it.

There are some hotel and fine-dining restaurants that expect a jacket and tie for dinner, although this rule is becoming a little more relaxed these days.

In the summer, loose-fitting lightweight clothes are definitely the order of the day—cotton being the ideal material. You will probably be doing significantly more walking than usual, so don't forget to pack comfortable sneakers or walking shoes. Your vacation is not the time to break in new shoes.

Sunstroke and sunburn are quite common, so prevent this by wearing plenty of sun block and drinking lots of water. To combat the heat, try this trick taken from *Tea with Tracey—The Woman's Survival Guide to Bermuda by Tracey Caswell:* "Fill an old Windex bottle with water and spray yourself and your clothes liberally throughout the day. If you don't have perspiration, create it." Or you could buy one of those battery-operated, portable fans that spray water.

Wearing a sun hat of some description is highly recommended. A fold-away rain jacket for the occasional shower is useful.

In the cooler months, generally around December to March, the temperatures don't require any thick winter coats, but you will need a jacket, a few sweaters, and long pants, especially for the evenings. Bring along a waterproof jacket for moped and scooter riding. The weather is changeable, so wearing layers is recommended.

A familiar sight around Hamilton during the summer is businessmen in Bermuda business shorts worn with long socks, shirt, tie, and jacket. Some do even in the winter, although this custom is generally not considered proper etiquette until after the May 24, Bermuda Day, public holiday. This wonderful tradition started with the military wearing khaki shorts. Adopting this style, Bermudians then refined it by wearing attractive colours. You will notice that the jacket or blazer is not the same colour as the shorts (to prevent the businessman from looking like a schoolboy), and the socks are folded over, knee-length. The secret to the shorts looking tailored is a three-inch hemline. Menswear stores profess they can always recognise new residents to Bermuda: The first year they wear blue or grey shorts, the second year they venture to burgundy and beige, and finally they move over in the third year to more daring pinks and yellows! Don't make the mistake some tourists do trying to copy this fashion by wearing knee-length socks with their casual holiday shorts, or pulling up their sports socks to somewhere midcalf.

## Banks and ATMs

Banks are usually open 9:30 A.M. to 3 P.M., and to 4:30 P.M. Fridays. Some branches are open limited Saturday hours. The two main banks are Bank of Bermuda and Bank of N.T. Butterfield, with main branches in Hamilton, St. George's, and Somerset.

### WHERE TO FIND AUTOMATED TELLER MACHINES (ATMS)

#### In Hamilton

**Bank of Butterfield**—3 bank branch locations: 1. Reid Street, 2. Front Street, 3. Bermudiana Road.

**Bank of Bermuda**—3 bank branch locations: 1. Par-la-Ville Road, 2. Church Street, 3. Head Office, Front Street.

Visitors' Service Bureau at Ferry Terminal

General Post Office, Church Street

Masters Building, 55 Front Street
Esso Automart, Richmond Road (open 24 hours)
Phoenix Centre, Reid Hall, Reid Street (second floor)
Washington Mall (ground floor)
Windsor Building, Queen Street (ground floor)
Marketplace (supermarket), Church Street
H.A. & E. Smith's (department store), Reid Street Level
#1 Shed, Front Street
#6 Shed, Front Street
Supermart (supermarket), Front Street
Trimingham's (department store), Reid Street Level

### Rest of Island ATMs
King's Square, St. George's
The Airport, St. George's
Rural Hill Plaza, Middle Road, Paget (next to Ice Queen takeout)
King Edward Memorial Hospital, Point Finger Road, Paget
Modern Mart, Paget
Bermuda College (Library), Paget
Shelly Bay Plaza, Hamilton Parish
Sonesta Beach Resort, South Shore, Southampton
Port Royal Esso Service Station, Middle Road, Southampton
Heron Bay Marketplace, Middle Road, Southampton
White & Son Ltd. (supermarket), Middle Road, Warwick
Warwick Service Station, Warwick
Harrington Hundreds (supermarket), South Shore Road, Smith's
Collector's Hill Apothecary, Smith's
Lindos Market, Watlington Road East, Devonshire
Marketplace (supermarket), Somerset
Somerset Village, Mangrove Bay
Gorham's Ltd., St. John's Road, Pembroke
Four Star Pizza, Flatts Village
Clocktower, Royal Naval Dockyard

### BERMUDA CLUB VISA
USAirways and VISA offer discounts and travel vouchers for joining Bermuda Club VISA. As a cardholder you will be entitled to receive discounts at restaurants, stores, and tours, plus travel certificates. You must be a U.S. resident to apply: call 1-800-847-7378 from the U.S. or 1-800-932-6262 from Bermuda.

# Newspapers

The local papers are well worth reading for "what's on" and store sales and to discover Bermuda's local news. The daily is the *Royal Gazette* (www.theroyalgazette.com). This paper inserts a free magazine (the *RG* ) once a month. The *Bermuda Sun* (www.bermudasun.org) is printed on Wednesdays and Fridays only. The *Mid-Ocean News* is available on Fridays. Foreign newspapers are sold at bookstores, the Phoenix Centre in Hamilton, and some hotel lobbies and gas stations.

# Magazines

For fascinating, up-to-date stories and information on all things Bermudian:

*RG Magazine*—Inserted free every month in the *Royal Gazette* newspaper (Tel. 295-5881, editor@logic.bm).

*Bermudian Magazine*—Published monthly and sold in Bermuda (Tel. 295-0695, berpub@logic.bm).

*Bermuda Magazine*—Published quarterly, available in Bermuda and distributed in the U.S. and Canada (subscription enquiries: Tel. 1-800-247-3620 or 616-377-3322).

For a detailed list of Bermuda business magazines, check chapter 7, "The Business Traveller."

# Local Radio Stations

**AM**
ZBM-1340
ZFB-1230
VSB-1160 (BBC World Service/Local Legislature)
VSB-1450 (Country & Western)
VSB-1280 (Religious)

**FM**
ZBM-89 (Adult 1970s, 1980s, and 1990s Music)
ZFB-95
VSB Mix-106.1

# TV Stations

Local: ZBM/CBS—channel 9; ZFB/ABC—channel 7; VSB/NBC—channel 11. The local news is broadcast at 7 P.M. and midnight. The local weather is broadcast on channel 4.

Many accommodations in this book are hooked up to full cable services. Bermuda cable offers all the usual U.S. stations, including CNN, CBS, ABC, and NBC. BBC World, shown on channel 8, is a 24-hour international news and information channel from London.

Don't want to miss your favourite sports game played on TV? **The Robin Hood Pub** (Tel. 295-3314) and **Flanagan's Irish Pub** (Tel. 295-8299) are both in Hamilton and both feature live games on television, usually on the weekends.

## Duty Free

Sold at wine and liquor stores, a wide variety of special packs of liquor, for export only, are substantially cheaper than regular bottles. If you purchase duty-free liquor it will be delivered to the airport or your ship when you depart. It must be purchased at least 24 hours prior to departure, and you will be asked for flight details. You won't be able to drink it until you are leaving the country (save receipts for proof of purchase).

There are two duty-free liquor stores at the airport: one next to USAirways and the other next to the British Airways first-class lounge.

### DUTY-FREE ALLOWANCES

**U.S. Visitors:** After 48 hours out of the U.S., may take back $400 worth of goods once every 30 days duty free, plus 100 cigars, 200 cigarettes, and 1 litre alcohol. Gifts bought over and above $400 and up to the value of $1,000 will be assessed at 10 percent of the retail value.

**Canadian Visitors:** 1. $50 after 24 hours (not including tobacco and alcoholic drinks). 2. $200 after 48 hours (including 200 cigarettes, 50 cigars, 400 grams of tobacco, and 40 oz. alcoholic drinks). 3. $500 after seven-day stay (includes same alcohol and tobacco in 2 above).

**British and European Union Visitors:** 1 litre spirits or 2 litres fortified wine, 2 litres table wine, 60 cc perfume, and 200 cigarettes, or 50 cigars, or 100 cigarillos, or 250 g tobacco. Other goods to the value of £145 (includes no more than 50 litres of beer).

**Duty-Free Tip:** For all countries, antiques (over 100 years old), prints, maps, coins, and stamps are all duty free. Also, Bermuda-made products are duty free.

**Duty-Free Mailing Gifts:** Residents of the U.S. may mail an unlimited number of presents home, duty free, with two stipulations. Each gift must be worth under $50, and no more than one may be sent to an individual on the same day. No tobacco, liquor, or perfume is allowed. This will not affect your $400 allowance. For further questions, contact the U.S. Customs Service (Tel. 293-8127). For Canadians, the total postal duty-free limit is a paltry $20.

## Airline Numbers While in Bermuda

- Air Canada, Tel. 293-1777
- American Airlines, daytime office Tel. 293-1420 (automated 24-hour number, 1-880-242-4444 for arrivals and departures; have flight numbers ready)
- British Airways, Tel. 1-800-AIRWAYS
- Continental Airlines, Tel. 1-800-231-0856
- Delta Airlines, Tel. 1-800-325-1999
- USAirways, Tel. 293-3072

## Postal Services

The government postal service runs from the main General Post Office (GPO) on Church Street in Hamilton (general enquiries Tel. 297-7893). There are also 13 post offices dotted around the country; their addresses are in the phone book, in the government blue pages.

Post offices are open 8 A.M. to 5 P.M. Monday to Friday; however, Somerset Bridge, Crawl, and St. David's sub-post offices close for lunch from 11:30 A.M. to 1 P.M. The GPO in Hamilton is also open on Saturdays from 8 A.M. to 12 P.M. International Data Express Mail needs to be mailed by 10:30 A.M. at the GPO for same-day dispatch.

**Perot's Post Office, Hamilton:** Bermuda's first-ever post office, Perot's Post Office, is on Queen Street in Hamilton, and this historic building, with its wood floors, high stools, and antiques, does not disappoint. An interesting tale about this post office entails an ex-prisoner from a convict ship. These ships were brought over from England during the 1800s, packed with convict labour used for the construction of the Royal Naval Dockyard. The prisoner, after his release from one of these convict ships, ran the first pony express service from Perot's Post Office. Originally, he had served his time for "borrowing" one of his father's horses. His father, who had wanted to teach him a lesson by calling in the law, was horrified when his son was sentenced to harsh convict labour. This prisoner was the only man ever allowed to remain in Bermuda after serving his sentence on a convict ship, probably because he was an upper-class gentleman.

## Nature Trails, Wildlife, Flora, and Fauna

If you are looking for peace and tranquillity, try exploring Bermuda's open spaces, parks, forts, nature reserves, trusts, and trails. And for the nature lover and ecotourist, Bermuda is like an immense lush secret garden waiting to be explored. Bermuda also has some of the oldest caves in the world; you'll be amazed at the stalactite and stalagmite formations at **Crystal Caves** (Tel. 293-0640) that took millions of years to evolve (for more information, check out "The East End," chapter 11).

To delight the senses, you will hear the melodic evening sound of the tiny tree frog or the daytime song of the kiskadee bird. Other birds include the bright red cardinal and bluebird. To encourage nesting, kind bird-lovers have placed bluebird boxes in strategic positions around the country.

You will see trees and flowers such as the flame-red royal poinciana tree, tropical hibiscus bushes used for hedges, bright purple morning glory flowers growing wild, pink and white oleander bushes, and overhanging purple and coral-pink bougainvillea bushes. A very interesting tree is the screw pine, which looks as if it's sprouting pineapples for fruit and has a multiple-root trunk. Trees also include paw-paw, loquat, grapefruit, lemon, and banana.

The native palm is the palmetto, whose fronds were used in earlier times for making hats and thatching roofs. As well as oleander and hibiscus, a bush used for hedges is the "match me if you can," so named because you can't match any of the leaves. Bermuda's (unofficial) national flower is the Bermudiana, a tiny purple flower that grows wild during April.

Nowhere will you smell anything quite as fragrant as the sweet-smelling frangipani tree's pink-and-white blossoms in summer. And, around Easter time, the fragrant white Easter lily blooms. The Easter lily was a major export during the 1800s, when literally millions of bulbs were shipped to Europe and as far away as Russia.

## WILDLIFE

Compared to other countries, there are hardly any mosquitoes in Bermuda, so your walks will usually be bite free. Here's some more good news: there are no snakes, poisonous spiders, or other scary animals. The little lizards don't bite and are more afraid of you than you are of them. The large toads are not very clever and tend to sit in the middle of the road on a rainy day, quickly becoming road-kill—try not to run them down, as they eat the roaches. At the other end of the spectrum, the whistling tree frogs are so small you probably won't get to see one (you'll hear them, though, at nighttime). Speaking of cockroaches—yes, I know they're horrible, but if you leave your fly-screen open and some food on the table, they'll come gliding in, so don't blame the hotel.

In the sea and on the beaches, steer clear of the Portuguese man-of-war (brilliant blue, gas-filled stinging jellyfish). If you spot one in the water or a dead one on the beach (it looks like an inflated blue balloon), give it a wide berth. Men-of-war are found March through June on the South

Shore. If stung, seek medical attention at the hospital: King Edward VII Memorial in Paget. In the meantime, remove the stinger (not with your hands). Applying vinegar (or meat tenderiser) to the area helps neutralise the sting. (In an emergency, Bermudians urinate on it!) Help can be found at Horseshoe Bay lifeguard station in the summer.

## TRAILS AND PARKS

From the road, it looks as though Bermuda has gobbled up most of its open spaces, leaving nowhere to walk. But if you venture out by boat, which, by the way, is the best way to view Bermuda, you can see lots of open spaces and parkland. Owing to the military land ownership in Bermuda, many open spaces have been saved from urbanisation—a good example of this being the magnificent walking trails of the South Shore, with their breathtaking views and unspoiled coastlines. In addition, strict building codes have prevented non-Bermudian hodgepodge house designs or high-rise buildings interrupting the skylines.

Save Open Spaces and The National Trust are two non-governmental watchdog organisations whose main function is to protect the landmass. Developments such as the Paget Marsh conservation and boardwalk project are rays of hope in preserving this overcrowded archipelago. Another ongoing conservation project is Nonsuch Island in the East End, which is being sustained with Bermuda's original endemic plant life (for tours, check out the Bermuda Biological Station for Research at www.bbsr.edu or Tel. 297-1880).

At 36 acres, the Botanical Gardens in Paget is one of the biggest landscaped areas and includes a fragrant garden for the blind, as well as a cactus and succulent greenhouse. In the East End there's the popular Perfumery Gardens and Nature Trail, and for a tour of more natural habitats, visit Spittal Pond, Blue Hole Park, Walsingham Nature Reserve, or Ferry Point Park. Spittal Pond is Bermuda's largest nature reserve and lots of fun to explore (note: not suitable for taking strollers around; see "The East End," chapter 11). At the West End you mustn't miss a visit to the Heydon Trust grounds and its 17th-century chapel. And if you're up to it, one of the most picturesque jaunts is the walk from Mangrove Bay to Royal Naval Dockyard (about two miles). This walk hugs the coastline most of the way (see "The West End," chapter 10).

Apart from the parks and trust lands, there is the Railway Trail, the forts, and the tribe roads.

## RAILWAY TRAIL

The public path known as the Railway Trail spans Bermuda from St. George's to Somerset. Walkers and joggers escape congested roads to view royal-mauve seas, white-roofed houses, and volcanic rock walls festooned with vibrant foliage. The sweet scent of fragrant flowers permeates the air.

Locally known as "Old Rattle and Shake," the train threaded its way from the West End to the East End and ran from 1931 to 1948. Said to be the most expensive railway track (per mile) ever built, and the slowest to be built (2.5 miles a year), the railway when completed was 22.5 miles long and had 22 steel bridges, 34 timber trestles, and 44 scheduled stops. During the 17 years it ran, some 14 million passengers were carried 4 trillion passenger miles—not bad for a 21-square-mile nation!

Sadly, in 1948 the train was sold, lock, stock, and track, to British Guyana. Considering today's heavy road congestion, it was a decision with little foresight. Sometimes, though, when a door is banged shut, a window opens, and in 1984 someone had the excellent idea of utilising the old tracks as a scenic trail.

Look out for the Railway Trail signs that hug the coastlines and Middle Road. For detailed maps and facts of the Railway Trail, check out the Department of Tourism's first-rate guides, available from Bermuda's tourist information spots. And for guided bicycle tours of the Railway Trail, call **Fantasea Bermuda Ltd.** (Tel. 236-1300, www.fantasea.bm, info@fantasea.bm).

## TRIBE ROADS

In the "Bermuda's Fascinating History" section ("Culture and Heritage," chapter 5), you'll find the background to how tribe roads developed in the early 1600s. Below are listed some of the prettier roads for walking that have not been paved, many of which intersect the scenic Railway Trail. Unfortunately, due to some rather nasty incidents, women should not walk the trails alone.

**Tribe Roads Number 4A** and **4B,** Paget to South Shore: Start at Hodgson's Ferry Stop on Harbour Road. Follow along Chapel Road to Middle Road, onto Tribe Road 4A, coming out at Southcote Road. At the end of Southcote Road, cross South Road (opposite Horizons hotel), onto **Tribe Road 4B,** which is then only a short distance to beautiful Elbow Beach. Tribe Road 4A also intersects the Railway Trail—going east to Paget Marsh or west to Warwick Pond and beyond.

**Tribe Roads Number 2** and **3,** Middle Road, Southampton: Two short tribe roads, which lead to a picturesque part of the Railway Trail. Watch local fishing boats bobbing below in Jews Bay. Either turn left onto Tribe Road 3 or travel straight ahead, up the steps, onto Tribe Road 2 and follow the sign to Gibbs Hill Lighthouse. Enjoy afternoon tea at the Lighthouse Tea Rooms.

**Tribe Road Number 7,** Warwick: Starts at Middle Road just before St. Anthony's Roman Catholic Church and takes you all the way through to Warwick Long Bay, cutting through the Railway Trail. This tribe road is used by Spicelands Horseback Riding Centre (Tel. 238-8212) for horse trail rides. Carolyn's Lunch Wagon is not far away (summer only).

**Tribe Road Number 3,** Paget: This tribe road starts opposite the Paraquet Restaurant on the South Road, adjacent to Loughlands Guest House. Keep going until the end (be considerate of private property on part of the walk), where you may join the Railway Trail on Ord Road.

## GUIDED NATURE TOURS

**Open House and Garden Tour:** An event organised once a year by the Garden Club of Bermuda, this gives you the chance to see some of the beautiful historic homes and gardens of Bermuda. Tours are offered during April and May on Wednesday, 1 P.M. to 4 P.M.; admission: adults $15, children $6, season ticket $60 (includes all houses in each group and free shuttle service between properties). Tickets are on sale in all the houses. There is a special price for groups of six or more, or senior groups, by prior arrangement. Pick up their leaflet at the Visitors' Bureau or call the Garden Club (Tel. 236-2009).

**Nature Walk & Talk:** During the November to March season, the Tourism Department organises nature walks throughout Bermuda. Check the Visitors' Bureau for details (Tel. 295-1480).

**Bermuda Lectures and Tours** (Tel. 234-4082): Walking tours cover Bermuda's unique history.

**Picture Hunting:** If your idea of a shoot is clicking with a telephoto lens (Bermuda has no hunting), then for island-wide photographic/nature tours contact Tamell Simons at **Native Adventures** (Tel. 295-2957/235-6515). For maximum enjoyment, tours are limited to six people at a time.

# 4

# Getting Around Bermuda

Due to the small size of Bermuda, visitors are unable to hire cars. In fact, to keep the number of vehicles on the road down, residents are only allowed one car per house. For this reason, as a visitor you must rely on public transport, taxis, bicycles, scooters and mopeds, or, of course, that old standby, your feet. Going everywhere by cab is obviously going to be too expensive for the budget-conscious traveller; however, there are alternative, cheaper forms of transport that usually run to strict timetables.

When you first land in Bermuda you can either catch a cab or board the prearranged airport transportation buses (Bermuda Hosts, Tel. 293-1334). You can't catch a regular bus, as they do not accept luggage.

## Buses (Tel. 292-3854, www.bermudabuses.com)

Bermuda's trademark pink-and-blue buses are both clean and convenient. During the day, buses run every 15 minutes. Travelling by bus is a great way to tour Bermuda, sitting high up and peeking over walls and hedges. Bus drivers are under a lot of pressure to keep to the timetable and are usually very punctual. To avoid annoying the driver, have your ticket or exact change ready before boarding the bus. If you need to transfer to another bus, request the transfer ticket upon boarding and don't detain the driver longer than necessary.

Bermuda is divided into 14 bus zones; each zone is two miles in length. There are two types of fare: 3 zone (3 zones or less) and 14 zone (4 to 14 zones). Bus schedules, passes, tokens, and tickets are all available from the Central Terminal on Washington Street in Hamilton. Tokens and transportation passes are also available at the airport as well as many hotels and guesthouses and from the Visitors' Service Bureaus in Hamilton, St. George's, and Dockyard. In addition, tokens and ticket books (15 tickets) are available at many sub-post offices. To save valuable vacation time and money, it's a good idea to purchase your passes as soon as you possibly can.

For sightseeing tours on Bermuda's buses, for groups of 20 people or more, you can call Tel. 292-6704.

### BUS TIPS

- Dollar bills are not accepted on the bus; exact change only.
- Buses also accept ferry tokens as fare, but ferries don't accept bus tokens or bus tickets—confused?
- Buses run less frequently on Sundays and public holidays and after 5 P.M. daily, so check your bus schedule for times.
- The cheapest and most convenient way to travel is to buy a Public Transportation Pass—see "Transportation Fares" below for prices.
- Buses do not allow luggage on board.
- Buses going west do not always go all the way to Dockyard; so if that's your destination, check with the driver before boarding.
- To help you navigate your journey, bus-stop poles are pink and blue-striped. The poles with a pink stripe at the top indicate buses going in the Hamilton direction. Poles blue-striped at the top indicate an out-of-Hamilton direction.

## Ferries (Tel. 295-4506, www.seaexpress.bm)

Catamaran and regular ferry services leave Hamilton for Somerset, Dockyard, Paget, Warwick, and St. George's. Ferries to St. George's run in the summertime only but drop you right in the heart of the historical town. For just a few dollars, the ferry takes you off the highways and byways, providing a tranquil view of the waterways, tiny inlets, and coves around Bermuda. This is one of the most charming and popular ways to see Bermuda, and the ferry operators are very friendly and cooperative, making sure the ferries run on time. They also assist you on and off with scooters and bikes and will call you when your stop is approaching, if you ask nicely.

# Transportation Fares

### BUS FARES

- Cash (exact change)—Adults, 3 zone: $3; 14 zone: $4.50. Children ages five-16, all zones: $1.
- Token—3 zone: $2.50; 14 zone: $4
- Tickets (15 per book)—Adults, 3 zone: $16; 14 zone: $25.50. Children, all zones: $7.
- Children under five—Free
- Bermudian seniors—Free
- Fare Savings—If you buy a book of 15 adult bus tickets (14 zone), instead of paying cash on the bus, you will save a total of $42. For even more savings buy a bus or ferry pass (see below).

### FERRY FARES

- Hamilton-Somerset-Dockyard Ferry—$4 one way (scooters an extra $4)
- Hamilton-Paget-Warwick Ferry—$2.50 one way
- Dockyard-St. George's Ferry (April to November only, five days a week)—$4 one way
- 15 tokens—Adults: $16. Children: $7.
- Children ages five-16—$1
- Children under five—Free
- Bermudian seniors—Free

### BUS AND FERRY PASSES (ALL ZONES)

- One-day pass—Adults: $11. Children ages five-15: $6.
- Three-day pass—Adults: $23. Children ages five-16: $11.
- Seven-day pass—Adults: $36. Children: $16.
- One calendar month's pass—$45
- Three-month pass—$120
- Children under five—Free

## Scooter and Moped Rentals

One way of discovering places off the beaten track is to rent a scooter or moped. Riding a scooter allows more flexibility and can be very pleasant and a lot of fun. However, accidents are a frequent occurrence (there are on average 400 tourists involved in scooter accidents a year, some serious). There are too many blind, narrow bends and speeding local bikers who swerve dangerously in and out of the traffic. It seems today nobody drives at the speed limit, and to compound the problem there is a lot of overtaking on blind corners. Due to the extremely high number of accidents on the roads, extreme caution should be taken and careful thought given to renting this form of transport.

If you *do* decide to rent a scooter, before you set out onto the roads make yourself familiar with the controls, especially the brakes. After a practise run, if you are too wobbly and unsure, change your mind about scooter rental; it could save your vacation enjoyment, and maybe your life.

- Driving is on the left-hand side, and the speed limit is 20 mph (35 kmh) and 15 mph in city limits, although generally vehicles drive somewhat faster.
- Helmets are compulsory and should never be worn with the strap unbuckled.
- Roundabouts (traffic islands) are designed to keep the traffic flowing, so it is important not to stop in the middle of one. The rules are not the same as for a four-way stop sign, as some American drivers seem to believe—it is not first come, first goes. On approaching a roundabout, always yield to traffic approaching from the right.
- If you are driving too slowly, you will hold up the rest of the traffic, so pull over every now and then to let others pass, especially in early-morning and evening rush hours—the locals will thank you for it. Consider avoiding these times altogether.
- One Bermudian tradition is to honk horns at passing friends on the street or at other vehicles, by way of a greeting. This can be distracting for novice riders.
- Bear in mind that if you do not lock your bike and it is stolen, some cycle liveries charge for reimbursement.

There are many scooter liveries dotted around Bermuda, and they are usually of similar price. Your guest accommodation will probably be only too glad to make rental arrangements. At the time of writing, one week's rental at **Eve's Cycle Livery** (Tel. 236-6247, evecycles@logic.bm) is $177 plus $15 insurance, for a double-seated scooter. They also can arrange group discounts of between 10 and 20 percent and provide a complimentary pick-up service. For a full list of liveries, check under "Cycles" in the Yellow Pages of the Bermuda Telephone Directory. From November to March, participating liveries and boat-tour operators offer 10-20 percent off their seasonal rates.

## SCOOTER TIPS

- Avoid driving in the rain. If a sudden downpour occurs, pull over at a bus shelter and wait for it to pass.
- Keep children's legs and feet safe and guard against muffler burn on legs. Better yet, don't ride with children.
- Ladies, tuck those long skirts under you, so they don't get caught up in the back wheel. Men, don't go topless on a scooter. First, it's an offence in Bermuda, and second, your pink skin will have no protection from road abrasions (known as road rash in Bermuda) if you fall.
- Some sections of the Railway Trail allow scooters. For example, the trail between Somerset (second turning after Somerset Bridge) and Cavello Bay is exceptionally scenic—note the beautiful wooden bridges overhead.
- Tracey Caswell has some practical tips for bike riders in her best-selling book *Tea with Tracey—The Woman's Survival Guide to Bermuda.* "Be wary of summer touring and 'moped thighs.' Bike-induced breezes will keep you cool, but the tops of your legs will scream 'SUNBURN' that night." She also advises: "Remember, if you leave your helmet with your bike, turn it top side up! Sudden showers happen often." To prevent theft, it is a good idea to lock your helmet inside your scooter helmet compartment.

## Bicycles

To differentiate between scooters and bicycles, Bermudians call bicycles "push bikes" and call scooters "bikes" or "cycles." Bicycling around Bermuda is a pleasant way of getting about, especially on the Railway Trail. The main roads are at times heavy with traffic, making cycling especially difficult with children. For bicycle rental, **Eve's Cycle Bike Shop,** 6 Seabright Avenue, Devonshire (Tel. 236-4491), charges $110 a week or $25 a day.

The literature for **Fantasea** guided bicycle tours (Tel. 236-1300, info@fantasea.bm, www.fantasea.bm) states, "Starts with a short boat ride, disembark at the Railway Trail where a tour guide and a 21-speed mountain bike with helmet awaits you. Relaxed pace, 3-hour tour, stopping at points of interest, and ending with a cool-down swim; then it's back on the cruise boat to round off an interesting day. Bring towel and wear swimsuit under your outfit."

**Bicycle Tip:** With hardly any traffic and flat roads, riding around the Royal Naval Dockyard at Bermuda's western tip is a pleasure. You can take your bicycle on the Somerset/Dockyard ferry.

## Taxis

The most frequently asked question for cab drivers is, "Why is the sea so blue in Bermuda?" Answer: Because the sand is pale pink and there is very little sediment (or pollution) in the clear ocean.

Taxi drivers take great pride in their cabs (don't slam the door) and are generally excellent ambassadors for Bermuda. The cabs with a tiny blue flag on them signify specially trained tour guides. Cabs are expensive: they cost $5 for the first mile and $1.20 for each additional mile. Rates escalate after midnight and cabs can be difficult to procure, particularly in St. George's or when it is raining.

For taxicabs call 295-4141. For minibuses and cabs in Somerset call 234-2344. St. George's minibus: 297-8199. Wheelchair taxi services: 235-2699 or cell 234-7003. For more taxi company numbers check the Yellow Pages under "Taxi Services."

## Nontrack Train (Tel. 236-5972)

The Bermuda Train on wheels seats 40 passengers and transports visitors around the West End's Royal Naval Dockyard during April to November and also the city centre for tours of Hamilton. Stops include the National Gallery at City Hall, Bermuda Underwater Exploration Institute, and the Cathedral on Church Street. This service is now run primarily for the cruise-ship passengers, but there are some seats for other visitors. The best thing to do is call the above number to find out.

## Horse-and-Carriage Rides

Cars didn't arrive in Bermuda until after the Second World War. Prior to then, the quiet of the sleepy roads was broken only by the clip-clop of a horse and carriage, or people travelled by bicycle or the short-lived train service. Gone forever are those halcyon days. As Mark Twain wrote, Bermuda was a great place for a jaded man to loaf in. Twain lived here and dreaded the idea of the arrival of the combustion engine, slicing through the peace as surely as a snake through paradise. Apparently, just before cars were made legal, a depression descended upon the people, as they instinctively knew that an age was ending forever. With today's road congestion and impatient drivers, many people feel there is no place for horses in Hamilton city anymore.

If you like, you can tour the city and back roads of Hamilton in a carriage: board on Front Street. The nicest rides (both for you and your horse) are in the cool of the evening.

**Shilo Ranch** (Tel. 236-6678), **Tucker's Carriages & Stables** (Tel. 236-7059), and **Terceira's Stables** (Tel. 236-3014) are three stables worth checking out.

# 5

# Culture and Heritage

## Bermuda's Fascinating History

Imagine a tiny group of islands, somewhere in the middle of the Atlantic Ocean, where not a single dwelling stands or inhabitant lives, where the pink beaches are void of footprints, the forests intact. Here the coves are free of hotels, the harbours free of ships, and only the seagulls circling the air break the dead silence. Such a nirvana did exist, and until the 1500s no human eyes had cast a greedy glance upon her shores.

This then is the start to Bermuda's history, a clean sheet in the evolution of a place so unspoilt that the fishes were unafraid of man, having never been plucked from the sparkling waters of the ocean. Bermuda was then a place unsullied by man's selfish quests.

Bermuda's 400-year history is fascinating, with many links to both the New World and the Old. And because of America's proximity, and Bermuda's early British-colony status, these two countries have played a major part in colouring Bermuda's heritage and traditions. Slavery too has been a major player in Bermuda's culture and history.

Peppered throughout this guidebook you will find vignettes of historical facts, especially in the references to historical buildings and the chapter on the old colonial town of St. George's in the East End. Bermuda is also a world-class site for fortifications and boasts some of the oldest and most interesting forts to be found anywhere.

If you are a history buff, or just like roaming around old towns, then St. George's is the place for you. The first buildings in St. George's were wooden and have not survived, but many of the first stone ones have. Unlike Williamsburg in the U.S., St. George's is not reconstructed but is a living history town much unchanged over the 400 years since settlement.

St. George's was the first town and capital of Bermuda, but in 1815, much to the chagrin of the people of St. George's, Hamilton became the new capital—due to its bigger harbour and central location. It was a blessing in disguise; the old town never recovered and was unable to modernise, therefore saving all of its old history for generations to come.

Bermuda's history is steeped in shipwrecks, pirates, and profiteers, and its accidental discovery as an inhabitable archipelago inspired its motto, *Quo Fata Ferunt* (whither the fates do carry us). But let us start at the beginning. . . .

## GEOLOGICAL BEGINNINGS

Bermuda was formed over 100 million years ago from a volcano. Don't worry, though; that volcano is long extinct. Six thousand years ago, the island was 300 square miles in landmass, but over the centuries the sea level rose to leave a fish-hook-shaped group of islands resting on a tabletop of rock just 21 square miles in area.

Gradually the sandy beaches were formed, but how did they become pink? They are created from the skeletons of tiny single-celled animals called red forams that live under the coral reef. When the red foram dies, its crimson skeleton mixes with white sand and broken seashells, creating a pink tinge. This pink glow is most prominent at sunset. When you come to Bermuda, take some sand in your hand and separate it with your fingers. You'll see for yourself the different blends and colours of shell.

## WHAT'S IN A NAME?

Bermuda was originally named after the Spanish explorer Juan de Bermudez, who sighted the isles around 1503 from his ship, *La Garza* (Spanish for "the Heron").

Mainly due to the treacherous coral reef that skirts the isles, where many a passing ship has floundered, Bermuda gained the reputation as a place to be avoided. And because of the haunting sounds of the cahow birds circling the shores, Bermuda became fearfully known as **Devils Isles.**

In the early 1600s, England was in the process of colonizing the Americas. Adventurers often formed investment companies and these businesses often saw the settlement of a country purely in financial terms. Just such an investment company in England, the Virginia Company, was in the process of colonizing Jamestown, Virginia. But in 1609, the news coming out of Jamestown was critical—they needed urgent supplies or the colonizers would perish. A fleet of ships, under the command of Sir George Somers, set out on a quest to help the people of Jamestown.

Some of the ships made it to Jamestown, and what they found there was devastation, as William Strachey wrote in 1610:

> Viewing the fort, we found the palisades torn down, the ports open, the gates off the hinges, and the empty houses (which owners had taken from them) rent up and burnt, rather than the dwellers would step into the woods, a stone's cast off from them, to fetch other firewood. And it is true, the Indians killed as fast without, if our men stirred but beyond the bounds of their blockhouse.

One ship didn't make it to Virginia. For three days and three nights, the flagship, the *Sea Venture,* was caught in a terrible hurricane. In a 1610 letter, which Shakespeare later read and based his last play *The Tempest* on, Strachey describes the storm as "roaring and beat[ing] all light from heaven; which like a hell of darkness turned black upon us . . . the sea swelled above the clouds, which gave battle unto heaven."

On Friday, July 28, 1609, the *Sea Venture* eventually became grounded off the eastern coast of Bermuda, stuck upright between two reefs. All 150 people aboard were thankfully able to come ashore, including Sir George Somers, the head of the Virginia Company.

The survivors stayed in Bermuda for nearly a year, building two ships, the *Deliverance* and *Patience,* out of indigenous cedar trees and the wreck of the *Sea Venture,* before once again setting sail for their original destination, Virginia. Initially, these lucky shipwreck survivors named Bermuda **"Virginiola,"** referring to their dearly departed Queen Elizabeth I ("The Virgin Queen").

This incredible adventure of survival ultimately led to the English colonisation of Bermuda in 1612, after the Virginia Company had sold Bermuda to a new collective group of colonisers—The Bermuda Company—for the ridiculous sum of £2,000, a bargain by any day's standards. And so, in honour of Sir George Somers, the island became **Somers Isles** (sometimes spelled "Summers," in reference to the balmy climate), before eventually reverting to its original name—**Bermuda.**

## POCAHONTAS

While the survivors toiled on their rescue ships, two babies were born: a girl, who was aptly named Bermuda, and a boy, Bermudas. The baby girl was the daughter of a man named John Rolfe, though, sadly, both wife and baby died.

Later, when he moved to Virginia, John Rolfe married native Indian princess Pocahontas—whom, you may have heard, was famous for saving John Smith and other starving settlers when she was 12 years old. Hollywood movies about Pocahontas and John Smith never mention the Bermuda connection, maybe because the ending is so sad.

"It is Pocahontas," Rolfe wrote (according to the Association for the Preservation of Virginia Antiquities), "to whom my hearty and best thoughts are, and have been a long time so entangled, and enthralled in so intricate a labyrinth that I [could not] unwind myself thereout." The wedding took place in the spring of 1614, in Virginia. It resulted in peace with the Native Americans long enough for the settlers to develop and expand their colony and plant themselves permanently in the newly inhabited Jamestown.

In 1613, John Rolfe introduced tobacco, which became the main economic support of Jamestown. And he took Pocahontas to England to become a fine English lady, but, unfortunately, she too died seven months later, leaving a baby son.

## SIR GEORGE SOMERS

Sir George Somers, who had been knighted by King James and was known as "a lamb on shore but a lion at sea," had tried to settle down to a landlubber's life in England and was even made mayor of Lyme Regis in Dorset (today twinned with St. George's), but the lure of the sea beckoned him back.

Now, on this latest seafaring mission to Virginia, his troubles knew no bounds. Out of his fleet of nine ships, his own ship was stuck in Bermuda, one had gone down with all hands onboard, another had only 10 men left out of 70, and yet another ship had the plague onboard. Only the surviving five ships made it to Virginia to aid the colonists there.

But in the spring of 1610, Sir George was unaware of the fate of the rest of his fleet. Although he had fallen in love with Bermuda, he concentrated on building not one but two ships, to take the survivors of the *Sea Venture* on to Virginia.

By the end of the first month in Bermuda, before building the two ships, the people had built a rough longboat, to see if a quick rescue could be attained. Eight men set off to find help but were never heard of again. A watch was organised to look out for their return, and they burnt fires on the hills, but by autumn they had given up all hope of seeing them again.

When Sir George finally arrived in Virginia and found the colonists starving, he at once turned around to return to Bermuda to collect more provisions. He never made the journey back to Virginia, as he died of a heart attack while in Bermuda. His nephew, Matthew, eager to inherit Sir George's money, set sail at once for England, leaving Somers' heart in Bermuda and taking the body with him for evidence of his death. Today, in Somers Garden in St. George's, a tomb marks the spot where his heart was buried.

## THE COLONIZATION OF BERMUDA

Tales of Sir George's amazing journey, and of how wonderful Bermuda was, filtered their way around London's high society. Consequently, a new Bermuda Company was formed and by the spring of 1612, the first 60 settlers of Bermuda set sail on the *Plough*.

The Bermuda Company ran Bermuda from England for nearly 70 years in return for Bermuda's first currencies: pearls, oil, tobacco, and a product from whales, used in the manufacture of perfume, called ambergris. Christopher Carter (one of the original men from the *Sea Venture* who had been left on the empty island with two other men, for two years) thought better of going ahead with a plot to hide some valuable ambergris he had found. In return for the ambergris, the Bermuda Company rewarded Carter with Cooper's Island. (Carter chose this particular island because he thought there was some Spanish treasure buried on it.)

Christopher Carter's life ended dramatically in 1623. He was partying onboard a visiting ship, the *Sea Flower*, when an explosion blew the vessel to smithereens. Carter's house still stands on Cooper's Island and is now a museum (Carter House, Tel. 297-1642), but, alas, the Spanish treasure was never found.

## THE EARLY DAYS

Since 1612 to this day, there has been an English governor of Bermuda, in the beginning to purely govern the people, and in more recent times, as an English figurehead. Each governor has enhanced Bermuda and brought his own individuality. The very first governor, Richard Moore, was a carpenter, a useful trade in a new colony. The second governor, Daniel Tucker, a sea captain, found the early settlers lazy, so he made the morning rounds beating a drum to wake everyone up. He also had a man hanged for stealing cheese, so life was tough.

Other governors left their mark, such as Samuel Day, who built the first governor's house in 1698 (now the Globe Hotel, Rogues and Runners museum, Tel. 297-1423), and Henry Pullein, a pirate who fooled the English government into thinking he was knowledgeable enough to be governor. Maybe the colony wasn't growing fast enough, because in 1738, Gov.

Alured Popple brought in a one-shilling tax on bachelors, in order to promote matrimony.

Reid Street in Hamilton is named after the governor who finally commissioned the building of Gibbs Hill Lighthouse in 1846, to help prevent any more ships foundering on the shores. (There are about 350 wrecks dotted around the reef.) You can visit the lighthouse in Southampton, open daily, 9 A.M.–5 P.M. (Tel. 238-0524), and a climb to the top will be rewarded with one of Bermuda's best panoramic views.

## HOG MONEY

The first coinage minted for Bermuda was made from 1616 to 1619 and was called "hog money." On one side the coins were decorated with a hog, to commemorate their existence found by the first settlers, and on the reverse was a picture of the *Sea Venture*. The hogs were a good source of food and easy to catch, so they soon disappeared. Hog money has been found on Bermuda's Castle Island and is extremely valuable. When ground is broken in Bermuda for the construction of buildings, a search for old bottles and coins is always first on the list. (Hey, they may just pay for the mortgage.)

## DIVIDING THE LAND

In 1616, Richard Norwood surveyed the land and divided it into shares. The members of the Bermuda Company owned the shares, and their names were used for the parishes, although the village of Somerset is named after Sir George Somers ("Somers Seat"), because of his fondness for that area. Southampton Parish was named after the third earl of Southampton (Henry Wriothesley), William Shakespeare's friend and patron.

The parishes were once called "tribes," derived from the old Latin term *tribus*, meaning division of land.

Norwood divided Bermuda into shares of 25 acres each, which ran vertically from shore to shore. A tribe constituted a landmass of 50 shares and was given a tribe name. Dividing the tribes were straight paths used by the general public and called tribe roads. In 1913, a Tribe Road Commission was appointed, and this led to a law that protected the 31 tribe roads left. Today, Warwick has seven tribe roads, Devonshire four, and Pembroke two. Paget, Southampton, and Sandys have six each. St. George's, Hamilton Parish, and Smith's have lost their tribe roads. Some of the prettier tribe roads intersect the old Railway Trail and are unpaved and worth walking. You will find details of walking the tribe roads in the "Nature Trails, Wildlife, Flora, and Fauna" section of chapter 3, "Once You're Here."

## SLAVERY

Unfortunately, the third governor, another ship's captain, Nathaniel Butler, introduced slavery into Bermuda. Slavery existed in Bermuda from 1616 to 1834. Many Bermudian slaves had trades, while others were house servants or worked in the fields. And many slaves worked side by side with the English colonists.

Slaves were also used in the colonisation of the Turks and Caicos Islands, where, every year for a century, men from Bermuda would go for the salt raking. Salt raking was carried out under harsh conditions, and the slaves spent long hours in the searing heat, boils festering to the bone from long hours standing in the salt water.

One Bermudian slave, Mary Prince, played a major role in the abolition of slavery. Her dramatic account of life as a slave, as told in Susanna Moodie's book *The History of Mary Prince* (1831), fostered an understanding of the hardships and atrocities suffered by slaves. Bermuda now has a museum in St. George's dedicated to black history—the Heritage Museum (Tel. 297-4126). Inside the museum you will read details of Bermuda's own *Amistad* (the U.S. ship whose slaves mutinied and then were set free after a lengthy court fight, as portrayed in Steven Spielberg's movie). Four years prior to the *Amistad* controversy, the American slave vessel *Enterprise* was thrown by a storm into the safe harbours of Hamilton. Slavery had been abolished in Bermuda by that time, so it was deemed that since the slaves were here, then they could be set free. A court case ensued, and the slaves—many of them children who had been snatched from their parents—were pronounced free to live in Bermuda.

Bermuda's black Friendly Societies and Lodges assisted the freed American slaves, and an exhibit dedicated to them is also housed in the Heritage Museum. These lodges also gave spiritual and financial support during the difficult years following emancipation.

On August 1, 1834, slavery was abolished and 4,000 slaves were liberated in Bermuda. Today, Bermuda celebrates August 1 every year with a public holiday and Cup Match cricket game between the West End and the East End.

## SEGREGATION

Up until 1959, tourists and residents were segregated. It seems amazing now, but black visitors had to stay in separate hotels. There was a great fuss at one of the large hotels when a black couple tried to check in. The couple refused to move, so after much discussion, they were allowed to stay. The unfortunate couple had to eat their meals in their rooms, and they weren't allowed to swim in the pool!

All that changed with a peacefully organised boycott of the movie theatres in 1959. A group of 20 or so ordinary but frustrated black citizens, after returning home from college in countries where segregation had been abolished, banded together and formed a secret organisation called the Progressive Group. In those days, anyone not toeing the line could be ruined economically by the powers that be; thus the need for absolute secrecy. It was a moment to be proud of in the history of Bermuda's suffrage when, without any trouble or riots, a peaceful demonstration by over 1,000 people outside the Island Theatre led to Bermuda's desegregation and on to further rights of the individual to sit anywhere in hotels and restaurants without fear of prosecution.

Also around that time a visiting famous actor, Hurd Hatfield (*The Picture of Dorian Gray*), refused to go on stage when he heard the audience would be segregated. It caused a huge fuss in England, and a governor was sent to help integrate Bermuda's people. The governor's wife did her part by inviting every black person she met to important functions.

### WITCHES AND WARLOCKS

Another dark period in the history of Bermuda was during the fourth governor's administration in 1642. The Scottish who arrived in Bermuda "educated" the local people about the witch scares of Europe, and Gov. Josias Forster encouraged these superstitions.

An animal suddenly sick, butter unable to be churned, babies dying at childbirth, a strange look here, or a coincidence there were all reasons a neighbour would use to accuse another of dealing with the devil and sorcery. The little colony became gripped in a hysterical witch hunt, and the persecution of so-called witches and warlocks would last for 46 years, much longer than the Salem trials in America.

In all, there were 16 witch and six warlock trials. Out of that number, six were found guilty (after enduring ducking trials and body searches for devil's marks). Of those, five were hanged, and a young woman was reprieved at the last minute because she was pregnant.

In her book, *Bermuda and the Supernatural,* Terry Tucker tells of the highly respected first land surveyor, Richard Norwood, and his daughter, Anne, who was tried for witchcraft in 1651. Although found not guilty, Anne was "bound over to be of good behaviour," then released in return for 200 pounds of tobacco.

In 1730, several years after the trials had ceased, a servant named Sally Bassett was burned at the stake for poisoning her employers, and not for witchcraft, as people like to believe. Even today, the elderly in Bermuda still call a hot day a real "Sally Bassett."

## EARLY PARLIAMENT

The new parliament first met in St. Peter's Church but soon moved to Bermuda's first stone structure, the State House in St. George's. The State House still stands and can be viewed Wednesdays between 10 A.M. and 4 P.M.

Initially, gunpowder was stored at the State House but was moved for safety and security reasons. In hindsight, this decision might have been a mistake, because in 1775 it was stolen in the dead of night from the gunpowder magazine near Governor Bruere's house. In those days, gunpowder was a very precious commodity, so much so that a very important letter from George Washington was sent to the people of Bermuda. This historic letter requested that supplies of gunpowder be sent to America, which was in urgent need of ammunition at the beginning of the War of Independence (1775-83). Although the Bermuda government refused him the gunpowder, it found its way into American hands through a group of sympathetic Bermudians in return for much-needed grain for the island. The letter from George Washington hangs on the wall of the Historical Society Museum in Queen Street, Hamilton (Tel. 295-2487).

## AMERICAN CIVIL WAR

In 1861, Queen Victoria declared that Britain would remain neutral during the American Civil War; however, that did not stop Bermuda from cashing in on the dozens of visiting Confederate ships needing carpenters, sailmakers, and all manner of ship repairs. Hamilton prospered so much that the farms were abandoned by labourers, who could earn several times their normal wages by working in the ports.

A display cabinet in the "Rogues and Runners Exhibit" at the National Trust Museum (Globe Hotel, built circa 1698) in St. George's contains Confederate memorabilia left over from the Civil War. According to the museum, Bermuda's sympathies were with the South during this war, and St. George's played a significant and prosperous role as a blockade-running, gunrunning port. During this era, sometimes as many as 150 ships could be seen there at one time, and many local fortunes were made running supplies to Charleston and Wilmington.

Also at that time, an attempt to foil the North was made by Dr. Joseph Blackburn, a Southerner, who was arrested by the authorities and jailed for the devilish plan of transporting infected clothing from yellow fever victims in Bermuda in the hope that he could spread this deadly disease through the Union cities.

Another American, W. R. Higginbotham, was one of Bermuda's unsung heroes. Much to the displeasure of the U.S. Congress, Bermuda aided the

Confederate blockade runners. The U.S. nearly initiated a trade embargo against Bermuda but Higginbotham persuaded them to drop this proposed bill, therefore staving off a possible nasty international incident.

After the North won, Bermuda's economy was stalled for some time, until later on when the agricultural market was successfully cultivated and even later, when tourism was founded.

## BERMUDA: THE GIBRALTAR OF THE WEST

From the very beginning of Bermuda's colonisation, it was apparent that Bermudians would have to protect their shores from invasion, firstly from Spain and later on from the Americas. At every possible entry into Bermuda, a garrison was constructed. Bermuda had such a strong ring of fortifications that no one ever successfully invaded. Early on, the Spanish tried to invade Bermuda but were fired upon from Castle Island Fort (its remains are still evident). This frightened the Spanish off, which was fortunate, as the Bermuda colonists had only one shot remaining in their arsenal.

Fortunes were made by Bermudians profiteering and pirating at every opportunity. In the 1700s, during the Spanish and French wars, King William III issued a "proclamation for the apprehension of pirates that do infest the seas." During America's War of Independence (1775-83), the Canadian War (1812), and the American Civil War (1861-65), Bermuda's fast ships were used for blockade running. And when Bermudians weren't profiteering from warships, much-needed supplies were obtained by looting ships wrecked off the coast. These wrecks were called "turtles in the net."

With the loss of the Americas after the War of Independence in 1783, Britain needed to have a strategic base between Canada and England, and Bermuda was in the ideal location. An eight-year survey was carried out, culminating in the purchase of Ireland Island at the western end of Bermuda and the construction of the Royal Naval Dockyard. Bermuda became the guardian of the sea, continuing England's 400-year reputation for having the finest navy in the world.

Work commenced on Dockyard in 1809, but progress was slow and laborious. To speed things up, convict ships from England were brought to Dockyard from 1826 to 1863. In all, 9,000 men came—some for minor offences such as stealing bread—living in atrocious conditions, many of them dying of yellow fever, which swept through Bermuda many times from the 17th to the 19th centuries. The death toll and harsh conditions led eventually to convict ships being abolished by the English Houses of Parliament, but not before 2,000 men had died building Dockyard, "the

Gibraltar of the West." In recent times, local divers have skimmed from the seabed beautiful carvings the convicts had created with their own hands. This original collection has been valued at around $1,000,000.

By the time World War II came around, America and Britain were old friends. America needed somewhere to protect its own shores and in 1941 secured land in Bermuda for the construction of an air force base at St. David's. An airfield was built and manned that gave the people of Bermuda a free jump-start to the tourist trade after the war. But by the end of the Cold War, there was not the same need for overseas bases, and so in 1995 the American, Canadian, and British bases were wound down and eventually closed, taking with them $50 million a year in Bermuda's revenue. The American airfield was handed over to Bermuda and the Canadian base is now a tourist spot.

Today, the Royal Naval Dockyard is a thriving tourist area and marina with shops, restaurants, art centre, and movie theatre. I wonder what those convicts would think of that?

## SALT, CEDAR, AND SAILORS

Bermuda has been innovative and entrepreneurial throughout the ages. As mentioned before, early life was hard and sometimes hungry. A ship washed upon the shores was fair game for a struggling people.

Bermuda first bartered in whale oil and tobacco leaves; later, fresh produce was shipped to the colder climates of North America. Onions were particularly famous for their crisp and sweet quality—that is, until refrigeration arrived, and also when a farmer in Texas named his farm Bermuda and started selling his own onions as "Bermuda" onions!

During the late 1800s Bermuda exported millions of fragrant Easter lilies, and to this day a bunch is still sent every Easter to the queen in England.

Bermuda was also famous for shipbuilding, and the Bermuda sloop was the fastest ship in the world.

Another export that was very successful for many years was hats made out of palmetto palm-tree fronds. A descendant of Christopher Carter from the *Sea Venture*, Martha Hayward, invented a hat that became popular with Queen Anne in 1702, and these trees were stripped bare to accommodate the demand. Another use of the palmetto was an alcoholic drink called "Bibbey." There were so many drunks around that a law had to be passed banning Bibbey, and a cage was built to house drunkards.

Out at sea, the Bermuda flag was known as the "sawed-stone jack" because of the Bermuda limestone the ships carried with them for the construction of houses. (When first dug from the ground, limestone is soft and can be sawed easily.) To this day, you can see Bermuda stone houses in the Turks and Caicos Islands. Every season during the 1700s the men left Bermuda for the salt raking, but by 1801 the Bahamas had claimed Turks and Caicos for their own. Bermuda had tried salt production at home (hence the name Salt Kettle Harbour in Paget Parish), but the process was found to be too time-consuming.

As well as limestone, cedar was a prominent feature in everyday life, and many products were carved out of these indigenous trees. Unfortunately, a cedar blight hit the island in the 1940s and wiped out nearly all the trees.

### SHE WORKS HARD FOR A LIVING . . .

Women have played a prominent role in Bermuda's development, although their accomplishments weren't always acknowledged by the menfolk. While the men were away at sea, it was the women who saw to the day-to-day running of the island, both at home and on the farms. Life was tough, and the women had to fight for the vote for many years. For centuries, only landowners had the right to vote, and women who owned land had to pass their vote to hubby. Women suffragettes fought long and hard to be granted rights to education and the vote, even resorting to withholding their parish taxes in protest. In a landmark case in 1932, the courts seized and auctioned off a group of suffragettes' furniture, but these enterprising women bid it back for each other.

Today, women hold many prominent positions in government and business. Many government ministers are women, and so is 54 percent of the workforce. And every Bermudian boy knows that Mama rules the roost at home.

### TOURISM

At the end of the 1800s, the tourist industry made a tentative beginning. Princess Louise, the daughter of Queen Victoria, found Bermuda to her taste, especially as she was living in the frigid winters of Canada with her husband, the governor-general. As royal tastes do, her arrival started a trend, and soon hotels and guesthouses began to pop up; one was named "The Princess" in her honour and is still there today (The Hamilton Princess).

Another famous visitor to Bermuda was Mark Twain, who made Bermuda his second home. He thought Bermuda was paradise and helped prevent cars from arriving on the island. Cars first appeared here as late as 1946. Twain spent his last summer in Bermuda, as did the Beatle John Lennon, accompanied by his son Sean, in 1980. The famous playwright Eugene O'Neil, whose daughter was born here and later married Charlie Chaplin, liked Bermuda so much that he rented a house. Modern-day famous residents include Michael Douglas, who has a Bermudian mother. Michael and his famous wife, Catherine Zeta Jones, are frequent visitors to Bermuda, where they own a house and he is a partner of the Ariel Sands Club in Devonshire.

Tourism plays a very important role in Bermuda today, but Bermuda also has a thriving business community where many offshore companies have set up shop to take advantage of her tax-friendly offshore status, bringing with them all the benefits of employment, along with the millions of dollars they pour into the community. Read all about Bermuda's business practices in chapter 7, "The Business Traveller."

The future of Bermuda is an unknown commodity, but from as far back as 1620, careful and considerate legislation has been enacted to protect the natural resources of this precious island. While other countries are grappling with sustainable development in the new millennium, Bermuda's forward-thinking government of the 1600s strictly regulated poaching, polluting, tree felling, overfishing, and turtle and bird protection. The result shows today in Bermuda's natural beauty, pollution-free waters, and unspoilt reefs.

### HERITAGE PASSPORT

Dotted around Bermuda are Tourist Boxes with handy-sized flyers with details on attractions and eateries. This is where you can pick up the free Bermuda "Heritage Passport" for discounts on six cultural attractions: Bermuda Underwater Exploration Institute, Fort St. Catherine, the National Trust, the Maritime Museum, the Aquarium, and the National Gallery.

## Local Words and Phrases

Apart from a few teenagers who seem to have their own language these days, you will not have any trouble understanding the people of Bermuda. Bermudians speak with a very nice accent, a mix of English, American, and a style all its own. Sometimes the older generation speaks an old English patois. "D" replaces "j" ("Bermujian"), "v" replaces "w" ("velcome"), and "v" is switched with "w" ("wapour"). "Um um" is used as a pause in a sentence, much like "err." (There's even a comedy show based on the funny happenings in politics and local goings-on called "Not the Um Um Show.")

Even though Bermuda has an English background, because America is so close, and due to the influence of TV and movies and Bermudians attending U.S. schools and colleges, Bermudians say "cookies" for biscuits, "garbage" for rubbish, and "vacation" for holiday. And the dollar is the currency of choice, not the pound sterling, as it once was. However, as in the U.K., "soccer" is referred to as "football," driving is on the left, and education is based on the English system, with all children wearing full school uniforms. Nevertheless, the influence of American education is great, and the middle-school system has now been adopted.

Afternoon tea is still a tradition in the hotels and tearooms, but due to the high cost of living, the average Bermudian holds down more than one job and hasn't time for these quaint traditions. It may be a slow pace of life for the visitor, but it isn't for local people, with rents costing anywhere from $3,000 per month to $18,000 for a two- or three-bedroom house. And to purchase a three-bedroom house costs about $500,000 and upwards.

As a visitor you'll probably be warned about "road rash." No, it's not some strange disease but skin abrasions from a scooter accident that can be extremely painful. The hospital will tell you to keep it dry, but Bermudians will advise you to jump into the sea immediately.

Here are some words and phrases you should avoid using in Bermuda, as they may offend: "Native/s" (instead of "Bermudians"), "Caribbean" (referring to the island being located there), "What?" (instead of "Pardon"), and "This is the way we do it" (as in, know-it-all).

Colloquial sayings can confuse, so here is a list of a few sayings you may be puzzled over.

1. "Where you to?" means "Where are you staying?" or "Where do you live?"

2. "Up the Country" means Somerset and the West End of Bermuda. ("Down the Country" means St. George's and the East End of Bermuda. "You live all the way up de Country?")

3. "Thank you very much" means "I'm in full agreement with your comments."

4. "Bermuda Time" means "If it starts at two, then that's the time to set out." (Rushing shortens your life anyway.)

5. "In'it?" means "Isn't it" (usually placed after a statement, not a question: "She's tall, in'it").

6. "Longtail" means single lady tourist.

7. "Blinds" means house shutters or sunglasses.

8. "Hey bye" means hello there. ("Bye" means boy, but girls often say this to each other too.)

9. "Ace boy/girl" means good friend. "He's my ace boy."

10. "Bredrin" (as in brethren) means good friend (usually male).

11. "Hot" means drunk. ("Half-hot" means getting there.)

12. "Micein" means daydreaming.

13. "Gribble" means in a bad mood.

14. "Tank rain" means a good pour-down that will fill your water tank. The rain pours onto the white roofs and is channelled into drains and

down to underground tanks. As long as your roof and tank are clean, the water is safe to drink, and great for hair-washing.

15. "Girt" means big.

16. "Onion" means one who was born Bermudian. ("He's a real onion.") Bermuda was once famous for exporting onions.

17. "Back o'Town" means the nontourist area behind Hamilton.

18. "Title" means surname.

19. "Expat" means expatriate, or "guest worker" (foreigner working in Bermuda on work permit).

20. "From away" means from overseas, usually America. ("I got that from away" or "He's from away." Bermudians are very well travelled and love to go shopping.)

21. "Rock Fever" means a feeling of being hemmed in (a bit like cabin fever). Cure: get off the island for a while.

## Festivals, Ceremonies, and Major Events

### BERMUDA FESTIVAL—JANUARY/FEBRUARY

Running January and February, the Bermuda Festival presents several international performing artists showcasing classical productions of dance and theatre. Some of these productions are staged in the Ruth Seaton James Auditorium, a state-of-the-art theatre located in the CedarBridge High School, Prospect, Devonshire. Mostly, though, productions are staged at Hamilton's City Hall.

Brochures and advance tickets are available from Bermuda Festival Ltd., P.O. Box HM 297, Hamilton, HM AX, Bermuda, or by calling Tel. 295-1291, fax 295-7403, bdafest@logic.bm, www.bermudafestival.com. The box office is open December 1-February 28 (Tel. 292-8572). Festival brochures can also be obtained from overseas travel agencies.

### ANNUAL STREET FEST—MARCH

This is an open-air festival held on the first or second weekend in March on Front Street in Hamilton, featuring Bermudian talent and sponsored by the Department of Tourism. Street theatre, Scottish dancers, African dancing, fashion shows, music, and a food court can all be found here. It is an excellent chance for you to capture the flavour of local and international culture.

### BERMUDA INTERNATIONAL FILM FESTIVAL—MARCH

Lights, cameras, action! The Bermuda International Film Festival (www.bermudafilmfest.com) is held annually in March, showcasing in-dependent feature-length films at both the Little Theatre and Liberty

Theatre in Hamilton. Tickets may be purchased at the Visitors' Service Bureau on Front Street, Hamilton, at bdafilm@logic.bm, or at 1-441-293-FILM.

### AGRICULTURAL EXHIBITION—APRIL

This event is known locally as the "Ag Show." If you are interested in local agricultural heritage and all things bright and beautiful, this is a fun-packed, entertaining, three-day event, held in April at the Botanical Gardens since 1940.

Competitions include horse shows/parades, fruit and vegetable growing, homemade food products, woodcraft and hobby exhibits, flowers, and artwork. Charitable food concessions may be found on site.

### EQUESTRIAN FESTIVAL —APRIL

This two-day horseback-riding festival is held every two years at the Botanical Gardens. Riders come from the U.S., Canada, England, and France. Team competitions allow five animals per team, comprising a novice, a pony, an intermediate rider, open, and international representative. Proceeds go to charity. For further information go to www.bef.bm.

### GOOD FRIDAY KITE FESTIVAL—APRIL

Colourful handmade and shop-bought kites of every shape and size fly from beautiful Horseshoe Bay—the place to be on Good Friday. The tradition of flying kites in Bermuda on Good Friday is said to have originated with a Sunday-school teacher taking his class on a hill and, with the aid of a kite rising heaven-bound, demonstrating Jesus' journey.

Festivities start around 11 A.M. and run through to 4 P.M. Family fun, entertainment, games, and kite competitions take place. Prizes are awarded for most original and most beautiful kites in the giant (minimum six foot) and smallest kite (maximum four inches) categories. Good Friday in Bermuda usually includes a traditional codfish-cake breakfast with hot-cross buns.

### PEPPERCORN CEREMONY—APRIL

During this unique, cultural, colourful ceremony in historical King's Square, St. George's, His Excellency the Governor receives one peppercorn for the rent of the State House (believed to be the oldest stone house in Bermuda) from the Masonic Lodge. This popular spectacle is held on the Wednesday closest to April 23.

### BEATING RETREAT CEREMONY—APRIL TO OCTOBER

This military musical ceremony is performed twice a month between April and October (excluding August) in Hamilton, St. George's, or Dockyard starting at 9 P.M. Under spotlights, the Bermuda Regiment Band (www.bermudaregiment.com) marches with the Bermuda Islands Pipe Band (bagpipes and all). It is very uplifting. The Bermuda Regiment Band has also successfully performed at the prestigious Edinburgh Tattoo in Scotland.

### BERMUDA DAY—MAY

The May 24 Heritage Parade features majorettes, Gombey African dancers, floats, and bands. Also organised are sporting activities such as the Bermuda Fitted Dinghy Races (St. George's harbour) and Bermuda Day Marathon (from Somerset to Hamilton).

A Bermuda fitted dinghy is only 14 feet long, but it has over 1,000 square feet of sail. During the dinghy race, the skipper is allowed to order any one of the crew overboard if he thinks the load is too heavy!

### GRAND ART FESTIVAL BY THE SEA—MAY

This is a community art-recognition day held in the middle of May, organised by the Masterworks Foundation (www.masterworksbermuda.com) to showcase local artwork for visitors and locals. Everything from chalk painting to prints to quick art is judged by professionals; there is also a "People's Choice" award.

### QUEEN'S BIRTHDAY—JUNE

In Bermuda, the queen's birthday is marked by a public holiday on the last Monday in June, with a parade and 21-gun salute in Hamilton.

Royal trivia: In Canada, once a British colony, Queen Victoria's birthday is celebrated with a public holiday and fireworks. In Australia, the queen's birthday is honoured with a public holiday. However, in England, where the royal family originates, there are no public holidays for any of the kings or queens—strange but true.

### CUP MATCH (SOMERS DAY AND EMANCIPATION DAY)—AUGUST

The rest of the world is envious of this one—two whole days off work and school the Thursday and Friday before the first Monday in August, for a cricket match between the East End and the West End. Matches alternate each year between the Somerset Cricket Club and the St. George's Cricket Club. Cup Match celebrates the emancipation of all slaves in Bermuda on August 1, 1834. Somers Day is celebrated in honour of Bermuda's accidental discovery by Sir George Somers.

### FESTIVAL OF THE AUGUST MOON—AUGUST

A romantic evening of music and dance under the stars is held at the Royal Naval Dockyard on the Saturday closest to the full moon in August.

There is free local entertainment of the highest calibre, and local food concessions are on hand. Check the local newspaper in August for details.

### CULTURE FEST—SEPTEMBER OR OCTOBER

Organised annually for the past few years, this celebration of ethnic music and food is held around September or October at the Royal Naval Dockyard. Popular with both locals and tourists alike, this event features international cuisine prepared by local vendors at reasonable prices. Also on display are arts and crafts stalls. Culture Fest is concluded with a sunset ceremony by the Bermuda Regiment and Bermuda Islands Pipe bands.

### JAZZ FESTIVAL—OCTOBER

This yearly festival of jazz music—first introduced by the Department of Tourism in October 1996—features top-name international performers. Some free performances are held at the Royal Naval Dockyard and St. George's. Previous shows boasted internationally acclaimed performers such as George Benson and Gladys Knight. Tickets to concerts are $60 general admission and $85 reserved. For further details go to www.bermudajazz.com.

### CONVENING OF PARLIAMENT—OCTOBER

This is a lot of pomp and ceremony to announce the convening of the Houses of Parliament, at the Cabinet Building on Front Street, Hamilton—held the second week of October. The governor of Bermuda reads a lengthy speech from the throne about Discussion Papers and Bills for the upcoming year.

Bermuda's government is based on the British system and first convened on August 1, 1620, making it the second-oldest in the Commonwealth, next to Britain.

### FLATTS FUN FESTIVAL—OCTOBER

Held in October, this celebration of Flatts Village heritage features music, dancing, food, arts and crafts, merchandise, races, a boat regatta, a ducking stool, a "greasy pole" competition, pole jostling, and fireworks. Flatts Village is home to the Bermuda Aquarium, Museum and Zoo (www.bamz.org) and is set in a picturesque harbour where the sea flows in rapidly from Harrington Sound. The name "Flatts" is thought to originate from an old English word for drying fish.

### REMEMBRANCE DAY—NOVEMBER

A public holiday and parade honouring war veterans is held on November 11, starting at 10:30 A.M. on Front Street, Hamilton, and ending with a simple wreath-laying ceremony at the Cenotaph. About 80 Bermudians lost their lives in World War I, 35 in World War II. Lest we forget . . .

## CHRISTMAS WALKABOUT IN THE OLDE TOWNE OF ST. GEORGE'S—DECEMBER

Victorian festivities begin on an evening in the early part of December (check local newspapers nearer the time for actual date). An old-fashioned Christmas is celebrated in this historic town with an open-house guided tour followed by yuletide merriment—flute, harpsichord, and clarinet music, costumed carollers, and performance speakers. Thirsty revellers can drink a cup of rum eggnog.

## CHRISTMAS BOAT PARADE—DECEMBER

Slotted for just before Christmas, this nighttime boat parade helps get Bermuda in the Christmas spirit—not an easy feat when the weather is warm and balmy. All types and sizes of Bermuda's boats are decorated with Christmas lights, characters, and decorations. The parade makes the circular water route twice around Albouy's Point, Hinson's Island, and Salt Kettle Harbour and can be viewed from vantage points on Front Street, Hamilton. A fireworks display rounds off this fun family evening.

## BOXING DAY—DECEMBER

Boxing Day is the day after Christmas Day. (No, it's not when the country watches the sport of boxing.) It originates from England, when on this day all the church charity money boxes were opened and then distributed to the poor. Later, it came to represent the rich giving their servants and tradespeople a Christmas bonus. Today, Boxing Day represents a day of rest and relaxation. This is also the traditional day for the African Gombey dancers to be out and about.

## LOWERING OF THE ONION—DECEMBER

This New Year's celebration, held December 31 at King's Square, features free live entertainment along with the Bermudian traditional lowering of the "Onion" (Bermudians are often known as "onions" due to the famous onions exported years ago). The evening ends in a fireworks display.

## OTHER MAJOR EVENTS THROUGHOUT THE YEAR

**Annual Magic Masquerade** (April); **Annual Gombey Festival** (May); Annual **Soca Concert** held at Dockyard (July); **Champion Cat and Dog Shows**

(biannual); **National Dance Theatre of Bermuda's Production** (August, odd years); **Bermuda Regiment Tattoo** (November).

## The Art Scene

Note: For theatre groups, go to chapter 8, "Theatres and Concerts" section.

There's a new awakening these days of both Bermuda's old artists and new budding ones. It may be a backlash against all those years of pretty pastel cottage scenes, or it may be a sign of modern times. Whatever the reason, art appreciation is in the eye of the beholder, and everyone has personal tastes. If it pleases you, then it's good art, and there's nothing further to say.

If it *is* pretty pastel cottages, flowers, and seascapes you want to purchase (and there's nothing wrong with that), then Carole Holding has made quite the cottage industry out of this type of work. Her paintings are always pleasant, never jar the eye, and provide a good memory of your Bermuda vacation. She has galleries all over the island (www.caroleholding.bm).

Another artist, Michael Swan, has three galleries: one in Hamilton, one at Dockyard, and another in St. George's (www.michaelswan.com). His work is also inspired by Bermuda's soft beauty, but his tone is more vivid than Holding's, and he uses airbrushes for his medium. Swan is a minimalist and usually paints corners of roofs and Bermudian architecture, creating angles, shapes, and shadows. His work brightens up the gloomiest of corners in your home and is available in poster form as well as print.

Jill Amos Raine's watercolours of cottages and landscapes are bright and full of intricate detail. She succeeds in capturing the essence of Bermuda's myriad colours; my favourite is *Dusk,* which is a hilltop view of old St. George's. Her gallery, Bermuda Memories, is in King's Square in St. George's.

Amy Evans' Bermuda scenes are true to form, incorporating intricate detail and fine brush strokes for buildings and broad strokes for plant and tree life.

Graham Foster's art is the opposite of pastel. His unusual abstract depictions of Bermuda scenes use lots of bold, vibrant colours. He says, "Ninety-five percent of what I paint is from imagination, so rather than paint scenes or people from life, I keep interesting images stored in some subconscious place in my memory to be used at a later date." Foster also creates unique and unusual sculptures. He sells his art during the summer at Wednesdays' Harbour Nights on Front Street and at some art galleries and department stores (www.grahamfoster.com).

Robert Bassett has a fascination with Bermuda Gombeys, who are tribal dancers originating from Africa, so his paintings are bright and rhythmic. In fact, Bassett is known as the "Poet of Colour." His work can be spotted at Regal Art Galleries in Hamilton and St. George's (www.grandpasart.com/robertbassett.htm).

Molly D. Smith's paintings use a pleasing combination of light and shadow and her paintings document Bermuda's heritage and historical properties.

Alfred Birdsey was a prolific watercolourist who painted impressions of Bermuda's landscape up until his death. His daughter, Jo Birdsey Linberg, who also paints, still keeps his gallery open in Paget.

Sharon Wilson's paintings of local people never give rise to any negative criticism. Her portraits of black children and families capture vignettes of real-life private moments perfectly. She says, "I paint the people who are the heartbeat of the island—people that the tourists don't often see." Sharon is also a children's book illustrator. She illustrated *The Day Gogo Went to Vote: South Africa,* by Elinor Batezat Sisilu (Little, Brown and Company). Nelson Mandela called this book "an inspiring, moving testament to the strength and courage of the South African people." To view her work, go to www.sharonwilsonart.com.

Daniel Dempster is a charcoal portrait artist and oil painter who can be seen many mornings at Rock Island Coffee Shop on Reid Street in Hamilton, sketching willing models. He describes charcoal as an "elegant, sensuous medium." His oil paintings of the waters around Bermuda are translucent: see *Summertide* at his Web site (www.liquidlight.com) for an amazing example.

Particularly popular with children is Elizabeth Mulderig, who illustrates the Bermuda *Tiny Tree Frog* book series. Her art is funky and original, using lots of purple and green tones.

Desmond Fountain (www.desmondfountain.com), a Fellow of the Royal Society of British Sculptors, is a sculptor whose work can be seen enhancing Bermuda's parishes and hotels. He specialises in children's bronze statues, but there is nothing statuesque about them, being both lifelike and fluid. Fountain sculpts from real life, not photos or body casts. You can spot his sculptures adorning the pond in front of City Hall on Church Street, in the mezzanine of the Fairmont Southampton Hotel, and in St. George's, where his famous statue of Sir George Somers, Bermuda's founding father, is located.

Other respected artists in Bermuda include Bruce Stuart, Sheilagh Head, Otto Trott, and Jason Jones. Bruce Stuart (www.brucestuart.com), in particular, takes ordinary everyday items and brings them to life on canvas. Stuart has exhibited in galleries in the U.S., Europe, and Mexico. His metamorphosis into new-age art is a real change from his previous cottage work; however, all of his award-winning work is both accomplished and pleasing to the eye. His new paintings are so luminous they are practically neon.

As well as in art galleries, you can find art for sale in the major department stores along Front Street in Hamilton. You can also view early Bermudian artwork and portraits at the museums and historical houses.

The above are just some of Bermuda's 500 or so artists, and I apologise to all those I left out.

## ART GALLERIES

**Bermuda National Gallery,** City Hall, Church Street, Hamilton (Tel. 295-9428, www.bng.bm). Open Mon.-Sat., 10 A.M.–4 P.M. Admission: free.

Frequently changed art exhibitions, both historic and contemporary from around the world, as well as Bermuda.

Tours: Guided tours each Thursday at 10 A.M. and a weekly lunchtime series on Wednesdays. There is a special Art & Architecture Tour available on Tuesdays from 10 A.M. to 1 P.M. Cost: $65 per person, which covers tour and lunch at Waterloo House Hotel (minimum eight people, maximum 15 people), and must be booked in advance.

There are also lectures and evening cultural and social events (see Web site for listings: www.bng.bm) and the gallery is also happy to prearrange special tours for groups.

**Masterworks Foundation Gallery,** 97 Front Street, Hamilton, and Masterworks at Colonial Gallery, Reid Street, Hamilton (Tel. 295-5580, www.bermuda.bm/masterworks). Open Mon.-Fri., 8:30 A.M.–5 P.M. This gallery has a high standard of art exhibitions, which are rotated every two weeks. Exhibits feature contributions from local and international artists.

**The Bermuda Arts Centre,** Dockyard (Tel. 234-2809). Open daily, 10 A.M.–5 P.M. There is an eclectic display of local exhibits in this friendly centre featuring an artists' studio operated by volunteers. Exhibits include paintings, ceramics, jewellery, sculpture, prints, and note cards.

**The Birdsey Studio,** 5 Stowe Hill, Paget (Tel. 236-6658). This studio features the work of Alfred Birdsey, the prolific artist whose daughter, Jo Birdsey Linberg, is carrying on his name.

**Garden Gallery,** 151 North Shore Road, Hamilton Parish (Tel. 293-0484). Open Mon.-Fri., 10 A.M.–1 P.M. Among other things, this gallery houses the island's largest collection of original oil paintings showcasing Bermudian life.

**The Desmond Fountain Gallery,** Emporium Building, 69 Front Street, Hamilton (Tel. 296-3518, sculpture@logic.bm, www.desmondfountain.com).

Desmond also has a private studio at Flatts Village, by appointment only (Tel. 292-3955). You can also view his internationally acclaimed, lifelike sculptures at **The Sculpture Gallery,** Fairmont Southampton Hotel.

### SPRING BREAK ARTS

During mid-March spring break through to March 31, the Department of Tourism sponsors a college students' arts programme—**Spring Break Arts**—that runs concurrently with Spring Break Sports. Along with painting, glass blowing, furniture making, and photography, there is an intensive tour of Bermuda's National Trust properties and art galleries. The hours students invest during their stay in Bermuda can be credited to their college degrees. There are special discounts for hotels, guesthouses, nightclubs, pubs, restaurants, and scooter rental. Contact the Department of Tourism for details (Tel. 292-0023).

## The Food Scene

Bermuda has a fine selection of expensive, medium-priced, and budget restaurants. You can grab a bite on the go from a deli or sample the delicious fare at lunch wagons dotted around the island. Is maybe having a pie and pint at one of the friendly pubs more your style? The choice is limitless—from quick snacks and light refreshments to traditional afternoon tea or dinner. As they say in Bermuda, "Pleasant appetite."

### BERMUDIAN DISHES

Fish dishes are very popular in Bermuda. Caught in the pristine waters, Bermuda fish is white and flaky. The catch of the day is always worth considering. Codfish and potatoes is the Sunday breakfast of choice for Bermudians. Or try the Bermuda tradition of fish chowder laced with Outerbridge's Sherry Pepper Sauce or Bermuda Rum—warm and hearty. Bermuda lobster is a real treat, and is available in the months that contain the letter "R."

Easter is codfish cake and banana breakfast time (usually served on a sweet currant bun), although this dish is available any time of the year, particularly on a Sunday.

At Christmastime, cassava pie is traditionally served. Made from cassava root and pork or chicken, this unique pie is delicious when served with chow chow (pickle chutney). Studies show that cassava root can prevent certain types of cancer, so it's good for you too.

Some dishes originate from the West Indies, such as Hopping John, which is mainly black-eyed peas and rice with seasoning.

Baked goods such as Johnny bread, a sort of flat tea biscuit (scone) served warm with butter or jam, are sold at local bakeries. Also, bread pudding made with bread slices and raisins, spiced with cinnamon, is a real Bermuda/English favourite.

Afternoon tea is traditionally served at 4 P.M., and many places offer it between 2 and 5 P.M. Traditional afternoon tea consists of scones (tea biscuits) with jam and cream spread thickly; thinly sliced quarter sandwiches (cucumber or smoked salmon usually); cakes; and, of course, a good-quality pot of tea.

Popular afternoon tea spots include:
- Waterloo House Hotel, Hamilton (Tel. 295-4480), daily 4-5 P.M.
- Mrs. Tea's Victorian Tea Room, Southampton (Tel. 234-1374), daily 2-5 P.M. (closed Monday)
- The Carriage House, St. George's (Tel. 297-1730), daily 2:30-4:30 P.M.
- Lighthouse Tea Rooms, Southampton (Tel. 238-8679), daily 2:30-5 P.M.

## LUNCH WAGONS

Dotted around the island, with food freshly made to order and especially convenient on the go, these popular lunch wagons usually serve fries, burgers, wonderful homemade fishcakes, fish sandwiches, "steakums" (wafer-thin slices of hot beef on a bread roll), sodas, and ice creams.

**Dinty's Wagon,** Elbow Beach (at the end of Tribe Road Number 4B, Paget) and also located on Front Street, Hamilton. Open throughout the day during summer season at Elbow Beach, and year round in Hamilton.

**Keith's Kitchen,** adjacent to Duncan & Decousto Building on Victoria Street, Hamilton. Open breakfast and lunch.

**Carolyn's,** opposite Warwick Long Bay (entrance nearest Hamilton), South Shore, Warwick (bright purple van). Open throughout the day, summer season only.

**Degraff's,** situated in Victoria Street parking lot behind City Hall, Hamilton. Open during lunch hours.

## DINE-A-ROUND PROGRAMME (NOVEMBER 1-MARCH 31)

From November to March, when Bermuda is at its uncrowded best, reserve your table at participating restaurants for the great-value "Dine-a-Round" menu. These cut-price menus are a good opportunity to try some of the otherwise expensive venues without breaking the bank.

Dine-a-Round menus offer two or three choices in each category: Starter, Entrée, and Dessert. Gratuities of 15 percent are usually included, but drinks are not included. Just ask your waiter for the Dine-a-Round menu or you can pick up a brochure at the tourist bureaus during the low season.

Here is an example of the restaurants participating in the Dine-a-Round programme, with set menus for under $30 per person:

The Carriage House (Tel. 297-1730), Chopsticks (Tel. 292-0791), Coconut Rock (Tel. 292-1043), Flanagan's Irish Pub (Tel. 295-8299), Freddies Restaurant (Tel. 297-1717), Freeport Seafood Restaurant (Tel. 234-1692), Frog & Onion Pub (Tel. 234-2900), Harbourfront (Tel. 295-4207), Henry VIII (Tel. 238-1977), The Hog Penny (Tel. 292-2534), La Trattoria (Tel. 292-7059), Little Venice (Tel. 295-3503), Lobster Pot (Tel. 292-6898), M.R. Onions (Tel. 292-5012), Portofino (Tel. 292-2375), Robin Hood Pub (Tel. 295-3314), Rosa's Cantina (Tel. 295-1912), Tio Pepe Restaurant (Tel. 238-1897), Waterfront Restaurant (Tel. 297-1515).

Oh, one last thing; always call ahead to confirm if a restaurant is open (and when it's closing), especially in the low season, and whether a jacket and tie is required for men.

## FOOD SHOPPING

There's no getting around it—food shopping here is expensive, especially compared to America. Prices are slightly higher than Canada, especially for frozen goods.

Wednesday is often 5 or 10 percent discount day in many of the supermarkets. The Marketplace chain of stores is in the marginally cheaper price range, as is Whites Supermarket in Warwick. Supermart and Miles Market in Hamilton sell specialty British food products, and prices reflect this. Supermarkets stay open on Sundays from 1 to 5 P.M.

Local foodstuffs for sale: Outerbridge's selection of soups, mustards, mayonnaise, and spicy sauces, including the famous Sherry Pepper Sauce used to flavour chowders, seafood, and Bloody Marys. There are also Fourways Soups (from Fourways Inn Restaurant), Henry VIII Pies, Linda Horton's Original Black Rum Cake, Matt Man's Pasta, Bermuda Honey, and Sallie's Bermuda Preserves.

Best buys for home-grown fruit and vegetables are at the stalls located on the side of the road (some are open only on the weekends). One stall, Luke's Farm in Southampton, just after Déjà Vu Antique Shop, is open Monday to Friday, 3 to 6:30 P.M., and sells only Bermuda-grown produce, depending on season—strawberries, carrots, broccoli, onions, cabbages, flowers, etc. Fresh fruit and vegetables are also sold every Saturday at Barnes Corner in Southampton. There is also a popular weekly farmers' market every Saturday morning at the Bull's Head car park in Hamilton.

In addition, fresh fish can be found from roadside vendors, usually on Fridays.

Below is an example of a basic five-day grocery shop from a Bermuda supermarket for a family of two adults and two children. Once you start adding "treaties" and alcohol to the list, then the price starts to soar. Prices include tax and are accurate at time of writing:

```
4 Loaves Bread @ $2.99 ea............................................$11.96
1 Packet Hot Dog Buns..................................................$3.44
1 Packet Burger Buns.....................................................$3.20
4 Large Cartons 2% Milk @ $3.30 ea.........................$13.20
Sugar Cubes ....................................................................$1.18
Jam.....................................................................................$2.82
Small butter.....................................................................$1.93
2 Doz. Eggs @ $2.47 per. Doz. ....................................$4.94
3 Cans Campbell's Soup @ $1.12 ea. .........................$3.36
Laundry Detergent........................................................$5.24
Wheetabix Cereal ..........................................................$3.60
Grape Nuts Cereal .........................................................$5.06
Spaghetti Sauce...............................................................$1.38
Spaghetti Strands...........................................................$1.86
Ground Beef ....................................................................$3.20
Cooked Sliced Meats .....................................................$5.74
Sausage Patties...............................................................$4.80
2 Packets Lean Cuisine @ $4.31 ea. ...........................$8.62
Lamb Stew........................................................................$4.54
Chicken Strips.................................................................$5.53
Frozen Chicken Wings ..................................................$5.23
DiGiorno Supreme Frozen Pizza................................$10.56
Packet Noodle & Sauce..................................................$2.15
Cooking Oil......................................................................$2.70
Can of Tuna .....................................................................$3.28
Instant Coffee .................................................................$2.53
Tea Bags ...........................................................................$5.04
Frozen Orange Juice .....................................................$2.82
Cola, 1 ltr. .......................................................................$2.65
Peanut Butter..................................................................$2.45
Microwave Popcorn ......................................................$3.21
Cranberry Juice .............................................................$4.46
Crackers............................................................................$2.93
Cheddar Cheese .............................................................$2.32
English Muffins...............................................................$4.54
```

Rice ................................................................$1.76
Frozen Veg., Mixed, 1 lb. ...................................$2.91
Apples............................................................$4.04
Oranges .........................................................$5.92
Bunch Bananas................................................$1.69
Bunch Grapes .................................................$3.44
Lettuce  .........................................................$2.99
Bunch Carrots.................................................$4.29
Potatoes, 5-lb. bag...........................................$4.99
Ketchup, Small Bottle ......................................$2.50
Banana Muffins................................................$4.08
Cheese Slices..................................................$2.55
**Total Food Shop** .....................................**$193.63**

Shopping Tip: In the supermarkets, the student check-out "baggers" in school uniforms rely on tips, as they don't receive a salary. Fifty cents a bag is generally given.

# 6

# The Sports Scene

Bermuda is extremely sports-minded—the mild climate enables year-round activities, and being surrounded by pristine blue water ensures that water sports are abundant. Bermuda is also a golf-lover's paradise, with eight top-notch golf courses (some of them private, some government run). There are also dozens of tennis courts; you can book one at any of the major hotels for between $20 and $30. Pat Rafter, the top-ranking pro-tennis champion, lives on the island and sometimes puts in an appearance at the exciting international **Bermuda XL Tennis Open,** held at the Coral Beach & Tennis Club (Tel. 236-2233) in April—a must-see for tennis enthusiasts.

Spectator sports include cricket, rugby, field hockey, and soccer. Soccer is popular and has been given a boost by Bermudian Shaun Goater, a Manchester City star player who has been awarded an MBE (Member of the Most Excellent British Empire) by the queen of England, HRH Elizabeth II, for his dedication to soccer and his work with young Bermudian players.

The Bermuda Football Association (Tel. 295-2199) promotes several soccer cup matches and competitions each Sunday during the winter months. The FA Challenge Cup is played throughout the season with the final in April. On September 1 is the Martonmere cup series, with the final being held in November. During Christmas week till January 3 the Dudley Eve Trophy is played out at several different locations, and the Friendship Shield starts in October, with the final in April.

Cricket is taken very, very seriously, especially at **Cup Match** in August. Cup Match celebrates the abolition of slavery and is a two-day event between the East End and West End.

Rugby season runs October to April, at the National Sports Club in Devonshire (Tel. 236-6994), culminating with the **World Rugby Classic** (www.worldrugby.bm) in November, where former international players over the age of 33 compete. There are a total of 11 matches over a three-day period. Since the Classic's inception, countries such as New Zealand, South Africa, and Wales have contributed over 500 international players.

## Introduction to Water Sports

Bermuda has superb water facilities. Go swimming in the clear warm azure sea, or, for the more active, take part in any of the fantastic water sports available. Try diving to the depths of Bermuda's reefs that teem with marine life: blue angelfish, sea fans, squirrelfish, butterflyfish, parrotfish, brain coral, and hundreds of other species. (This is particularly fascinating and especially precious when you consider that Jamaica's reef is now over 90 percent dead through overfishing.)

Detailed in this book is a water sport for everyone's taste and pocket: snorkelling, diving, fishing, boating, parasailing, kayaking, bell diving, and personal-watercraft riding. Or just take a relaxing cruise to enjoy the beauty and serenity of the island—the perfect way to wind down. Prices for water sports and cruises can be as low as $25 and as high as $100 per person, but most cruises and rentals are good value for money and very well organised.

Note: Many water sports are not available during the low season or on less than calm days. To avoid disappointment, call ahead to see if your favourite water sport is offered.

*For full details of water sport activities, go to the "Water Sports" and "Guided Tours and Cruises" sections in chapters 8 through 12.*

### SNORKELLING

Snorkelling is a cheap, safe, and easily mastered activity. Bermuda's snorkelling is world class, offering pristine waters, colourful tropical fish, and water temperatures ranging from an average of 62 degrees (17 degrees C) in spring, 73 degrees (23 degrees C) in fall, to a high of 83 degrees (28 degrees C) in summer.

Bermuda is surrounded by a living, breathing, coral-reef necklace wherein lie three centuries of shipwrecks to identify, with at least one within snorkelling distance—the *Pollockshields* off Elbow Beach. Most good snorkelling is within easy reach of the shore, in relatively shallow depths.

Bermuda also has possibly some of the best soft coral in the world. Conservation is taken seriously, so please help preserve the reef by not standing on, touching, or breaking off any parts of it.

No matter how rough the weather, there is always a sheltered cove somewhere that is calm enough for snorkelling. Check the wind direction, either by phoning the weather phone numbers 977 and 977-2 or by checking the newspapers or television weather cable channel (if available at your accommodations), and go snorkelling at the opposite side of the island to the direction of the wind; i.e., if there is a northeast wind go snorkelling in the southwest.

There are even more chances of spotting brightly coloured fish on cloudy days, as they tend not to hide behind the reef or rocks on these days. Don't worry about the rain either; it's still clear under the water. In the months *outside* of June, July, August, and September, the visibility is optimum, as there is less plankton in the water, plus there are less people to scare away the fish. Most people need to wear a wetsuit during the cooler water-temperature months. It may be useful to note that fall water temperatures (October and November) are higher than spring temperatures (March and April) by about 5-10 degrees.

## SUPER SNORKELLING SPOTS
### (COURTESY OF AVID SNORKELLER MARTIN WALSH)

1. Elbow Beach, Paget, near the *Pollockshields* shipwreck (between Elbow Beach Hotel and Coco Reef Resort along the South Shore). Approximately 350-metre swim out to wreck.

2. Tobacco Bay, St. George's. There are far more fish outside the rocks (to the right as you look out to sea from the beach) than inside the rocks, where most visitors usually snorkel.

3. In the rocky crevices around the fort at St. Catherine's Bay, St. George's.

4. In the rocks between Tobacco Bay and Achilles Bay, just before St. Catherine's Fort in St. George's.

5. Church Bay, South Shore. Popular bay, especially with beginners. Find an abundance of fish, including many species of brightly coloured parrotfish in the shallow depths.

6. Bailey's Bay. Although not a typical tourist spot, a great place for snorkelling. From the public dock, loop back around the headland on North Shore or swim out to the far side of the islands just offshore.

Martin's Moustache Tip: Men with moustaches should apply a touch of Vaseline first. This gives the snorkelling mask a better seal and prevents leaks.

Safety Tip: If you ever find yourself caught in a tide's undercurrent or riptide, rather than wearing yourself out swimming against the tide, swim to the side of the current until you are in safer waters, after which time you can swim safely into shore. So remember: Swim to the side to survive.

## SCUBA DIVING

Scuba diving is another excellent way to discover Bermuda's fascinating underwater world. *Rodales Scuba Diving* magazine voted Bermuda the number-one destination for wreck diving in the Caribbean/Atlantic region. With over 350 historic shipwrecks in warm, pristine waters, year-round diving is Bermuda's best-kept secret. And the Gulf Stream, insulating the waters from the north and creating mild, warm, calm waters, gives Bermuda a subtropical climate and creates ideal conditions for the diving enthusiast.

The Department of Tourism (Tel. 292-0023) promotes a super Shipwreck Certificate Programme for those who complete a dive on any of the six most popular wrecks. Participants receive parchment-paper certificates decorated with an image of the original ship and outlining the ship's history.

Diving Tip: It is unsafe to dive up to 24 hours before your flight home, as you could get the "bends."

Historical Note: An early type of business was the stripping and looting of the many reef-bound shipwrecks on Bermuda's shores. This free bootie trade was known as catching a "turtle in the net." Please don't plunder the ships when diving today. Leave everything intact for the next generation.

## WINDSURFING

Bermuda's windsurfers are passionate about their sport. They often can be overheard bragging about their fastest speeds and size of board. And nothing, absolutely nothing, can detain them from rushing to the shore, wetsuit on, sailboard to the ready, when, head cocked to one side, they feel the call of the wind—much like ancient sailors, with only their wits to rely on when trying to predict hurricanes.

The best months in Bermuda for windsurfing are October through April. The best areas are anywhere along the North Shore or Shelly Bay, Somerset Long Bay, or Horseshoe Bay. For sailboard rental go to Windjammer Watersports in the "Water Sports" section of chapter 10, "The West End," and Blue Hole Waters in the East End (chapter 11).

## WATER-SKIING

Water-skiing is allowed in the protected waters of the Great Sound, Castle Harbour, Ferry Reach, Ely's Harbour, Riddells Bay, Hamilton Harbour,

Mangrove Bay, Spanish Point, and the calm waters of Harrington Sound. You can go water-skiing at Island Water Skiing at the Grotto Bay Beach Hotel in Hamilton Parish (Tel. 293-2915) or at the Bermuda Waterski Centre at Somerset Bridge in Somerset (Tel. 234-3354).

### FISHING

Bermuda has world-class reef and deep-sea fishing, with several charter fishing boats for hire. However, the price is not cheap, so it depends on how passionate you are about your fishing as to whether or not you should go. Charges for groups are around $600. If you are not with a group, charter boats will usually charge you $100 per person for a half-day trip, but the more people going out, the cheaper it is. Many Bermudians fish off the bridges (where allowed) and rocks, spending a relaxing day along the many miles of shoreline. To learn more you may enjoy Graham Faiella's book *Fishing in Bermuda*.

Protected species include marine turtles, porpoises, whales, dolphins, corals of all kinds, conchs, and sea fans. Special minimum-fish-size regulation rulers are available from local marinas or the Department of Agriculture and Fisheries, Botanical Gardens, 169 South Shore Road, Paget (Tel. 234-3642).

**Game Fishing Competitions:** Enter your catches year round with the Bermuda Department of Tourism. No entry fee or license is required. Catches can earn an Award of Merit, a Citation, or, to encourage conservation, a Certificate of Release (Tel. 238-0112).

### KAYAKING

Get away from it all on a kayak tour, where you won't be disturbed by the noise of a boat engine, and you can observe the water and surroundings at a leisurely pace. Popular with stressed-out tourists, this low-tech sport encourages us to enjoy nature in what is a rising trend in inexpensive soft-adventure travel. For kayak rentals, try **Blue Water Divers** (Tel. 234-1034), **Windjammer Watersports** (Tel. 234-3082), **Fantasea Bermuda Ltd.** (Tel. 236-1300), or **Blue Hole Water Sports** (Tel. 293-2915). For kayak tours, try **Kayak Bermuda** (Tel. 50-KAYAK).

## Jogging, Races, and Marathons

Due to the lack of sidewalks, conditions for jogging are less than ideal on Bermuda's narrow main roads. Once off the thoroughfare, the trails that hug the South Shore coastline and the Railway Trail are two scenic places to jog. A safe and scenic place to jog is the Botanical Gardens in Paget.

If running or jogging is too fast for you, then check out the **Walking Club of Bermuda** (www.walk.free.bm) walks. Bermuda's most famous walk is the "End-to-End" pledge jaunt held in May each year, where walkers go from one end of Bermuda to the other, following the Railway Trails and raising money for charity in the process. Leading up to the main walk are several shorter practice walks of between six and 15 miles.

If you wish to go on an organised jog, the **Mid-Atlantic Athletic Club** (P.O. Box HM 1745, Hamilton, HM GX, Bermuda) gathers at 6 P.M. in front of Camden House, at the Berry Hill Road entrance of the Botanical Gardens in Paget, from the first Tuesday in April until the last Tuesday in October. (There is no entry fee for this fun run.)

The club also organises the annual "Princess to Princess" Race. Route: Fairmont Princess Hotel Hamilton to Fairmont Southampton (7.2 miles).

In late September the **Bermuda Triathlon Association** (Suite #547, 48 Par-La-Ville Road, Hamilton, HM 11) organises the yearly Bermuda Triathlon. This race combines a one-mile swim, 15-mile cycling leg, and six-mile run, attracting top international triathletes competing for $100,000 in prize money.

The **Bermuda International Race Weekend** (www.bermudatracknfield.com), held in January, is a race festival that includes the men's and women's Bank of Butterfield Mile. There is a $10,000 cash prize for the fastest competitor less than four minutes. Even the children get to have a chance with races for under 12 (awards only) and under 18 ($100 cash prize). Other races on this weekend include the Bermuda Marathon, Half Marathon, and 10K race. There are cash prizes for winners and record breakers. For further enquiries, call the Race Committee (Tel. 296-0951).

In March, the Aquarium in Flatts Village (Tel. 293-2727) sponsors the annual "Zoom Around The Sound." Cycle, run, walk, in-line skate, or push a stroller (staggered starts) around Harrington Sound (approximately 7.2 miles). Entry fees apply for both Bermuda Zoological Society members and nonmembers.

For information and registration forms about year-round races, marathons, and the Bermuda International Race Weekend, contact the **Bermuda Track and Field Association,** P.O. Box DV 397, Devonshire, Bermuda, DV BX (www.bermudatracknfield.com). Forms can also be picked up from Sportseller, Washington Mall, Hamilton (Tel. 295-2692) or The Pro Shop, Reid Street, Hamilton (Tel. 292-7487).

## Tennis

In 1874, Miss Mary Ewing Outerbridge, an American sportswoman, introduced the game of tennis to the United States from Bermuda! She purchased tennis equipment from British army officers in Bermuda and set up the first U.S. tennis court on the grounds of the Staten Island Cricket Club in New York.

Today, there are over 100 courts in Bermuda, some of which are at the hotels, allowing visitors to use them at reasonable rates (tennis coaches are on hand for expert tuition). Tennis whites are usually worn. Courts available to nonguests include **Sonesta Beach Resort** (Tel. 238-8200), **Elbow Beach Hotel** (Tel. 236-3535), **Grotto Bay Hotel** (Tel. 293-8333), **Horizons and Cottages** (Tel. 236-0048), **Fairmont Southampton** (Tel. 238-8000), **Coco Reef Resort** (Tel. 236-5416), and **Cambridge Beaches** (Tel. 234-0331).

The **Government Tennis Stadium** is located at 2 Marsh Folly Road, Pembroke. Court fees are $8 per hour (daytime) and $8 plus $16 for lights, per hour (nighttime). Call in advance (Tel. 292-0105). This stadium is host to the Heineken Open played in April, the All Bermuda Tennis Club Members' Tournament in September, and the All Bermuda Tennis Club Open in October.

The **Port Royal Tennis Club,** Port Royal, Southampton, provides four plexipaved courts (Tel. 238-9070).

Tennis tournaments are held throughout the year. For details contact the Bermuda Lawn Tennis Association, P.O. Box HM 341, Hamilton, HM BX (Tel. 296-0834; blta@northrock.bm). During April, the XL group of companies sponsors an exciting world-class tennis tournament, the Bermuda XL Open, held at the **Coral Beach & Tennis Club** (Tel. 236-2233).

## Horseback Riding

If you reside in a country where there are acres and acres of farmland and wide expanses of fields, you may find horseback riding in Bermuda a little restricting, but the views astride your horse are more than adequate compensation.

**Spicelands,** Middle Road, Warwick (Tel. 238-8212), has beach trails for novice riders throughout the day costing $60 per person for over an hour's ride. Sunrise ride starts at 6:30 A.M. every day and takes you right on the beach. To assist your guide, inform the stables whether you or your family members are experienced or novice riders. Trail rides start punctually. Spicelands also offers private rides for experienced riders: cost $120. Riders trot, canter, and go on the beach.

## Harness Racing

Harness racing takes place at the National Equestrian Centre, Vesey Street, Devonshire, from late September to the end of March. For enquiries, call the

**Horse & Pony Driving Club** (Tel. 291-RACE). The entry fee is $7 (children under 12 free) and there's an on-site snack bar. No gambling is permitted.

## Golf

People say Bermuda is a golfer's paradise. There are numerous courses to discover, often challenging, and often located near forts and along the coastline. Golfing greens are in peak condition during the months of January and February, although warm breezes and superb views make this a perfect outdoor sport year round. Bermuda's golf clubs are so popular it is really difficult to get tee times during the summer, so book as early as possible.

Proper golf attire is required at all clubs. Wear Bermuda-length shorts— no jeans, gym shorts, or cut-offs allowed. Golf carts are mandatory at Fairmont Southampton Club and Tucker's Point Club (private club), and on weekends and public holidays at Port Royal, Ocean View, and St. George's clubs (see below for further details). And bring your own golf balls, as in Bermuda they cost double the price of U.S. balls.

During the months of October to March there are a variety of tournaments for all levels of ability. For information contact **Bermuda Golf Association** (Tel. 295-5772).

There are three public government courses: **Port Royal Golf Course,** Southampton (Tel. 234-0974), **St. George's Golf Club,** St. George's (Tel. 297-8353), and **Ocean View Golf Course,** Devonshire (Tel. 295-9093). The Information Hotline number for booking tee time or to prepurchase a reservation is 295-6500 (VISA or MasterCard required). Call 234-GOLF for an ID number for government golf passes.

Other nonprivate clubs popular with avid golfers are **Belmont Hills Golf Club** (Tel. 236-6400), which has a totally updated golf course, and **Fairmont Southampton Golf Club** (Tel. 238-0446).

In Bermuda, private clubs require an introduction by a member. Enquire at your hotel for one.

### GOLF CLUBS

Golf fees run anywhere from $25 to $80 (some private clubs, such as the Mid Ocean, cost even more), depending on club and number of holes. Electric or gas golf carts, which are mandatory in some clubs, cost around $40 to rent. The government golf clubs have three-day passes from $130 to $200, depending on number of courses. Many clubs offer discounted rates for sunset golf.

**Port Royal Golf Course,** Southampton (Tel. 234-0974). 18 holes. Green fees are higher during weekends and holidays.

**St. George's Golf Club** (Tel. 297-8353). 9 or 18 holes. Sunset golf available.

**Ocean View Golf Club,** Devonshire (Tel. 295-9092). 9 or 18 holes. Sunset golf available after 3:45 P.M. April-October and after 2:30 P.M. November-March.

**Horizons** (Cottage Colony) Course, Paget (Tel. 236-0048). 9 holes.

**Princess Golf Club** at the Princess Hotel, Southampton (Tel. 238-0446). Course right across from the South Shore beaches (may be useful for the nonplaying members of the family). 9 or 18 holes.

**Mid Ocean** (private club), Tucker's Town (Tel. 293-0330). Monday, Wednesday, and Friday for nonclub members.

**Riddell's Bay** (private club), Riddell's Bay, Warwick (Tel. 238-1060). 18 holes. Limited times allotted to tourists.

**Belmont Hills Golf Club,** Warwick (Tel. 236-6400). 18 holes.

**Tucker's Point Golf Club** (private club), Tucker's Town (Tel. 298-6959). Exclusive club—costs $75,000 to join! 18 holes.

### GOLF DRIVING RANGE

**Bermuda Golf Academy & Driving Range,** Industrial Park Road, off Middle Road, Southampton (Tel. 238-8800). Open daily, 8 A.M.–11 P.M. Golf range with 40 bays (25 covered), 3,000-square-foot putting surface, 320-yard driving range, and 18-hole putting green. Prices: $4 (day), $5 (night)—token entitles you to 45 balls. On-site 18-hole minigolf game and children's jungle gym ideal for families. Reasonably priced clubhouse/restaurant and bar on grounds.

On a final golfing note, did you know that the 19th hole is the bar you visit after a game of 18 holes? Now that's a watering hole!

## Squash

The **Bermuda Squash Club & Bermuda Squash Racquets Association,** Middle Road, Devonshire (Reservations 292-6881). Open for nonmembers Mon.-Fri., 10 A.M.–10 P.M. and Sat.-Sun., 10 A.M.–5 P.M. Rates: Nonmembers $10 plus $5 court fee. Bar available. This squash club has air conditioning in the bathrooms but not on the courts, so it can be a bit tough going on hot days.

Club Night: Social event on Friday evening for a nominal fee. Sign the register and have several 20-minute games. The Bermuda Squash Racquets Association also sponsors the Bermuda Open Squash Tournament, usually held in September for top international competing players.

## Spring Break Sports

For savings during the month of March, students are invited to join the sports and leisure activities geared towards them. Participating sports include tennis, soccer, track and field, lacrosse, golf, field hockey, and rugby. Special rates are available for hotels, guesthouses, night-clubs, pubs, restaurants, and scooter rental. Contact Department of Tourism for details (Tel. 292-0023).

## Other Annual Sporting Events

Merrill Lynch Shoot-Out (golf, held in September); Bermuda Mixed Foursomes Golf Championship (April); Bermuda International Open Golf Championship for Men (October); Bermuda Easter Lily Invitational Pro-Am Golf Tournament for Ladies (March); Newport-Bermuda Race (yacht racing held in June in even years); Daytona-Bermuda Yacht Race (held in May, odd years); Bermuda 1-2 Single-Handed Race (yachting, held in June, odd years); Marion-Bermuda Cruising Yacht Race (June, odd years); Non-Mariners Race (held at Sandys Boat Club in Mangrove Bay, Somerset, first Sunday in August)—amusing sea-fest of sailing vessels designed to sink; the winner is the one that sinks first!

# 7

# The Business Traveller

There are many reasons you may be contemplating a business trip to Bermuda. For instance, you may wish to carry out business with any one of the 13,300 international companies registered in Bermuda, 350 of which have a physical presence. Maybe you are coming to a conference or visiting a branch office, or perhaps you are contemplating opening an offshore company. This chapter, as well as explaining the inside track to offshore business in Bermuda, highlights hotels, restaurants, and business facilities, all with an eye to decreasing the costs of your business trip.

## All This in Such a Small Space

As an offshore jurisdiction, Bermuda is strategically positioned for the new millennium. It has a gross domestic product of more than $2 billion, is a leading captive insurance jurisdiction with insurance company assets of over $100 billion, and continues to deregulate its telecommunications industry.

Due to stringent restrictions, Bermuda has a discreet, quality business reputation, with money-laundering incidences a rare occurrence. But don't let that persuade you that Bermuda doesn't have a pro-business attitude. The government emphasises commercial freedom, with relaxed taxation policies helping to make Bermuda globally competitive. And what better place to conduct business than where the weather permits year-round golf?

## CUTTING COSTS

In today's fast-track world, enabling technologies such as videoconferencing, e-mail, conference calling, and the information superhighway means that business travel is monitored and reduced. Today's cost-conscious companies are putting business travellers under tighter restrictions. American Express business surveys show that as companies budget and track their travel expenses, there is a "marked trend away from upscale accommodations and a movement toward greater use of moderate and economy rooms." And "companies very often set guidelines that define 'reasonable' meal expenses."

In short, gone are the days of lavish expense accounts.

# A Bermuda Invention: The Offshore Business Jurisdiction

Bermuda may be a small group of islands in the middle of the Atlantic Ocean; nevertheless, it has a considerable overseas business presence, where multimillion-dollar transactions are carried out on a daily basis. Bermuda has never received financial aid from Great Britain or any other country and is completely self-sufficient.

Until quite recently, tourism was Bermuda's main source of income. During the last few years, the exponential growth in international companies residing here has overtaken that income, and with new office blocks springing up regularly, that trend does not seem to be abating. According to the Bermuda Stock Exchange, Bermuda's total market capitalisation exceeds $50 billion.

Bermuda's international sector requires regular air links, hotels, and a sophisticated infrastructure in order to carry out daily business. It is evident that the international-company sector and tourism are inextricably linked—one needing the other to survive.

## INTERNATIONAL COMPANIES RESIDING IN BERMUDA

Bermuda is the world's largest market for catastrophe reinsurance, with a 32 percent market share. And because of the insurance expertise located here, Standard and Poor's has described Bermuda as the "insurance laboratory of the world," with 1,500 insurance companies registered here.

The first international corporation in Bermuda, American International Group (AIG), established itself over 50 years ago, mainly due to Bermuda's use of British law, proximity to the U.S., and tax neutrality.

(Bermuda does not impose a tax on capital gains, withholdings, profits, income [both corporate and personal], or gifts.) Since that time, many other large corporations have followed suit, including Johnson Higgins, Aon Risk, XL, RenaissanceRe, and Centre Solutions (formerly CentreRe).

Sophisticated telecommunications (Cable & Wireless has had a presence for over 100 years) and state-of-the-art computer technology are other factors attracting companies to these shores. On a technology note, in a study on "information-age literacy," Bermuda came second, directly behind the U.S., in terms of the number of radios, telephones, and televisions per capita. Other studies show that Bermuda has one of the highest rates of personal computers per capita and one of the highest Internet-account ratios in the world.

According to the Bermuda Chamber of Commerce, apart from convenience and accessibility by air, the primary reasons international companies come to Bermuda are:

1. The ability to operate in a largely tax-free society (taxes are based on consumption, not income, and international companies save money on foreign earnings). Note: U.S. companies still have to pay U.S. taxes on sales that occur in the U.S., and American employees have to pay taxes on their income too.

2. Political stability.

3. A user-friendly regulatory system (a business may be incorporated quickly in Bermuda, once all the paperwork is in place).

4. The respected and established British-style judicial system.

5. The existing infrastructure and expertise.

6. A highly literate work force.

7. Bermuda's physical beauty.

## Types of Companies

There are three main categories of business in Bermuda: "Local," "Exempt," and "Permit" (see below for detailed explanations). Also, according to the Ministry of Finance, Bermuda is emerging as a domicile for trust companies. This growth in trusts, whether for asset protection or estate planning, is already reckoned to be estimated somewhere in the region of $200 billion in assets.

Due to laws enacted in 1988, the U.S. also benefits from the creation of "Foreign Sales Corporations," incorporated in Bermuda and explained later in in this chapter. Bermuda has also set up a neutral Arbitration Committee, and BIBA (Bermuda International Business Association) can act as appointing authority with respect to international arbitration in a commercial dispute.

It takes approximately three to five days from the receipt of all required documentation to incorporate a company and, according to the chartered accounting firm of Ernst & Young (www.ey.com/bermuda), costs about $4,500 for legal fees, etc.

All these offshore companies create one critical thing for Bermuda—a healthy economic climate. In a working population of around 35,000 (8,000 of whom are non-Bermudian), there are about 6,500 jobs in Bermuda as a direct result of international business, with another 6,500 jobs indirectly related. In addition, this healthy economic climate is manifested by the trickle-down effect of consumer spending on lawyers, accountants, computer equipment, hospitality services, housing, etc. Of course, the downside for Bermuda is that it loses its slow pace of living, putting stresses on the roads and housing, not to mention its ecology and people.

Here is a rundown on the different types of companies in Bermuda and the laws governing them.

## LOCAL COMPANY

A local company is a company incorporated in Bermuda that can trade within Bermuda, and abroad, with the stipulation that at least 60 percent of the company is Bermudian owned (known in Bermuda as the 60/40 rule).

## EXEMPT COMPANY

An exempt company, otherwise known as an offshore company, is one that is based in Bermuda in order to trade globally or with other exempt companies. These foreign-owned companies are exempt from Bermudian ownership rules (although up to 20 percent Bermudian ownership is allowed) and are not subject to exchange controls or stamp duties. Exempt companies cannot trade within Bermuda. They are free of taxes until the year 2016, after which time the tax laws are to be reassessed by the government. The fact that Bermuda does not have income tax or capital-gains tax lures many overseas companies, although there are annual company fees charged, along with the option to be treated as a local company with respect to Bermuda's employee payroll taxes. The Bermuda Registrar of Companies incorporates exempt companies upon approval by the Bermuda Monetary Authority.

Exempt companies are currently the bedrock of the Bermudian economy (tourism now comes second economically). Major exempt companies in Bermuda tend to be of the insurance and catastrophe-liability ilk, and include such insurance giants as ACE and XL.

## PERMIT COMPANY

Another type of business in Bermuda is a permit company. That is a company that is incorporated outside of Bermuda but can apply for a permit to be allowed to trade from Bermuda. A permit company license is obtained through the Ministry of Finance.

## FOREIGN SALES CORPORATIONS

To promote export of United States manufactured equipment, U.S. Foreign Sales Corporations (FSCs) can be incorporated and organised in Bermuda. An FSC based in Bermuda benefits from the following: fast incorporation (an FSC may be incorporated within 48 hours); no franchise tax, income tax, capital-transfer tax, estate duty, inheritance tax, or profits tax; favourable exchange controls in any currency; and protection against bankruptcy by the creation of "purpose" trusts.

## SHIPPING REGISTER

Bermuda is also a leading jurisdiction for shipping corporations. The Bermuda Shipping Register dates back to 1789 and has registered international vessels such as tankers and yachts. Ships flying the Bermuda flag, under the 1986 U.S. Tax Code, are exempt from the 4 percent freight tax levied on goods imported to the U.S.

## TECHNOLOGY PARK

Because of the relatively recent 5 percent increase in available land—due to the U.S., Canadian, and British military forces leaving the island—Bermuda is in the process of creating a "Technology Island" by encouraging technology-based companies to reside here. Bids from local and overseas companies, especially in new technologies such as electronic commerce and data storage, are being considered.

For further information on the new Business/Technology Park, you can contact the Bermuda Land Development Company, Andrews Drive, St. David's, DD BX, Bermuda (Tel. 293-5712, Fax 293-5714).

## THE FINE PRINT

- Know your geography. Don't ever make the mistake of saying you've "always wanted to do business in the Caribbean." Bermuda is in the middle of the Atlantic Ocean, 1,000 miles from the nearest Caribbean shore.

- Bermuda can be conservative. The big companies often wait for the little companies to try out new ideas. This is a good "back-door" approach.
- Do not underestimate the progress and sophistication of Bermuda's technology.
- Do not walk through an office area ignoring the support staff.
- Do not wear Bermuda shorts for business meetings unless you conduct business in Bermuda on a very regular basis.
- The American Society of Travel Writers recommends these items every business traveller should carry: a good pair of walking shoes; a photocopy of the first page of your passport (carried separately from passport) and photocopies of your credit cards, medical prescriptions, and eyeglass prescription; plastic zipper bags; a pocket flashlight; spare camera batteries; and your address book.

## Accommodations

Due to the healthy business climate and the increase in business visitors, more and more hotels in Bermuda are gearing their services towards the business traveller. Conference rooms, data ports, fax machines—these are some of the facilities modern business executives anticipate today. But all these services come at added costs. Are you the type of business traveller who insists on staying in first-class business accommodations with room service, early checkout facilities, business centres, etc.? Or can you manage with your laptop and Internet connection, provided you are close to the city and have a clean, comfortable room to stay in? There are several advantages to staying in one of the smaller properties. They can offer comfort, quiet, cooking facilities, the personal touch, and, of course, savings.

Regardless of which type of accommodation you are staying at, you should always enquire about corporate rates or, if required, special group rates. Ask about what facilities are available for businessmen and women. Do they have rooms close to an office or office equipment? Do they charge for local calls as well as long distance? If they have a spa or gym, is it included in the room rate or is it an extra expense? Is tax and service charge included in the room rate or is it an extra expense? How close is the hotel to the city of Hamilton and what transport is available? Being prepared will save you considerable time and money. For off-season savings, November to March is when you'll find lower room rates.

Most of the accommodations listed in this chapter are located in and around Hamilton and geared towards the business traveller. Highlighted also are accommodations outside Hamilton that have special business facilities.

The recently opened **Wharf Executive Suites Hotel** is an example of a Bermuda hotel geared towards busy business executives. They offer a 24-hour concierge service as well as in-room high-speed Internet access. This business hotel is located across from Hamilton Harbour and is a short seven-minute ferry ride from downtown (see below for full details).

### HIGHER-PRICED ACCOMMODATIONS IN AND AROUND HAMILTON

Note: To get deals on rooms at the large resort hotels in Bermuda, go to the "Package Deals" section in chapter 2, "Before You Leave Home."

**Fairmont Hamilton Princess** (Hamilton Harbour), Pitts Bay Road, Pembroke (Tel. 295-3000, Toll-free: U.S. 1-800-223-1818, Canada 1-800-268-7176, Fax 295-1914, Hamilton@fairmont.com, www.princessbermuda.com). Walk to Hamilton: Five minutes.

Readers of *Successful Meetings* magazine voted for this charming harbour-front hotel and the magazine gave it their Pinnacle Award. Because of its city location, the Princess specialises in caring for business clients. It assists the business traveller with express check-in and check-out and has two special business floors offering rooms with full business facilities: speakerphones, voicemail, work desk, and cable TV. Foreign newspapers, business magazines, concierge staff for special requests, computers, fax, copy machines, and typing and photocopying services are also available. This hotel offers wireless Internet connections in all public areas and guest rooms. There are several meeting rooms (three large, four small), plus reception lounges and banquet facilities with multimedia equipment for hire. The Princess has undergone a conference-room upgrade and can accommodate from 20 to 300 persons inside and up to 500 people outside on the terraces, patios, and gardens. There is also a daily ferry service to its sister hotel, the Fairmont Southampton, which is located close to Bermuda's idyllic beaches on the South Shore.

**Single or double room rates:** $349 to $699 (depending on month or category of room), plus service charge and tax. Corporate rates upon request.

Author's note: Currently, this hotel is Hamilton's most popular business hotel.

### MEDIUM-PRICED ACCOMMODATIONS IN AND AROUND HAMILTON

**Rosedon Hotel,** Pitts Bay Road, Pembroke (Tel. 295-1640, Fax 295-5904, Toll-free U.S. 1-800-742-5008, rosedon@logic.bm, www.rosedonbermuda.com). Walk to Hamilton: Five minutes.

From the road, the Rosedon Hotel is deceptive. This 10-room white manor house looks stately; however, it hides a secret tropical garden where an additional 33 rooms with cedar balconies are nestled unobtrusively amongst the greenery. The Rosedon has full modern facilities and a year-round swimming pool. All rooms have private bath, reverse-cycle air-conditioning unit, telephone (with voicemail), radio, cable TV, Internet connection, coffee maker, refrigerator, ceiling fan, iron and ironing board, hair dryer, and wall safe. Rosedon also has an unusual "honour bar" lounge, where the guests are trusted to pour and pay for their own drinks. There isn't a restaurant, but breakfast, lunch, and afternoon tea can be served in your room, on your patio, or poolside. An early 6:30 A.M. continental breakfast is served in the lobby for business visitors. The corporate plan for business visitors offers "best room available" at time of booking.

**Double room rates:** $220 to $318 (depending on month), plus service charge and tax.

Author's note: Gracious and elegant with lots of facilities. Hotel Manager Muriel Richardson is a previous winner of Bermuda Tourism's "Manager of the Year" award.

**Royal Palms Hotel,** Rosemont Avenue, Pembroke (Tel. 292-1854, Fax 292-1946, Toll-free: U.S. 1-800-678-0783, Canada 1-800-799-0824, rpalms@logic.bm, www.royalpalms.bm). Walk to Hamilton: Eight minutes.

Situated on the outskirts of Hamilton, the Royal Palms has been catering to business travellers for many years. Accommodations are either in the main manor house or on-site cottages. The lush garden has a pool and patio area. There is an excellent restaurant where you can dine for lunch and dinner. All rooms are air-conditioned with cable TV and private bathroom. Some rooms have kitchen facilities. Recent additions include new minisuites and two new cottages. For the convenience of the business traveller, there are Internet and modem hookups in all rooms, and direct-dial telephones with voicemail.

**Double room rates:** $165 to $305 (depending on month), plus service charge and tax. Rate includes continental breakfast.

Author's note: Old World charm with modern-day amenities.

**Waterloo House,** Pitts Bay Road, Pembroke (Tel. 295-4480, Fax 295-2585, Toll-free U.S. 1-800-468-4100, reservations@waterloohouse.bm, www.bermudasbest.com). Walk to Hamilton: Three minutes.

This beautiful harbour-side hotel, very close to Hamilton, has a peaceful flowered courtyard where you can wind down with a cocktail after work. The hotel's dining room overlooks the harbour; plus there is an outside courtyard restaurant where you can view the comings and goings of visiting yachts. Every room is fully air-conditioned and has cable TV and a private terrace.

There is a small conference room for business visitors. Guests have use of facilities at the Coral Beach Tennis Club.

**Double room rates:** $210 to $255 (depending on month), plus service charge and tax. Rate includes breakfast and afternoon tea.

Author's note: Very attractive Bermudian-style hotel with excellent reputation.

**Rosemont Guest Apartments & Suites,** 41 Rosemont Avenue, Pembroke, HM 08 (Tel. 292-1055, Fax 295-3913, Toll-free: U.S. 1-800-367-0040, Canada 1-800-267-0040, rosemont@logic.bm, www.rosemont.bm). Walk to Hamilton: 10 minutes.

The Rosemont is clean, bright, modern, and within walking distance of Hamilton and offers quality service. The price may be medium but the quality is not—the owners, Barbara and Cyril Cooper, were voted by Bermuda Tourism as "Hotelier of the Year" (1999).

The hotel provides complimentary newspapers and morning coffee, modem hookups, coin-operated snack machines, and soft drink and laundry machines. In addition, if needed, they will arrange golf, tennis, cruises, cycle rentals, and barbecue rentals. Facilities include a pool, reverse-cycle air-conditioning, colour cable TV with movie channel, daily maid service, private patio or balcony, wheelchair accessibility, fully equipped kitchens, and sea views.

**Standard double room rates:** $156 to $170 plus service charge and tax. Corporate rates upon request.

Author's note: Excellent value for money, and proven reputation.

## BUDGET-PRICED ACCOMMODATIONS IN AND AROUND HAMILTON

Note: For a list of budget properties to rent, go to "Private House and Apartment Rentals" in chapter 2, "Before You Leave Home."

**The Oxford House,** Woodbourne Avenue, Pembroke (Tel. 295-0503, Fax 295-0250, Toll-free: U.S. 1-800-548-7758, Canada 1-800-272-2306, oxford@bermuda.com, www.oxfordhouse.com). Walk to Hamilton: One minute.

Of all the accommodations in Hamilton, this small guest property is in the most convenient situation for city offices, stores, and restaurants. Because of its proximity to the city, the business traveller can save considerably on taxi fares. The proprietor, Mrs. Ann Smith, has been catering to business clients for several years and many of her guests are repeat visitors. Oxford House is elegantly furnished throughout, and many of the rooms with antique furniture are still bright and cheery. It is a recipient of the Department of Tourism's "Cedar Tree Merit Award" for good housekeeping.

There are 12 rooms, all of which boast air-conditioning, cable TVs, coffee/tea makers, and private bathrooms. Golf can be arranged if desired.

**Single room rates:** $143 to $156, **double room rates:** $168 to $180, plus service charge and tax. Room rates include a substantial home-baked continental breakfast.

Author's note: Cosy, well-run hotel, very convenient for the city.

### HIGHER-PRICED ACCOMMODATIONS
### OUTSIDE OF HAMILTON

The following hotels will require you to procure taxis and/or public transport if carrying out business in Hamilton, but I have included them because they offer good facilities for business travellers.

**Wharf Executive Suites Hotel,** Harbour Road, Paget (Tel. 232-5700 or 1-866-STAY BDA [782-9232], www.bermudaresorthotels.com). Seven-minute ferry ride to Hamilton or 10-minute taxicab ride, depending on rush-hour traffic congestion.

Overlooking Hamilton Harbour and the immaculate skyline of Hamilton city centre, the Wharf has 15 luxury suites and five one-bedroom suites, all with sea views and all with kitchens and work centres including two-line speakerphone, fax machine, printer, copier, and high-speed Internet access. This hotel offers personalised 24-hour concierge services.

**Double room rates:** $210 to $395 (depending on month and suite), plus service charge and tax. Monthly and yearly rates available.

Author's note: This hotel is specifically designed with the business traveller in mind.

**The Fairmont Southampton,** South Shore, Southampton (Tel. 238-8000, Fax 238-8968, Toll-free: U.S. 1-800-223-1818, Canada 1-800-268-7176, www.fairmont.com). Distance to Hamilton: 20-30 minutes.

The Fairmont Southampton (previously called the Southampton Princess) is one of Bermuda's largest hotels and has several conference and reception rooms. Its main feature for business purposes is a huge 7,400-square-foot amphitheatre with sophisticated multimedia sound and projection equipment. This hotel also has its own golf course and previously won the "Gold Tee Award" by subscribers of *Successful Meetings* magazine.

**Standard single or double room rates:** $219 to $459 (depending on month), plus service charge and tax.

Author's note: Excellent business facilities. Good place to wind down after work or to bring along the family.

**Sonesta Beach Resort,** South Shore, Southampton (P.O. Box HM 1070, Hamilton, HM EX) (Tel. 238-8122, Fax 238-8463, Sales Office in Boston, Tel. 1-617-421-5470, Toll-free U.S. 1-800-SONESTA, www.sonesta.com/bermuda).

Distance to Hamilton: 20-30 minutes. (Note: Due to damage sustained by Hurricane Fabian, this hotel will be closed for repairs until May 2004.)

Sonesta deals extensively with group-related business travel. This 400-room hotel has meeting facilities to accommodate from 15 to 350 people and has been the winner of the Pinnacle Award for seven years in a row. Sonesta boasts the only large hotel directly on the beach, and certainly its location is its best selling point.

**Double room rates:** $160 to $425 (depending on month and category of room), plus service charge and tax. 30 percent discount if you arrive on a Sunday or Monday. Other discounts include fourth and fifth nights free depending on month.

Author's note: Sonesta caters regularly to groups and has experienced conference and meetings staff on hand.

**Elbow Beach Hotel,** Paget (P.O. Box HM 455, Hamilton, HM BX) (Tel. 236-3535, Fax 236-8043, Toll-free U.S. 1-800-344-3526, Reservations: 1-800-223-7434, www.mandarinoriental.com/bermuda). Distance to Hamilton: 15 minutes.

Set a little ways back from a long stretch of private sandy beach, the Elbow is one of Bermuda's largest hotels and has seven theatre-style meeting rooms, as well as classroom and banquet facilities, which offer a full range of audio-visual equipment and accommodate 10-300 guests. There is a business centre open 9 A.M. to 5 P.M. and the hotel has 24-hour room service—a service not easily found in Bermuda. Each room has free Internet connection.

**Noncorporate double room rates:** $295 to $575 (depending on month and category of room), plus service charge and tax. Corporate rates for local companies.

Author's note: The only four-star hotel in Bermuda.

**Ariel Sands Beach Club,** Devonshire (P.O. Box HM 334, Hamilton, HM BX) (Tel. 236-1010, Toll-free: U.S. 1-800-468-6610, Canada 1-800-267-7600, www.arielsands.com). Distance to Hamilton: 10 minutes.

For a truly Bermudian experience, you can stay at a luxury cottage colony. Cottage colonies in Bermuda consist of a main clubhouse with dining room, bordered by a group of tiny cottages set in landscaped gardens with private beach and/or pool. Although they usually just cater to tourists, the Ariel Sands Club, owned by actor Michael Douglas, caters to business visitors as well. The on-the-beach massage treatment to relieve the day's strains might tempt you as well.

**Noncorporate double room rates:** $210 to $375 (depending on month), plus service charge and tax. Breakfast included. Corporate rates for local companies.

Author's note: If Ariel Sands is good enough for visitors Jack Nicholson, Michael Douglas, and Catherine Zeta Jones, then it's good enough for you.

## MEDIUM-PRICED ACCOMMODATIONS
## OUTSIDE OF HAMILTON

**Grotto Bay Beach Hotel & Tennis Club,** 11 Blue Hole Hill, Hamilton Parish, CR 04 (Tel. 293-8333, Fax 293-2306, Toll-free: U.S. 1-800-582-3190, Canada 1-800-463-0851, Lsgrottobay@logic.bm, www.grottobaybeach.com). Distance to Hamilton: 20 minutes.

Only one mile from the airport (seven to Hamilton), this is a 201-room hotel (including three suites, each with two double bedrooms, three baths, and living room) in 11 separate lodges that overlook the bay with a private beach. There are four tennis courts, water sports, a bar, and main dining room for meals. Convention groups of up to 200 are catered to, with three meeting or function rooms available at no extra charge. Poolside barbecues and tennis tournaments can be arranged. Audio-visual equipment is on site. Secretarial services are available.

**Noncorporate double room rates:** $189 to $220 (depending on month), plus service charge and tax. Corporate rates in the low season.

Author's note: Very handy for airport, but quite a drive to Hamilton (remember, the speed limit is 20 mph here). Good place to get in some after-work tennis and water sports.

## BUDGET-PRICED ACCOMMODATIONS
## OUTSIDE OF HAMILTON

Budget accommodations that are close to Hamilton: **Edgehill Manor Guest House** and **La Casa Del Masa Guest Apartments,** as detailed in chapter 8, "The City of Hamilton."

Located in Paget, close to the South Shore and only a 10-minute bus or cab ride away from Hamilton, is **Paraquet Guest Apartments** (full details in "Budget-Priced Accommodations," chapter 9, "The South Shore"). **Serendipity Apartments** in Paget is detailed in chapter 12, "The Rest of the Island."

# Taking Care of Business: What You'll Need

The following is a general guide to what the businessperson requires to enter Bermuda, and the services and restaurants he or she may wish to utilise while here.

Reminder: Bermuda's area code is (441). When dialling from North America, a "1" precedes the area code. If calling from England, "001" precedes the number.

## PERMITS

1. Business travellers can now work in Bermuda for six days (and can visit three weeks in total) with the permission of a sponsoring company and the Immigration Department.

2. If an overseas branch of a Bermudian company employs you, you can work 15 days (five-week total visit allowed).

3. In cases (1) and (2), the sponsoring company must fill out an Immigration Department's Visitor Form.

4. Business visitors can also apply for a three-month work permit. Visitors without a sponsoring company must get permission from Immigration. Call the Work Permit Officer (Tel. 297-7940).

5. If you are bringing in technical and professional staff for a group-related function, you will need to apply for a work permit.

6. Permission is required from Immigration and Customs if you wish to bring in conference goods and materials with the intent to sell and/or solicit orders. Declared presentation items will not be subject to duty if they are marked clearly: *"Presentation items to be taken out of Bermuda again by individuals."*

## SALESMAN'S PERMIT REGULATIONS

Source: Bermuda Chamber of Commerce.

Application for a Salesman's Permit is made through the Bermuda Chamber of Commerce, P.O. Box HM 655, Hamilton, HM CX, Bermuda (Tel. 295-4201, Fax 292-5779, bcc@logic.bm). Note: You can download the application form from the Chamber of Commerce Web site: www.bermudacommerce.com.

The Salesman's Permit application and fee must be received 21 working days prior to the trip. The total cost of a Salesman's Permit ($370 per annum) includes the permit from the Immigration Office together with administration and processing charges. Cheques should be made payable to "Bermuda Chamber of Commerce." The chamber accepts either a company cheque or a bank draft.

A deposit is required on all product goods and samples that must be declared upon arrival in Bermuda at Customs, along with a complete invoice. This deposit will be refunded at the Customs office in Hamilton on the date of departure from Bermuda. The Bermuda Chamber of Commerce office will assist the salesperson in setting up appointments. Salespeople with a sole Bermuda agent can apply for an annual Salesman's Permit. Upon arrival in Bermuda, permits must be collected from the Bermuda Chamber of Commerce, 1 Point Pleasant Road, Hamilton, HM 11 (Tel. 295-4201, Fax 292-5779).

Neither the Customs office nor the Bermuda Chamber of Commerce are open on the weekends or public holidays, so salespersons must make their arrangements well in advance.

## DATA PORTS

These are not available in many hotels. To counteract this inconvenience, bring along a jack-splitter, so that you can simultaneously use the telephone and your laptop.

## CLOTHING

During the summer you can spot the visiting businessmen; they're the ones feeling a little hot under the collar due to their long pants. Bermudian men are lucky to wear tailored Bermuda shorts for work. Due to the hot, humid conditions, the business traveller should at least wear lightweight suits and short-sleeved shirts.

If you are a frequent business visitor to Bermuda (and only if you are), and would like to outfit yourself in Bermudian business attire, the best course of action is to ask a Bermudian friend or acquaintance to accompany you to an outfitters. He will guide you in making the correct purchases. This is important if you wish to avoid being the target of good-natured humour. English Sports Store has reasonably priced Bermuda business shorts and shirts and Marks & Spencer's sells a very smart lightweight business blazer.

If planning to get a few swings in, bring proper golfing attire, as Bermuda is rather conservative about what to wear on the course. (An exception to this is the Bermuda Golf Academy Driving Range in Southampton; see "The Sports Scene," chapter 6). You will also find that golf shirts are very handy and acceptable as smart-casual wear. A lightweight rain jacket will come in handy and can be purchased from Island Trading Ltd., Spurling Hill, Hamilton (Tel. 292-0400) or from a few of the Front Street, Hamilton stores. Swimwear is a must. Even if you don't think you'll want to take a dip, the crystal-clear Bermuda seas or the hotel pool are bound to entice you, and what a great way to relax at the end of a hectic business day. Don't forget sunglasses and sunscreen: summer or winter you will need these.

## TRANSPORT

Taxis are a must when you are in a hurry, buses when you have more time, ferries when you want to enjoy leisurely travel, and scooters for convenience. See below for taxi rates and turn to "Getting Around Bermuda," chapter 4, for details on other forms of transport.

## AIRPORT TRANSPORTATION BUSES

The services below can be arranged at the airport or prior to arrival by fax or phone. Prearranged airport transfer costs anything from $5 to $15 per person.

**Bee Line** (Tel. 293-0303, Fax 293-8015, www.beelinetransportltd.com)
**Bermuda Hosts** (Tel. 293-1334, Fax 293-1335, www.bermudahosts.bm)
**Flood Transport** (Tel. 295-3589, Fax 295-3588)

## TAXIS

Cabs cost $5 the first mile, $1.20 each additional mile (taxis that hold more than four people cost a little more). They add 25 percent for more than four people and 25 percent for midnight-6 A.M., Sundays, and public holidays. Luggage is 25 cents per piece on the roof or in the trunk. Tours: $30 per hour, maximum four people, or $42 for five to six people.

Cabs often don't have radio contacts, so if you have ordered a taxi, make sure you are waiting outside for it, as they won't hang around for long, thinking you've been picked up by another cab.

**Bermuda Radio Cabs:** Tel. 294-4141; Group Sales: Tel. 295-0041
**Bermuda Industrial Union Cabs:** Tel. 292-4476
**Bermuda Taxi Operators:** Tel. 292-5600
**Bermuda Taxi Services:** Tel. 295-8294
**Wheelchair Cabs:** Tel. 236-1456
**Sandys Taxi Services** (for the West End): Tel. 234-2344

## MINIBUS SERVICES

Rates: $3 to $5 per person. Hamilton/Pembroke/Devonshire area, 7 A.M.–midnight (Tel. 234-8986, 234-1825, or 235-5299). St. George's/St. David's area, 7:30 A.M.–10 P.M. (Tel. 297-8492 or 297-8199). Somerset/West End area: Sandys Mini-Cabs, Hook & Ladder Lane (Tel. 234-2344).

## LEISURE ACTIVITIES

Stress reduction is an important component of the business trip. Unwinding after busy business transactions is easy on an island geared towards travel and leisure. You could take a leisurely walk along a cliff path. Or you'll find swimming in the ocean or hotel pool a great rejuvenator. Just have a quick half-hour to fill? Then you may want to check out the art galleries and exhibitions at City Hall, Church Street, open Mon.-Sat. 10 A.M.–4 P.M., admission free (www.bermudanationalgallery.com). Check out "The Sports Scene," chapter 6, for squash, tennis, golf, etc.

Other Bermudian stress-busters: Tour the Botanical Gardens in Paget, rent a boat, take a ferry ride, enjoy a glass-bottom boat tour, ramble over a fort, swim with the dolphins at Dolphin Quest at the Royal Naval Dockyard, have a leisurely afternoon tea, go snorkelling or diving, go for Sunday brunch, take in a show, watch sports on TV at an informal pub, or indulge in a facial or massage.

## Dining

On the run? Then check out the "Budget-Priced Eateries" in chapter 8, "The City of Hamilton." For good-value, healthy, and fresh pasta meals both to take out and sit in, you can't beat **Pasta Basta** on Elliott Street in Hamilton (Tel. 295-9785). But if you want to have a sit-down meal, especially when entertaining prospective clients, you need to know where there are restaurants with a good reputation.

The following is a sample of restaurants catering to the corporate client. It is usually wise to make advance reservations. These and other restaurants are outlined in more detail in chapter 8, "The City of Hamilton."

### BUSINESS LUNCHES IN HAMILTON

Restaurants popular with businesspeople for lunch in Hamilton are **La Trattoria** (Tel. 292-7059), the **Little Venice** (Tel. 295-3503), and **Portofino** (Tel. 292-2375)—three good Italian eateries.

**The Monte Carlo** (Tel. 295-5453). Upscale restaurant always busy with the business crowd.

**Harbourfront Restaurant,** Front Street (Tel. 295-4207). Subdued interior makes an ideal atmosphere for a business lunch.

**Fresco's Restaurant and Wine Bar** (previously Chancery Wine Bar), Chancery Lane (Tel. 295-5058). Mediterranean menu with Bermudian flavours; CNBC and Bloomberg on TV keep business clients in tune with what's happening in the business world.

### BUSINESS DINNERS

When dining or entertaining in the evening, you could select one of Bermuda's many pubs. If you need to splurge on a restaurant, try one of the following for prices that aren't through the roof.

### HIGHER-PRICED RESTAURANTS INSIDE HAMILTON FOR DINNER

**La Coquille Restaurant & Bar,** East Broadway (waterside) (Tel. 292-6122). Situated in the Bermuda Underwater Exploration Institute building.

**Ascots,** (Royal Palms Hotel), 24 Rosemont Avenue, Pembroke (Tel. 295-9644). Award-winning restaurant set in an English country garden.

*Sunset, courtesy of Bermuda Tourism*

*Dolphin Quest at the Southampton Princess, courtesy of Bermuda Tourism*

*Ferry to Paget, courtesy of Bermuda Tourism*

*Playing Golf, courtesy of Bermuda Tourism*

*Island Hopping, courtesy of Bermuda Tourism*

*Gombey Dancers, courtesy of Bermuda Tourism*

*Horseshoe Bay on the South Shore, courtesy of Bermuda Tourism*

*City Hall (in the City of Hamilton), courtesy of Bermuda Tourism*

*Businessmen (wearing Bermuda business attire), courtesy of Bermuda Tourism*

*Snorkelling, courtesy of Bermuda Tourism*

*Pink and Blue Bus, courtesy of Bermuda Tourism*

*Lunch Wagon, courtesy of Bermuda Tourism*

*Concert in the Park, Victoria Park, Hamilton, courtesy of Bermuda Tourism*

*The* Deliverance *(full-sized replica of boat that shipwrecked survivors made to get to Virginia in 1610) in St. George's, courtesy of Bermuda Tourism*

*Waterville Historical House, Paget, courtesy of Bermuda Tourism*

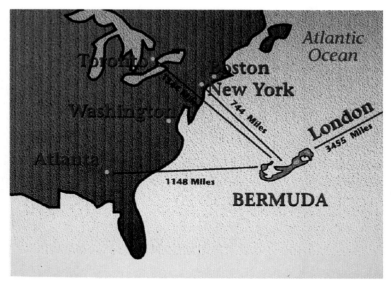

*Location, Location, Location, courtesy of Bermuda Tourism*

*Munro Beach, courtesy of Catherine Harriott*

*Cumberland House, courtesy of Catherine Harriott*

*Royal Naval Dockyard, courtesy of Catherine Harriott*

*Children's Playground (at the Royal Naval Dockyard), courtesy of Catherine Harriott*

*Railway Trail Sign, courtesy of Catherine Harriott*

*Warwick Long Bay on the South Shore, courtesy of Catherine Harriott*

*Child's Paradise, courtesy of Catherine Harriott*

*Telephone Box, courtesy of Catherine Harriott*

*Sunset in September, courtesy of Catherine Harriott*

*Children's Playground (at Warwick Long Bay on the South Shore), courtesy of Catherine Harriott*

*State House (oldest stone building where Parliament met during the 1600s), courtesy of Catherine Harriott*

*Midway, courtesy of Catherine Harriott*

*Sign to St. George's Preservation Area, courtesy of Catherine Harriott*

*The Little Chapel at Heydon Trust, courtesy of Catherine Harriott*

*Flowers on a Frangipani Tree, courtesy of Catherine Harriott*

*Mini Golf Adventure, courtesy of Catherine Harriott*

*Sign to Fort Scaur, courtesy of Catherine Harriott*

*Non-Track Red and Green Train (Royal Naval Dockyard), courtesy of Catherine Harriott*

*Welcome to Bermuda, (Sign Outside Airport), courtesy of Catherine Harriott*

*Taylor House, courtesy of Catherine Harriott*

*Afternoon Tea Anyone?, courtesy of Catherine Harriott*

*Morning Glory, courtesy of Catherine Harriott*

*Rosedon Hotel, courtesy of Rosedon Hotel*

**The Wellington Room & Poinciana Terrace,** Waterloo House Hotel, Pitts Bay Road, Pembroke (Tel. 295-4480). This restaurant set in a pretty hotel opposite the harbour (great place for afternoon tea as well) has won AAA's Five-Star Diamond Award for four years running.

### HIGHER-PRICED RESTAURANTS JUST OUTSIDE HAMILTON FOR DINNER

**Café Lido** (Elbow Beach Hotel), Paget (Tel. 236-9884). Impressive beachside views and service (see chapter 9, "The South Shore," for more details).

### MEDIUM-PRICED RESTAURANTS INSIDE HAMILTON FOR DINNER

**Port O'Call,** 87 Front Street (Tel. 295-5373)—seafood, nautical theme; **Portofino,** Bermudiana Road (Tel. 292-2375)—Italian; **La Trattoria,** Washington Lane (Tel. 292-7059)—Italian; **Red Carpet,** 37 Reid Street (Tel. 295-6774)—Continental; **Chopsticks,** Reid Street (Tel. 292-0791)—Chinese; **Lobster Pot & Boathouse Bar,** Bermudiana Road (Tel. 292-6898)—Fish; M.R. Onions (Tel. 292-5012)—American/Bermudian.

### MEDIUM-PRICED RESTAURANTS JUST OUTSIDE HAMILTON FOR DINNER

**Aqua Seaside Restaurant** (Ariel Sands Beach Club), South Shore Road, Devonshire (Tel. 236-1010)—seaside restaurant and bar; **North Rock Brewing Company,** South Shore Road, Devonshire (Tel. 236-6633)—brew pub and restaurant.

### COFFEE STOPS

Hooked on caffeine? Then you need to know where to grab a decent cup of java. Try **Caffè Latte,** 1 Washington Mall, Hamilton (Tel. 296-1188), and 8 York Street, St. George's (Tel. 297-8196), or **Rock Island Coffee,** 48 Reid Street, Hamilton (Tel. 296-5241).

## Where to Find . . .

### EVENT AND TOUR PLANNERS

Event planners take the work out of organising everything from hotel rooms to tours and events.

**Meyer Destination Management,** Somers Wharf, St. George's (Tel. 295-9733, Fax 292-8251, carlaf@stgeorges.meyer.bm, www.meyer.bm).

**Destination Bermuda,** Washington Mall, Hamilton (Tel. 292-2325, Fax 292-2252, jveney@cdt.bm).

**Select Sites Group,** Suite 764, 48 Par-La-Ville Road, Hamilton (Tel. 292-9741, Fax 292-2770, ssgbda@logic.bm).

**Bermuda Escapes** (Tel. 236-4034, www.bermudaescapes.com). Provides vacation packages for the business visitor including ticket sales for performances.

**Magic Moments** (Tel. 296-8848). Party store specialising in organising theme parties: Mardi Gras, Country and Western, and Hawaiian. They also have 1970s supplies such as lava lamps, disco balls, fog machines, platform shoes, Afro wigs, etc.

**Party ideas for group and incentive travellers:** Diving trip, jazz picnic, kayaking trip, tea party, Bermuda Regiment Band, art gallery tour, Gombey dancers, horseback trail, snorkelling trip, buggy rides (especially evening), cruise to private island, pub tour, ferry ride, glass-bottom boat tour, or beach barbecue.

## PHONE CARDS

Prepaid phone cards from **Cable & Wireless** are sold at their Hamilton office on the corner of Burnaby and Church Street, or at retail outlets around the island. Cards are sold in $10, $25, or $50 denominations.

Discount telephone rates are from Monday to Sunday, 9 P.M.–7 A.M. (Canada), 6 P.M.–7 A.M. (U.K.), and 7 P.M.–7 A.M. (U.S.). Callback services cannot be used in Bermuda. Bermuda time is Greenwich Mean Time minus four hours: one hour ahead of New York, Boston, and Toronto; four hours behind London; 12 hours behind Hong Kong; and five hours behind Paris.

## CELLULAR HOOK-UP

To hook up your Verizon cell phone, call Bermuda Telephone Company (**BTC**, Tel. 292-6032). Rates are $30 activation plus $5 per day. Calls cost 60 cents daytime and 35 cents 7 P.M.–7 A.M. Overseas calls cost extra.

## CELLULAR RENTAL

Upon arrival you can rent a cell phone at the airport, next to the British Airways check-in (Tel. 297-4663). Rates are $35 activation, $8 per day, plus cost of local and long-distance calls.

Or **Internet Lane** (Tel. 296-9972, Fax 296-9217) rents out prepaid cell phones for $2 per day and you can load the phones with any amount up to $100.

## LOCAL E-MAIL HOOK-UP

For those of you bringing in laptops with modems (and who isn't these days?) and wishing to hook up with local e-mail, try **Logic Communications** (Tel. 292-HELP, Fax 295-1149, www.logic.bm). Rates are $29 per week.

The airport also has an Internet Lounge, located in the Departure Lounge, offering high-speed Internet facilities. And there are Internet-surfing and e-mail-checking facilities in Hamilton at **Internet Lane,** 11 The Walkway, off Reid Street (Tel. 296-9972), **Print Express** on Burnaby Street (Tel. 295-3950), and **Twice Told Tales** bookstore on Parliament Street (Tel. 296-1995), as well as **Flanagan's Irish Pub & Restaurant** on Front Street (Tel. 295-8299).

Tip: Bring an electric extension cord and a long phone wire, so that you can use your laptop in any convenient position, either at a desk or in bed.

## BANKS

There are three licensed banks in Bermuda (with branches throughout the island), with balance sheet assets in excess of $15 billion and assets under management of around $75 billion. On all bank accounts, the English common law rule of confidentiality predominates.

**Bank of Bermuda Limited,** 6 Front Street, Hamilton (Tel. 295-4000).

**Bank of N.T. Butterfield,** 65 Front Street, Hamilton (Tel. 295-1111).

**Bermuda Commercial Bank Limited,** 44 Church Street, Hamilton (Tel. 295-5678).

For keeping up to date with financial information and business news, a Bloomberg computer is available for use in the hallway of Washington Mall in Hamilton.

## LAWYERS

To open an offshore business in Bermuda you will need the services of a corporate lawyer. There are numerous lawyers in Bermuda; for a detailed list, check out the Bermuda Yellow Pages under "Barristers & Attorneys." Here are some sample listings:

**Appleby, Spurling & Kempe** (Tel. 295-2244, Fax 292-8666, www.ask.bm)

**Conyers, Dill & Pearman** (Tel. 295-1422, Fax 292-4720, info@cdp.bm, www.cdp.bm)

**Cox, Hallet & Wilkinson** (Tel. 295-4630, Fax 292-7880, cw@cw.bm)

**Marshall, Diel & Myers** (Tel. 295-7105, Fax 292-6814, info@law.bm, www.law.bm)

**Mello, Jones & Martin** (Tel. 292-1345, Fax 292-2277, mjm@mjm.bm, www.mjm.bm)

**Moniz & George** (Tel. 295-8607, Fax 292-8454)

## U.S. CHEQUE CASHING

Many stores now accept U.S. cheques for purchases. If you need to cash a cheque, go to **Bermuda Financial Network,** 133 Front Street, Hamilton (Tel. 292-1799, support@easypay.bm). They are also a representative for American Express and will help with any queries cardholders may have.

## FAX MACHINES

There are public fax machines in the Departure Lounge at the airport and at the Visitors' Service Bureau offices. Also, in Hamilton: General Post Office, Church Street; Cable & Wireless, Church Street; and Numbers 1 and 6 Passenger Terminals, Front Street.

## PHOTOCOPIERS

**Internet Lane,** 11 The Walkway, off Reid Street, Hamilton (Tel. 296-9972); **The Business Centre,** Washington Mall, Hamilton (Tel. 292-3458); **Mailboxes Unlimited,** 48 Par-La-Ville Road, Hamilton (Tel. 292-6563), Middle Road, and Church Street, Hamilton (Tel. 292-5656); **Pronto Print,** 44 Victoria Street, Hamilton (Tel. 295-0183); and **Bermuda National Library,** 13 Queen Street, Hamilton (Tel. 295-2905).

## COMPUTER TECHNOLOGY

Check out **The Computer Centre** (Tel. 292-1779, idmac@ibm.net), **ACT** (Tel. 295-1616, info@act.bm, www.act.bm), or **Gateway Systems Ltd.,** 10 Queen Street, Hamilton (Tel. 292-0341, Fax 292-0455).

## SECRETARIAL SERVICES

Most of the larger resort hotels offer secretarial services; if not, there are several secretarial agencies in Hamilton. All the agencies charge the same rate per hour (so temps won't shop around for higher salaries). Many agencies offer shorthand services as well as the usual typing and computer desktop services. Two of the top agencies are **Business Services of Bermuda,** Church Street, Hamilton (Tel. 295-5175) and **Professional Consultants,** 18 Queen Street, Hamilton (Tel. 295-1847). Check out the Bermuda Yellow Pages under "Secretarial Services" for more agencies.

## CONFERENCE FACILITIES AND BOARDROOMS

Note: Meetings in Bermuda are U.S. tax-deductible.

**Bermuda Underwater Exploration Institute** (Tel. 292-7219)—theatre auditorium for large groups.

**Fairmont Southampton** (Tel. 238-8000)—facilities for meetings of 14 to 1,500 people. State-of-the-art amphitheatre. One large and one medium convention room, one boardroom, and eight small break-out rooms.

**Hamilton Princess** (Tel. 295-3000)—three large meeting rooms plus four small break-out rooms.

**Chamber of Commerce** (Tel. 295-4201)—one boardroom fits 50 people.

**Bermuda Insurance Institute** (Tel. 295-1596)—one boardroom fits 50 people, one boardroom fits 25, and a small one fits 15 people.

## GROUP BOAT CHARTERS

**Bermuda Island Cruises** (Tel. 292-8652, info@bic.bm, www.bicbda.bm). Will arrange anything you require for group-related travel, from musical entertainment to glass-bottom boat tours and trips to private islands.

**Andrea Christine Charters** (Tel. 236-1487, Cell 237-3048, Fax 292-5783). Luxury motor yacht cruises available for hourly or daily cocktail, luncheon, and dinner cruises. This 60-foot boat has air-conditioning, heating, television, VCR, and stereo system.

**Jessie James Cruises** (Tel. 296-5801, Fax 296-7088, www.jessiejames.bm). 57-foot motor yacht available for sightseeing, swimming, snorkelling, cocktails, buffet dinners, parties, etc.—maximum capacity is 40 people. Also 31-foot *Seaquest* available for sightseeing, snorkelling, glass-bottom, and cocktail cruises—maximum capacity is 20 people for cruising and 16 people for snorkelling.

**Longtail Boat** (Tel. 296-5263, Fax 296-9908, mvlongtail@hotmail.com). Buffet-style parties and water-shuttle services available.

**Coral Sea Cruises,** King's Square, St. George's (Tel. 235-2425, bevans@northrock.bm, www.charterbermuda.com). 60-foot glass-bottom cruiser tour available for lunch and dinner cruises, corporate cruises, wedding receptions, sunset cruises, and formal dinners.

**Fantasea Bermuda Ltd.** (Tel. 236-1300 or 236-6339, info@fantasea.bm, www.fantasea.bm). Offers group services for sailing, snorkel trips, kayak safaris, bike tours, dive charters, beach parties, and catamaran and cocktail cruises to private island.

**Blue Safari Tours** (Tel. 236-5599, Cell 734-9098, info@bluewatersafari.com, www.bluewatersafari.com). Private charters for minimum of two hours, includes swimming and/or snorkelling. Beer and wine and towels onboard. Picnics can be arranged upon request.

**Tam-Marina Group Charters** (Tel. 236-0127). Splash out on a luxury yacht cruise for either your business or vacation group. *Lady Tamara* licensed for 250 passengers, rates from $990 (up to 70 people for one hour) to $2,660 (125-250 people for three hours). *Lady Erica* licensed for 70 passengers, rates from $457 (20 people for one hour) to $1,495 (20 people for six hours)—add $5-$25 charge (depending on hours) for each extra passenger. Add to rates: $35 corporation tax, bridge openings $50 per hour, snorkelling equipment, karaoke equipment, bar and drink charges. Add 20 percent to boat rate for public holidays.

## VIDEOCONFERENCING

**Cable & Wireless** has facilities in Hamilton (Tel. 297-7000). Or try **Bermuda Technologies Ltd.** (Tel. 296-7000).

## INVESTIGATIONS

Many companies these days utilise the services of a private investigator to double-check potential business partners or prospective employees. It could save you lots of money and hassle in the long run. Check the Bermuda Yellow Pages (www.bermudayp.com) under "Private Investigations."

Or you could subscribe to the **Offshore Business** Web site to search for fraud court cases in Bermuda and other offshore jurisdictions (www.offshorebusiness.com). This service is not free but well worth it for serious business executives doing due-diligence background checks.

## COURIERS IN HAMILTON

For local and overseas shipping: **IBC,** Dallas Building, Park Road (Tel. 295-2467); **FedEx Express,** 25 Serpentine Road (Tel. 295-3854); **DHL,** Washington Mall, 16 Church Street (Tel. 295-3300); **Sprint International Express,** Commerce Building, Third Floor, 54 Reid Street (Tel. 296-7866); **Mailboxes Unlimited** (agents for UPS, IBC, DHL, and TNT plus regular air or surface mail), two locations: 48 Par-La-Ville Road (Tel. 292-6563) and 12 Church Street (Tel. 296-5656).

## DRY CLEANERS

**Just Shirts** (they do everything else too), Par-La-Ville Road, next to M.R. Onions restaurant (Tel. 292-5366). Just Shirts provides a delivery service. Wednesday is discount day. They also have two other convenient drop-off locations at their packing and shipping courier outlets—see **Mailboxes Unlimited** in the courier section above.

## SHOE REPAIR

**Heel Sew Quick,** 34 Church Street, Hamilton (Tel. 295-1559). Also drop-off service at the **East End Florist,** York Street, St. George's (near the police station).

## FITNESS CENTRES

**The Total Fitness Centre,** Brunswick Street, Hamilton (Tel. 295-0087). Use of facilities for one day, $15 walk-in rate. This entitles you to use of state-of-the-art weight room, whirlpool, showers, towels, and gym. The rate for one week is $60. If you wish to join in an aerobics class, then the charge is $12. Princes Deli, an excellent place to grab lunch, is also in the building.

**The Olympic Club,** 13 Dundonald Street, Hamilton (Tel. 292-4095, Fax 296-1000). Popular gym and exercise club. Daily rate for visitors: $12. Weekly rate: $35. Includes gym, workout equipment, and classes.

**SeaView Health & Fitness Centre,** 9 North Shore Road, Devonshire (Tel. 292-7266). Fitness centre featuring Cybex and Trotter exercise equipment, Stairmasters, Freeclimbers, and strength equipment. Daily rate for visitors: $12. Weekly rate: $65. Personal trainers available upon request.

## NIGHTSPOTS

Nightspots popular with business visitors are **The Deep** night-club at Elbow Beach Hotel on the South Shore, and **The Hog Penny** (pub) and **Blue Juice Disco and Bar** in Hamilton. Sports fans will enjoy **Flanagan's Irish Pub** or **Robin Hood Pub & Restaurant.** See "Nightlife" in chapter 8, "The City of Hamilton," for full details on these and other clubs.

## READING MATERIAL

Overseas newspapers are available at most pharmacies and some hotel lobbies. Here is a list of business magazines and publications:

***Bermuda Business Visitor:*** Magazine, available both in Bermuda and North America. Jam-packed guide includes a candid look at the island, giving facts, tips, and opinions on Bermuda's business community. Published by Bermuda Marketing Ltd. On sale in the U.S. at magazine stores or e-mail cbarclay@bm.bm for order details.

***The Bottom Line:*** Quarterly, free magazine with several in-depth articles on the Bermudian international business market, local business profiles, and technology features. Available at retail outlets in Bermuda or call Crown Communications (Tel. 295-5881).

***Bermudian Business:*** Business magazine, especially focused on the catastrophe insurance market, accounting, and financial services. Affiliated with the *Bermudian Magazine* and published quarterly by Bermudian Publishing Co. (Tel. 295-0695, berpub@logic.bm).

***Who's Who:*** Compilation of some of the top business and government people in Bermuda. Published by Bermuda Marketing Ltd. and sold at bookstores and retail outlets.

*Bermuda Facts and Figures:* Every business traveller should know about the market they are visiting. A printed digest of statistics is available from the Bermuda Government Department of Statistics: Global House, 43 Church Street, Hamilton, HM 12 (Tel. 297-7711), or The Bermuda Library on Queen Street.

## Business Web Sites

**Bermuda Directory** (lists names, addresses, telephone numbers, and e-mail addresses): www.netlinkbermuda.com
**Bermuda Inc.:** www.bermuda-inc.com
**Bermuda Insurance Institute:** www.bermuda-insurance.org
**Bermuda International Business Association (BIBA):** www.biba.org
**Bermuda Monetary Authority:** www.bma.bm
**Bermuda Stock Exchange:** www.bsx.com
**Bermuda Yellow Pages:** www.bermudayp.com
**Chamber of Commerce:** www.bermudacommerce.com
**Computer Society of Bermuda:** www.csb.bm
**Executive Relocation Services:** www.bermudarelocate.com
**Law firms:** www.hg.org/firms-bermuda.html
**Offshore Newsletter** (covering business-related and legal matters in offshore jurisdictions including Bermuda; subscription charge): www.offshorebusiness.com
**Rims** (Risk & Insurance Management Society): www.rims.org

## Handy Phone Numbers

**Attorney General:** Tel. 292-2463, Fax 292-3608
**Bermuda Archives:** Tel. 297-7737, Fax 292-2349
**Bermuda Employer's Council:** Tel. 295-5070, Fax 295-1966
**Bermuda Insurance Institute (BII):** Tel. 295-1596, Fax 295-3532
**Bermuda International Business Association (BIBA):** Tel. 292-0632, Fax 292-1797
**Bermuda Monetary Authority** (among other things, is responsible for processing applications for incorporation): Tel. 295-5278, Fax 292-7471
**Bermuda's Group & Incentive Service:** Tel. 236-1633, Fax 236-1662
**Bermuda Stock Exchange:** Tel. 292-7212 or 7213, Fax 292-7619 (the world's first offshore, fully electronic stock exchange with over 100 companies listed, and with a market capitalisation in excess of $25 billion)
**Bermuda Tourism, Group & Incentive Sales Department:** (U.S.) 1-800-223-6106 ext. 213; (Europe) 171-771-7001

**Chamber of Commerce (International Companies Division):** Tel. 295-4201, Fax 292-5779

**Customs Department:** Tel. 295-4816, Fax 295-5392

**Department of Technology & Information:** Tel. 292-6832, Fax 295-5267

**Government (Central Switchboard):** Tel. 295-5151

**Executive Relocation Ltd.:** Tel. 232-0059, Fax 232-0060 (contact Iris Doughty, who assists in the smooth transition of executives and their families relocating to Bermuda)

**Immigration Department:** Tel. 295-5151, Fax 295-4115 (Work Permit Office: Tel. 297-7940)

**Institute of Chartered Accounts of Bermuda (ICAB):** Tel. 292-7479, Fax 295-3121

**Ministry of Finance:** Tel. 295-5151, Fax 295-5727

**Registrar of Companies:** Tel. 297-7579, Fax 292-6640

**Visitors' Service Bureau (Tourist Information):** Tel. 295-1480 (next to Ferry Terminal, Front Street)

# 8

# The City of Hamilton

Hamilton city centre, Bermuda's bustling shopping hub and capital since 1815, is basically squashed into one colourful, busy square mile—not your typical sprawling metropolis. You'll hear people talk about Front Street a great deal, especially when it comes to shopping and entertainment. Overlooking the harbour, Front Street is Hamilton's main street full of stores, clubs, and restaurants.

The friendliest person in Bermuda is Johnny Barnes, who can be spotted every weekday morning at the Crow Lane Roundabout in Hamilton, waving to commuters between the hours of 5:30 and 10:30, come rain or shine. Just a few yards away, a statue in his honour can be seen waving anytime.

## 1. Transport

If you need to catch a bus out of Hamilton, the main Bus Terminal is on Church Street, next to City Hall. From the cashier's booth you can purchase bus passes, tickets, and tokens to practically anywhere on the island. You can also transfer to any destination with a transfer ticket purchased on your last bus.

The main ferry terminal at Albouys Point is at the end of Front Street (adjacent to the Visitors' Bureau). Albouys Point is also where many glass-bottom boat cruises set sail. The Somerset ferry goes to Dockyard via Somerset, with other little scenic stops along the way, and you can take your scooter or bike aboard. There are also ferries to Paget, Warwick (and St. George's in the summer) landing at five different stops along Harbour Road.

Bus and ferry passes: One-day, three-day, seven-day, monthly, or three-monthly passes are good money-savers. For full details on buses and ferries check out chapter 4, "Getting Around Bermuda."

You can grab a cab at taxi stands along Front Street and Church Street, or by calling 295-4141.

Getting about Hamilton is made a lot easier with the red and green non-track train service that transports passengers around the main roads, taking in sights such as the National Gallery, Historical Society, Anglican Cathedral, and the Bermuda Underwater Exploration Institute. A similar train has been successfully in operation at the Royal Naval Dockyard, and by extending the service to Hamilton it gives city visitors the convenience of seeing the sights without getting too worn out. However, this service is usually reserved for cruise-ship passengers, so it may be wise to book ahead by calling Tel. 236-5972.

## 2. Accommodations

### HIGHER-PRICED ACCOMMODATIONS
Note: To get deals on rooms at the large resort hotels in Bermuda, go to the "Package Deals" section in chapter 2, "Before You Leave Home."

**Fairmont Hamilton Princess** (Hamilton Harbour), Pitts Bay Road, Pembroke (Tel. 295-3000, Fax 295-1914, Toll-free: U.S. 1-800-223-1818, Canada 1-800-268-7176, Hamilton@fairmont.com, www.princessbermuda.com).

The Princess, as it is locally known, is definitely on many people's list of favourite places to stay and dine. Built in 1884, it was in the forefront of Bermuda's tourism beginnings, no doubt enhanced by visits from royalty at the time. With over 400 rooms, the Hamilton Princess is currently Hamilton's largest property. As you enter the lobby, polished tiled floors and a unique indoor wall garden with trickling waterfalls give you a grand first impression. Turn right for the reception area or left for views of seafront gardens with fishponds intersected with tiny wooden bridges.

Water sports can be arranged from the Princess's private deepwater dock, or you can relax by the outdoor freshwater and saltwater swimming pools. This hotel has three restaurants—see the "Higher-Priced Restaurants" guide below. (There is also a meal exchange programme with the Fairmont Southampton Princess, on the South Shore.) The Princess also has night-club entertainment during the summer months in the Gazebo Lounge.

There is a daily ferry to its sister hotel, the Fairmont Southampton, on the South Shore, where guests can take advantage of the beach, play tennis, and play a round of golf.

**Single or double room rates:** $349 to $699 (depending on month and category of room), plus service charge and tax.

**Waterloo House** (Hamilton Harbour), Pitts Bay Road, Pembroke (Tel. 295-4480, Fax 295-2585, Toll-free: U.S. 1-800-468-4100, reservations@ waterloohouse.bm, www.waterloohouse.com).

Member of the prestigious Relais and Chateau chain of hotels, this peach-coloured hotel with flower-filled window boxes and Old World service is located very close to shops and restaurants. In the centre of the hotel is a peaceful courtyard bursting with plant life where you can wind down with a cocktail. Freshly baked cakes are served at afternoon tea between 4 and 5 in the dining room overlooking the harbour. The restaurant has been a winner of AAA's Five-Star Diamond Award for four years running. Every room has air-conditioning, cable TV, hair dryers, fax and Internet access, and private terrace with sea, pool, or garden views (some of the deluxe ones have Jacuzzi tubs). There's a small heated pool and hotel boat for cruises and picnics. Guests also have full use of facilities at the Coral Beach Club in Paget.

**Double room rates:** $210 to $650 (depending on month and category of room), plus service charge and tax.

## MEDIUM-PRICED ACCOMMODATIONS

**Rosedon Hotel,** Pitts Bay Road, Pembroke (Tel. 295-1640, Fax 295-5904, Toll-free: U.S. 1-800-742-5008, rosedon@logic.bm, www.rosedonbermuda.com).

Once a private residence (this was the first home in Bermuda to be lit by gas lamps), the Rosedon is now a friendly hotel, well run, with all modern facilities and a year-round swimming pool. All rooms have private bath, reverse-cycle air-conditioning unit, radio, cable TV, coffee maker, refrigerator, ceiling fan, iron and ironing board, hair dryer, and wall safe.

**Double room rates:** $220 to $318 (depending on month), plus service charge and tax. Afternoon tea is served daily and is included in the EP (European Plan) room rate. Full-course breakfast and afternoon tea are included in the BP (Breakfast Plan) rate.

**Royal Palms Hotel,** Rosemont Avenue, Pembroke (Tel. 292-1854, Fax 292-1946, Toll-free: U.S. 1-800-678-0783, Canada 1-800-799-0824, rpalms@logic.bm, www.royalpalms.bm).

The Royal Palms is a traditional Bermudian hotel with lush tropical gardens overlooking the pool and patio area. Accommodations are either in the main manor house or on-site cottages. This hotel has an excellent restaurant, Ascots, where you can dine for lunch and dinner. All rooms are air-conditioned, with cable TV and private bathroom; some have kitchen facilities.

**Double room rates:** $165 to $305 (depending on month), plus service charge and tax. Rates include continental breakfast.

**Rosemont Guest Apartments,** Rosemont Avenue, Pembroke (P.O. Box HM 37, Hamilton, HM AX, Tel. 292-1055, Fax 295-3913, Toll-free: U.S. 1-800-367-0040, Canada 1-800-661-8363, rosemont@logic.bm, www.rosemont.bm).

Overlooking Hamilton Harbour, set in pleasant gardens and yet only five minutes' walk from Hamilton city centre, Rosemont consists of 37 self-contained units; clean and modern; each with private patio or balcony, cable TV, kitchen, full bath, and reverse-cycle air-conditioning. Winner of the 1999 VIP (Visitors Industry Partnership) award; nothing is too much trouble for the guests at Rosemont. Washer/dryer available 24 hours, along with ironing boards and irons. No charge for local phone calls. Adjoining rooms available on request. Complimentary morning coffee and newspaper. Nice pool with diving board and patio area.

**Standard double room rates:** $156 to $170 (depending on month and whether poolside or garden area), plus service charge and tax. Suites cost more.

**The Oxford House,** Woodbourne Avenue, Pembroke (Tel. 295-0503, Fax 295-0250, Toll-free: U.S. 1-800-548-7758, Canada 1-800-272-2306, oxford@bermuda.com, www.oxfordhouse.com).

Small but well-run guesthouse on the outskirts of the city. Handy for shops and restaurants, this is a charming and tastefully decorated property. Winner of the "Cedar Tree Merit Award" for good housekeeping. There are 12 rooms, all of which boast air-conditioning, cable TVs, coffee/tea makers, and private baths. Golf can be arranged if desired.

**Double room rates:** $168 to $180, plus service charge and tax. Rates include substantial home-baked continental breakfast.

### BUDGET-PRICED ACCOMMODATIONS

Note: For a list of budget properties to rent, go to "Private House and Apartment Rentals" in chapter 2, "Before You Leave Home."

There is no such thing as "roughing it" in Bermuda, so "budget" in this book represents great value for the money.

**Edgehill Manor Guest House,** Rosemont Avenue, Pembroke (P.O. Box HM 1048, Hamilton, HM EX, Tel. 295-7124, Fax 295-3850, edgehill@bermuda.com, www.bermuda.com/edgehill).

Colonial-style guesthouse convenient to Hamilton's shopping and restaurants yet located in quiet residential area. Guestrooms have private balconies or private terrace, cable TV, air-conditioning, safe, microwave, and refrigerator.

**Double room rates:** $150 to $182 (depending on season), plus service charge and tax. Rates include sumptuous home-baked continental breakfast.

**La Casa Del Masa Guest Apartments,** Eve's Hill Lane, Pembroke Park, Pembroke West (Tel. 292-8726, Fax 295-4447, Toll-free: U.S. 1-800-637-4116, lac@bspl.bm).

High on a hill, close to the city, with sweeping views of the North Shore and the Great Sound, extending to the western tip of the island. Self-contained apartment complex with fully equipped kitchens. Decorated in the modern style, each attractive apartment has two double beds and full bathroom, cable TV, and air-conditioning. After a day's shopping in the city, what could be better than a relaxing soak in the outdoor whirlpool or a dip in the pool? Complimentary rum swizzle (cocktail) on arrival.

**Double room rates:** $100 to $150 (depending on season), plus service charge and tax. Honeymoon specials available.

## 3. Restaurants

### HIGHER-PRICED RESTAURANTS

Reservations are recommended at the following restaurants. Dress is smart-casual during the day, with a jacket and tie usually expected for men in the evening.

**La Coquille Restaurant & Bar,** at the Bermuda Underwater Exploration Institute (BUEI), Foot of the Lane (Tel. 292-6122). Open for lunch noon-2:20, dinner 6:30-10. Overlooking Hamilton Harbour, this spacious restaurant has French Provincial cuisine. Featured on Sunday between 9:30 and 2:30 is a popular breakfast buffet: cereals, fruit, pastries, omelettes and eggs Benedict made to order, scrambled eggs, sausage, bacon, and Bermuda codfish and potatoes. Afterwards, take a tour of the BUEI for $10.50 per person. Boat moorings available.

**Ascots Restaurant,** at the Royal Palms Hotel, corner of Rosemont Avenue and Richmond Road, Pembroke (Tel. 295-9644). Open for lunch and dinner. Award-winning restaurant with good reputation. Lunchtime is particularly popular, so reservations are recommended. Dine inside in the country-style restaurant or outside in the tropical garden.

**The Wellington Room & Poinciana Terrace,** Waterloo House Hotel, Pitts Bay Road, Pembroke (Tel. 295-4480). Open for lunch noon-2:30, dinner 7-9:30. Traditional Bermudian harbourside restaurant with old-fashioned service and peaceful ambience.

**The Monte Carlo,** Victoria Street, behind City Hall (Tel. 295-5453). Open for lunch noon-3, dinner 6-10:30 (Sun. dinner only). South-of-France-style, cedar-beamed fine restaurant with every menu selection Cuisine Du Soleil. Complimentary rosemary focaccia topped with olive-paste tapenade with your meal.

**Harbourfront Restaurant,** Front Street, opposite Ferry Terminal (Tel. 292-4207). Open for lunch Mon.-Sat. from 11:30, dinner from 6. This nautical restaurant overlooking Hamilton Harbour is famous for its Sushi Happy Hour and business lunch menu.

**Fresco's Restaurant and Wine Bar** (formerly Chancery Wine Bar), Chancery Lane (Tel. 295-5058). Open for lunch and dinner. The term *fresco* means a picture painted in wet limestone on a wall or ceiling and, true to its name, Fresco's has a wall-to-wall garden fresco painted by local artist Nick Minugh. The cuisine is Mediterranean, with lots of choices for vegetarians as well as seafood, chicken, and meat dishes. Inside or covered courtyard dining.

**Port O'Call,** 87 Front Street (Tel. 295-5373). Open for lunch Mon.-Fri. 11:30-3, dinner from 5 (Sun. 6:30). Another nautical-theme restaurant—you actually feel as if you are onboard ship—with attentive service and good seafood selection.

**Barracuda Grill,** 5 Burnaby Hill (above The Hog Penny, Tel. 292-1609, www.barracuda-grill.com). Previously Fisherman's Reef. Open every night for dinner 5:30-10, weekdays for lunch noon-3. Seafood and chop restaurant decorated in warm hues. Example entrée: Rockfish and Lobster: Pan Seared Rockfish Fillet with Butter Poached Maine Lobster Meat, Truffled Avocado Green Onion Risotto Steamed Aspiration, and Lemon-Caper-Tarragon Beurre Monte. The bar offers wine by the glass—over 20 types.

**Fairmont Hamilton Princess Hotel** (Tel. 295-3000). There are three main restaurants at the Princess: **Heritage Court** open for breakfast, lunch, and dinner (closes at 1 A.M.). **Harbourview Ballroom,** a spacious restaurant overlooking Hamilton Harbour. Or you might enjoy sitting around the pool at the Mediterranean Bistro, **Harley's,** which overlooks the harbour too. Harley is the name of the person who first built the hotel, and he was lucky enough to have HRH Princess Louise, Queen Victoria's daughter, stay here, and with some clever 19th-century marketing, he promptly changed the hotel's name to the Princess.

## MEDIUM-PRICED RESTAURANTS

**Fine Dine-In** (Tel. 295-9998, www.finedinein.com). Open Sun.-Thur. 5:30-10:30 P.M. and Fri.-Sat. 5:50-11 P.M. Here's a neat idea that first surfaced in the

Cayman Islands and is now available in Bermuda: a food pick-up and delivery service delivering everywhere from Gibb's Hill Lighthouse in Southampton all the way to Grotto Bay in the east, as well as areas in between. Choose a dinner from their restaurant menu book with selections from 18 midpriced restaurants and Fine Dine-In will place your order, pick it up, and deliver it right to your hotel room, office, home, or even boat. They carry the food in thermal delivery packs, keeping it hot on the journey to your door.

**Bistro 12,** entrance either on 12 Reid Street or Front Street (Tel. 295-5130). Open every day except Sun. 7 A.M.–5 P.M. Courtyard dining at its best. Decorated with a fountain centrepiece, this pleasantly pink courtyard café is just the pause you need from busy shopping. Satisfy your appetite with homemade soups, pastas, fruit plates, gourmet sandwiches, and daily blackboard specials. Seating also available inside.

**Rosa's Cantina,** 121 Front Street (Tel. 295-1912). Open daily noon-1 A.M. Lively Mexican restaurant serving a variety of south-of-the-border dishes: three-bean salads, guacamole, burritos, fajitas, and excellent barbecued spare ribs. Inside or balcony dining.

**M.R. Onions,** Par-la-Ville Road (Tel. 292-5012). Open for lunch Mon.-Fri. noon-2:30, dinner nightly 5-10. Happy Hour Mon.-Sun. 5-7 P.M. ). Early Bird Specials 5-6 P.M. Open public holidays for dinner. This popular restaurant is very accommodating and friendly, with a relaxed atmosphere. The name M.R. Onions translated into Bermudian is "him are onions," meaning he is a born Bermudian. Delicious freshly baked breads and pastries baked on premises. M.R. Onions is also a cybercafé.

**Lobster Pot & Boathouse Bar,** Bermudiana Road (Tel. 292-6898). Open for lunch Mon.-Sat. 11:30-3, dinner 6-11. Informal seafood restaurant with good reputation and friendly service.

**Spring Garden Restaurant & Bar,** Washington Lane (Tel. 295-7416). Open for lunch 11:30-3:30, dinner 6:30-10, bar open from 10 A.M. Happy Hour 5-7 P.M. Closed Sun. For those of you who need a reminder— Bermuda is not in the Caribbean. For those of you looking for a taste of the Caribbean, you could try the Spring Garden Restaurant. Menu items offered: Barbadian flying fish, oxtail soup, beef stew, rack of lamb, and chicken dishes. The owner, Victor Alleyne, says he is trying to fill a void by bringing Caribbean food to Bermuda.

**D'Mikado Seafood House & Grill,** Pier 6, 28 Front Street (Tel. 292-6566, Fax 295-0580). Open Tues.-Sun. noon-3 A.M. (No lunch Sun.) Japanese and sushi bar restaurant with teppanyaki chef. This large restaurant overlooking Hamilton Harbour holds up to 120 people and is popular with cruise-ship visitors.

**House of India,** Park View Plaza, 57 North Street, opposite Transport Control Department (TCD) (Tel. 295-6450). Open for lunch Mon.-Fri. 11-2:30, dinner Sat.-Sun. 5:30-11. Takeout: Mon.-Fri. 11 A.M.–10 P.M., Sat.-Sun. 5-10 P.M. Delivery: in town only for lunch specials. Traditional Indian cuisine such as chicken tandoori, chicken tikka masala (boneless chicken cooked in a tomato cream sauce), and samosa (stuffed vegetables rolled in special pastry).

**Surf & Turf Restaurant,** 22 Richmond Road (Tel. 296-7067). Open seven days (full bar open to 1 A.M.). Large portions and friendly service make this a popular place to dine.

## ITALIAN

**Pasta Basta,** 1 Elliott Street (Tel. 295-9785). Open Mon.-Fri. 11:45 A.M.–11 P.M., Sat.-Sun. 5-11 P.M. Casual, modern, friendly, and bright eatery serving fresh and healthy Italian food at reasonable prices. On the menu: Fettuccine Pasta Basta with cheese, cream, and mushrooms (with or without chicken) and penne chicken pepporanta with diced sweet peppers, pineapple, and onion. Weight-watchers' and health-watchers' pasta specials served. Famous for their fresh and crisp salad bar. All items available for takeout.

**La Trattoria,** Washington Lane (Tel. 292-7059). Open for lunch Mon.-Sat. 11:30-3:30, dinner 6-11 (Sun. from 5:30). "The Trat," as this lively Italian eatery is locally known, serves tasty pasta dishes in a pleasant atmosphere. Children particularly enjoy the cosy booths and friendly service. Rooster wine pitchers add to the ambience (you can purchase them at the restaurant, in various sizes). Dishes include a large selection of pizzas, lasagne, cannelloni, fettuccine, and chicken cacciatore. Try a round of the delicious bruschetta bread. Dessert tray very tempting; offers some of the best chocolate-smothered profiteroles on the island. Takeout store opposite restaurant (Tel. 295-1877), open Mon.-Sat. 11:30 A.M.–10:30 P.M.

**Portofino,** Bermudiana Road (Tel. 295-6090 or 292-2375). Open daily 11:30 A.M.–4 P.M. and 6 P.M.–midnight. Very popular Italian restaurant (reservations recommended) with excellent service and warm atmosphere. Appetisers such as Verdura Arrosto (roasted peppers, zucchini, eggplant, and mushrooms with olive oil, capers, and shaved romano cheese). Entrées include Linguini al Pesto (in green sauce made of basil, pine nuts, garlic, olive oil, and parmesan cheese) or Crespelle Fattore (mushrooms, spinach, and chicken blended in béchamel, folded in pancake topped with tomato sauce and mozzarella). Also, 17 varieties of 10-inch pizza available. Portofino takeout (Tel. 296-0606) open Mon.-Fri. 11 A.M.–10 P.M., Sat.-Sun. from 4 P.M.

**The Little Venice,** Bermudiana Road (Tel. 295-3503). Open for lunch Mon.-Fri. 11:30-2:15, dinner Mon.-Sun. 6-10. The good thing about all the Italian restaurants in Bermuda is that you are guaranteed great service and fine classic cuisine. The Little Venice is one of Bermuda's favourites.

**Primavera Restaurant,** Front Street West, 69 Pitts Bay Road, near Hamilton Princess Hotel (Tel. 295-2167, www.primaverarestaurant.com). Open for lunch Mon.-Fri. 11:45-2:30, dinner 6:30-10:30. Elegant Italian restaurant with fresh Italian dishes and lots of seafood specialties. Upstairs from Primavera is the **Omakase Sushi Bar.**

**Tuscany Restaurant, Pizzeria & Bar,** Bermuda House Lane, 95 Front Street (Tel. 292-4507). Open for lunch Mon.-Sat. 12:45-2:30, dinner 6-10:30. Super Italian restaurant specialising in Tuscan dishes. Pasta, fish, meat, and pizza dishes such as Pesce alla Livornese (shrimp, scallop, mussels, and fish cooked in their juice with a little tomato and white wine). Or how about Ravioli with Porcini Mushroom Sauce (ravioli filled with sautéed zucchini and ricotta cheese tossed in a porcini mushroom sauce)? Open beam-and-slate ceiling and painted fresco adds to Italian ambience.

**Four Star Pizza** (takeout and delivery), four locations: Hamilton (Tel. 295-5555), Flatts Village (Tel. 292-9111), Somerset (Tel. 234-2626), and Warwick (Tel. 232-0123). Open Mon.-Thur. 11 A.M.–11 P.M., Fri.-Sat. to midnight, Sun. 1-10 P.M. (winter hours vary). They said it couldn't be done: a chain of pizza restaurants in Bermuda. Four Star's success proved you shouldn't listen to the naysayers. 10- or 14-inch pizzas. Varieties: Bermudian (with onions, of course), bacon cheeseburger (bacon, hamburger, and extra cheese), pepperoni supreme, meat lovers', veggie (automatically includes hot peppers, so decline these if you don't like hot stuff), Deluxe, and Super Deluxe. Also spicy chicken wings.

## CHINESE

**L'Oriental,** located above the Little Venice Restaurant, 32 Bermudiana Road (Tel. 296-4477). Open for lunch Mon.-Fri. 11-2.15, dinner Mon.-Sun. 6-10. Classic sushi, teppanyaki, and fusion dishes served in this Asian and Thai restaurant with a relaxed atmosphere. Extensive and inventive menu including such dishes as Wok Seared Giant Scallops with wild mushroom infusion pasta; or Smoked Tomato Concasse and Snow Pea Shoots; or Fricassee of Shrimp made with ginger, peppers, Savoy cabbage, and allspice berries, with Asian lemongrass rice in a rice-paper basket.

**The Wok,** 10 Bermudiana Road (Tel. 295-7789/91). Open Mon.-Fri. 8 A.M.–midnight, Sat. from 9 A.M., Sun. 4-11 P.M. Choice of Chinese or Western traditional dishes such as chicken, beef, pork, and fish Chinese meals, chow mein, and a selection of fried rice dishes. Takeout only. Popular daily lunch buffet served.

**Chopsticks Restaurant,** 88 Reid Street (Tel. 292-0791). Open for lunch daily 11:30-2:30, dinner 5-11. Appetising and healthy, regional Chinese and specialties of Thailand. Good lunch menu at fairly reasonable prices. Great takeout and parties-to-go menus also.

**The Sung Sing,** 57 Victoria Street, corner of Victoria and Court Street (Tel. 296-8758). Open Mon.-Sat. 11:30 A.M.–midnight, Sun. and public holidays 4-9 P.M.

Casual takeout Chinese serving traditional Chinese and Cantonese fare: orange chicken, seafood curry, sesame chicken, and teriyaki dishes.

### PUBS AND TAVERNS

Note: See also "Clubs and Pubs" and "Happy Hours in Hamilton" in "Nightlife" below.

The concept of the public house, or "pub," as it is generally called, comes from jolly old England. Unlike bars, the pub is usually a family-friendly place with a clean and polished décor. There's usually good food served at good prices, and Bermuda's pubs often have the added advantage of having balcony seating, where people-watching is a favourite sport.

**Pickled Onion,** Front Street (Tel. 295-2263). Open Mon.-Sat. 11:30 A.M.–1 A.M., Sun. noon-1 A.M. Busy pub and restaurant with upstairs balcony dining serving pub-style meals. Lunch and dinner seafood specials, hot sandwiches, homemade soups, kids' menus, and daily lunch specials. Winner of "Best of Bermuda" award.

**The Hog Penny Restaurant & Pub,** 5 Burnaby Hill (Tel. 292-2534). Open seven days. Low season: noon-9 P.M. (lunch served noon-3, dinner served 6-9). Summer: 11:30 A.M.–1 A.M. (lunch 11:30-3:30, dinner 5:30-10:30). Fine example of attractive English traditional-style pub, with cosy booths surrounded by polished woodwork. Serves a variety of dishes including halibut, English "bangers and mash" (sausage and potato), shepherd's pie, and Angus prime rib with Yorkshire pudding. A good selection of desserts such as English sherry trifle. "Early Bird" dinner specials for the budget-conscious.

For those interested in TV trivia, the late David Allen, travel writer and minister of tourism, tells us the Hog Penny supposedly has close ties with the famous Boston pub the Bull & Finch, which the popular show "Cheers" was based on. The Hog Penny in Bermuda was initially the model for the Bull & Finch, which in turn was the model for "Cheers"!

**Coconut Rock,** Williams House, downstairs, on Reid Street (Tel. 292-1043). Open for lunch Mon.-Fri. 11:30-2:30, dinner 6-10:30, bar open till 1 A.M. A lively, popular pub with the latest videos and music to entertain you as you enjoy a curry, pasta, or selection from the burger bar.

**The Beach,** 103 Front Street (Tel. 292-0219). Open Mon.-Sat. 11 A.M.–3 A.M., Sun., noon-3 A.M. As the name indicates, this is a beach-theme pub, decked out in sea and sand décor. Prices for pub grub are reasonable, and they claim the drinks are the cheapest on Front Street. Munchies include nachos, tacos, piled-high sandwiches, and salads. According to the management, The Beach promises free advice daily on finance, real estate, politics, and sex.

**Robin Hood Pub & Restaurant,** Richmond Road, Pembroke (Tel. 295-3314). Open Mon.-Sat. 11 A.M.–1 A.M., Sun. noon-1 A.M. The "Hood" is a popular meeting place for young people, with nine TVs and two satellite dishes for all U.S. sporting events. This is a favourite hangout of English expatriates, crowded and rowdy during English soccer matches. Famous for its pizza and burgers, or try the curry on Sunday nights. Hootie and the Blowfish—whose song "Tucker's Town" from the album *Fairweather Johnson* is based on their Bermuda experience—make the Robin Hood their local hangout when they are in town.

**The Porch,** Front Street (Tel. 292-4737). Open Mon.-Fri. 11:30 A.M.–10 P.M., Sat. 5-11 P.M. Inside or balcony eating overlooking Front Street. Good food at reasonable prices—steak, ribs, seafood, chicken, etc. Fireplace adds to ambience in winter.

## BUDGET-PRICED EATERIES

**Picnics** are enjoyable and a great money-saver any mealtime. To save you the trouble of preparing them, try these handy, mouthwatering, takeout salad and buffet bars at the following supermarkets: **Supermart** on Front Street and **Marketplace** on Church Street (opposite the Anglican Cathedral).

**Café Acoreano,** The Russell Eve Building, 2 Washington Street (Tel. 296-0402). Open Mon.-Fri. 6.30 A.M.–5:30 P.M., Sun. 11 A.M.–6 P.M. The people of Portugal and the Azores Islands have resided in Bermuda for over 100 years, and their food and pastries have become a popular feature at local fairs and festivals. This Portuguese coffee shop and pastry store, conveniently positioned adjacent to the Bus Terminal on Church Street, enables you to taste Portuguese foods year round. They have a whole range of addictive pastries, huge soft donuts, and custards in flaky pastry as well as sandwiches, rolls, and pies.

**Caffe Latte,** 1 Washington Mall (Tel. 296-1188) and 8 York Street, St. George's (Tel. 297-8196, www.caffelatte.bm). Serves 40 varieties of coffee, including cappuccino, iced coffees, and, of course, latte. They also sell sandwiches and pastries.

**Take 5,** Washington Mall (Tel. 295-4903). Open Mon.-Sat. 7 A.M.–4 P.M. Moderately priced eatery with a brisk lunch trade serving breakfast, lunch, and light refreshments.

**The Grand Central Deli,** 4 Washington Street (Tel. 296-9462). Open Mon.-Fri. 7 A.M.–3 P.M., Sat. 8 A.M.–2 P.M. Closed Sun. Opposite the Bus Terminal, this Brooklyn-style deli serves up bagels, Reuben sandwiches, foot-long hot dogs, and New York cheesecake.

**The Lemon Tree Café,** 7 Queen Street (Tel. 292-0235). Open Mon-Thur. 7 A.M.–4 P.M., Fri. to 3 P.M. Happy Hour Thur.-Fri. 5-9 P.M. Closed Sat.-Sun. (This building was previously the site of the Scottish Wool Shop.) The Lemon Tree serves lemon cheesecake, lemon pie, sandwiches, soups, salads, gourmet coffees, and pastries. The chef was the executive chef at a top local hotel for 18 years. There is terrace seating for up to 40 people in a section of Par-La-Ville Park next door.

**Paradiso Café,** Washington Mall, Reid Street entrance (Tel. 295-3263). Open Mon.-Sat. 7 A.M.–5 P.M. Busy corner café (replaced Four Ways Café). Sandwiches, cakes, tarts, salads, Danishes, croissants, muffins, soup and sandwich specials, bagels, and coffee bar serving gourmet coffees.

**Fresco's Deli Express,** Front Street (Tel. 295-0449). Previously Pinks Deli. Open for breakfast, lunch, and dinner. Overlooking Hamilton Harbour with inside (seats 85) or balcony dining, this deli is owned by the operators of Fresco's Restaurant (see above in "Higher-Priced Restaurants") but is much more affordable, with speedy service and lots of deli and vegetarian fare.

**Café on the Terrace,** A. S. Coopers Department Store, Second Floor, Front Street (Tel. 296-5265). Open during store lunchtime hours. Outside dining on the patio, overlooking Hamilton Harbour and Front Street. Sandwiches, salads, etc. Great place for people-watching.

**The Windsor Garden Restaurant,** Windsor Building, Queen Street (Tel. 295-4085). Open Mon.-Sat. 7 A.M.–4 P.M. Set inside a modern mall, this busy eatery decorated in cool greens serves breakfast and lunch. Offers delectable desserts and tasty salads. This café is especially popular for breakfast.

**Rock Island Coffee,** 48 Reid Street (Tel. 296-2347). Open Mon.-Fri. 7 A.M.–6 P.M., Sat. from 8 A.M. New York meets Bermuda at Rock Island, a small arty place with comfortable couches and funky furniture specialising in delicious coffees. As well as the 12-15 different international coffees on hand, Rock Island has fresh-baked goods such as moist pumpkin cake. Seating inside or out.

**The Hungry Bear Espresso Bar & Café,** Chancery Lane (Tel. 292-2353). Open Mon.-Fri. 8 A.M.–4 P.M. Bright and cheery café serving Green Mountain specialty coffees as well as bagels, rolls, sandwiches, cakes, etc. The service is pleasant, the food is always fresh and tasty, and the prices are reasonable.

**Kathy's Kaffee,** ground floor at back of Emporium Building, off Front Street (Tel. 295-5203). Open Mon.-Fri. 8 A.M.–4 A.M., Sat. from 9 A.M. Popular meeting place with good service and convenient opening hours for late-night revellers. Read free magazines or study the hand-painted Bermudian mural on the wall while indulging in sinfully delicious homemade desserts. Breakfast specials include a fat-free power breakfast. Also serves sandwiches, burgers (and veggie burgers), codfish sandwiches, gyros, rotis, hot chocolate with piles of whipped cream, and homemade Bailey's ice cream. The rockfish and banana sandwich is particularly good.

**The Spot Restaurant,** Burnaby Street (Tel. 292-6293). Open Mon.-Sat. 6:30 A.M.–7 P.M. Very busy family-run diner, popular with locals for breakfasts and fast-food lunches.

**Brothers Café,** Trimingham's, Front Street (Tel. 295-1183). Open Mon.-Sat. 9:30 A.M.–4:30 P.M., lunch 11:30-3. Coffee shop located inside Trimingham's Department Store.

**Monty's Restaurant,** 75 Pitts Bay Road (Tel. 295-5759). Open Mon.-Sat. 7:30 A.M.–3 P.M. and 5:30-10 P.M. Sunday codfish breakfast with Johnny bread: 7:30 A.M.–2:30 P.M. Busy diner (smoke free) serves soups, salads, sandwiches, burgers, fish meals, curries, and homemade desserts. Decorated in a bright and airy style. The prices are right and the portions are big. (Maybe they should consider renaming it "The Full Monty"?)

**Kentucky Fried Chicken** (KFC), Queen Street (Tel. 296-4532). Open Mon.-Sat. 11 A.M.–10 P.M., Sun. 11 A.M.–9 P.M. The only fast-food franchise in Bermuda (in place before government policy disallowed any further fast-food restaurants). Serves KFC's familiar chicken, fries, spicy chicken strips, hot wings, coleslaw, and sodas. Prices are a little more expensive than in the U.S.

**Princes Deli & Bakery,** 22 Brunswick Street, located in lobby of Total Fitness Centre (Tel. 295-0098). Open weekdays 8 A.M.–4 P.M. Hamilton's best-kept secret—bright, clean, spacious, modern deli decorated in cool whites, serving hot and cold fresh food. Daily lunch specials. Generous portions and pleasant service. Take out or sit in and watch CNN on TV.

**The Ice Queen at the Little Theatre,** Corner of Queen and Church Street (also located at Rural Hill Plaza, Paget) (Tel. 292-6497). Open seven days 10 A.M.–10 P.M. This popular fast-food restaurant serves burgers, fries, chicken pieces, excellent fish sandwiches, and fish dinners. 11 varieties of ice cream, sundaes, and banana splits. Handy for snacks before and after a visit to the Little Theatre cinema.

**Mannie's Soul Food Express,** 18 Washington Lane (side of Washington Mall, Tel. 295-3890). Open Mon.-Fri. 6 A.M.–3 P.M., Sat. to 2 P.M. Down-home cooking. Select from buffet items to take out, such as curried beef, barbecued chicken, and macaroni and cheese.

**The Hickory Stick,** Clarendon House (Tel. 292-1781). Open Mon.-Fri. 6:30 A.M.–4 P.M. Busy deli serving freshly made subs, sandwiches, salads, Bermuda fare, and daily specials. Popular with the business crowd because of their speedy service and good-size portions. Some seating available.

**The Double-Dip,** 119 Front Street (Tel. 292-3503). Open Mon.-Wed. 11 A.M.–9 P.M., Thur.-Sat. to 10 P.M. It's nearly impossible to pass by this ice-cream parlour, especially if you have children in tow. Sit-in or takeout ice creams and quick snacks.

**La Baguette,** 16 Burnaby Street (Tel. 296-1129). Open Mon.-Fri. 9 A.M.–6 P.M., Sat. 8 A.M.–2 P.M. Colourfully designed French deli offering gourmet sandwiches, baps, focaccia, or minibaguettes. Meats include leberkase, bludwurst, bratwurst, salami, salmon cognac paté, etc.

**Crow Lane Bakery,** Church Street, opposite City Hall (Tel. 292-2220). Open Mon.-Sat. 6 A.M.–6 P.M. Selection of crisp fresh-baked breads and cakes. This bakery has a breakfast to go that serves coffee; small orange juice; Danish, muffin, or coffee roll; and newspaper for $3.75 (served from 7 A.M.).

**East Meets West,** 27 Bermudiana Arcade, Second Floor (Tel. 295-8580). Open Mon. Fri. 9 A.M.–3 P.M. and 5-10 P.M., Sat. 9 A.M.–10 P.M., Sun. 5-10 P.M. Tasty, spicy Indian cuisine, freshly made by Indian chefs. Extensive menu, including curries, rice dishes, and Balti dishes with Naan breads. Balti is a type of curry from "Baltistan" famous in Birmingham, England. This spotless restaurant features a clay oven heated from the bottom with coals.

## 4. Sightseeing

Your first port of call in Hamilton should be the Visitors' Bureau Tourist Information office (Tel. 295-1480) on Front Street (next to the Ferry Terminal). Find out about what's happening the week you are staying, pick up some bus tickets and any information booklets and special-offer vouchers, and you're ready to go exploring the city.

**Perot's Post Office,** 11 Queen Street (Tel. 295-5151). Open Mon.-Fri. 9 A.M.–5 P.M. Situated at the entranceway to Par-La-Ville Park (once the garden of the original postmaster, W. B. Perot). Wood floors and beamed ceilings add to the Old World atmosphere of Bermuda's first post office, where Mr. Perot presigned sheets of stamps so he could spend more time in his beloved garden. These stamps are now very valuable; one sold for $185,000 in 1991!

**Par-La-Ville Park,** entrance on Par-La-Ville Road or Church Street. Open daily. A peaceful haven in the middle of the city bustle. Pathways curl around the park, leading to flower gardens, tropical trees, and bushes. Par-La-Ville Park is where many local workers "brown bag" it lunchtimes and where you can enjoy a leisurely afternoon tea at the Lemon Tree Café (see above in "Budget-Priced Eateries").

**Bermuda Anglican Cathedral Tower,** Church Street. Open daily, 8 A.M.–4:30 P.M. Small admission charge. William Hay of Edinburgh designed this renovated gothic monument. A climb to the top (150 steps) will be rewarded by a sweeping panoramic view of Hamilton. Contrary to popular belief, this, and not Gibbs Hill Lighthouse, is Bermuda's tallest building.

**Bank of Bermuda Coin Collection,** Mezzanine, 6 Front Street. Open Mon.-Thur. 9:30 A.M.–3 P.M., Fri. to 4:40 P.M. British and Bermudian coins dating back as far as 1603 to the present time. Don't miss the Hog Money, the first money minted for Bermuda and the oldest British colonial coins.

**Bermuda Historical Society,** Queen Street (Tel. 295-2487). Open Mon.-Fri. 9:30 A.M.–3:30 P.M., closed all public holidays. Take a glance at early Bermudian life in this colonial museum located at Par-la-Ville house, a Georgian-style historical home and library. Collectibles from Bermuda, America, and England, such as china, furniture, and coins, are on display. A beautiful carved wooden sea chest that belonged to Sir George Somers in 1609 sits near the entrance.

**Bermuda National Gallery,** City Hall, Church Street, Hamilton (Tel. 295-9428, www.bng.bm). Open Mon.-Sat. 10 A.M.–4 P.M. Admission: free. City Hall is one of Bermuda's finest buildings. This magnificent, gleaming white structure, located in the middle of Church Street, is topped by a miniature replica of the *Sea Venture* (Bermuda's founding ship), in use as a weathervane. Housed here are splendid, frequently changed art exhibitions, both historic and contemporary, from around the world as well as Bermuda. For a description of their tours, go to chapter 5, "Culture and Heritage," in the "Art Galleries" section.

**Ocean Discovery Centre, Bermuda Underwater Exploration Institute (BUEI),** East Broadway (Tel. 292-7219, www.buei.org). Open daily 9 A.M.–5 P.M. Closed Christmas Day. Admission: $10.50 adults, $5.50 children ages seven-17, $8.40 seniors, and free for children six and under.

This is a $20 million educational and entertaining institution devoted to underwater research and the sustainable development of the sea. BUEI's purpose is "to educate and entertain our visitors about the mysteries of the deep oceans, using a combination of interactive, computer driven exhibits, films and displays." The BUEI is especially fascinating for undersea-diving enthusiasts.

The institute also has a 148-seat auditorium used for presentations on oceanography and related topics on the marine environment.

**Barrs Park,** Harbour Front (next door to Royal Yacht Club). This waterfront park is a good place to take a picnic lunch and watch the sailboats at the Yacht Club.

**Victoria Park,** entrance on Washington Street or Cedar Avenue. Open daily. Park with ancient palm trees, tropical plants, and Victorian bandstand. (See "Concerts in the Park," under "Theatres and Concerts," below.)

**Fort Hamilton,** end of Church Street (follow signs to fort on Happy Valley Road). Open daily 9:30 A.M.–5 P.M. Pleasant walk around this magnificent fort with impressive views of Hamilton. Lush green variety of subtropical plants in the moat. Every Monday at noon (Nov. through Mar.), a "skirling" (bagpipe-playing) ceremony with Scottish band pipers and highland dancers takes place by the ramparts. Find **Victoria's Castle** tearoom (Tel. 237-3160) for refreshments at the fort.

**Sessions House/Houses of Parliament,** 21 Parliament Street (Tel. 292-7408). Open Mon.-Fri. 9 A.M.–5 P.M. (closed 12:30-2 P.M. ). The original building was built in 1817, and later additions of the clock tower and colonnade were made in 1887. Parliament meets on Fridays at 10 A.M. from late October through July and can be viewed from the Visitors' Gallery.

## 5. Guided Tours and Cruises

During the November-to-March season, the Department of Tourism arranges city tours. Find details at the Visitors' Bureau (Tel. 295-1480) or check the local daily paper, *The Royal Gazette.* With regards to the tours and cruises below, it is always wise to call ahead to see if any changes have taken place since the time of this writing.

**Bermuda Island Cruises' "Don't Stop the Carnival"** (Tel. 292-8652, bic@logic.bm, www.bermuda.com/bic). Departs at 7 P.M., returning 10:30 P.M., May-Oct., Tues.-Sat. Board the party boat at Albouys Point for a fun cruise to private Hawkins Island. An open bar, live music, and delicious island buffet await you as you warm up for a show packed with comedy, music, and dancing. Reservations are recommended. Call ahead to arrange group discounts. Families are welcome.

**Fantasea Bermuda Ltd.,** Hamilton (Tel. 236-1300, or Tel. 238-1833 for diving enquiries, www.fantasea.bm). Many cruises offered, including catamaran, sightseeing, snorkelling, champagne evening cruise, whale watching, ecotours, and scuba diving. Self-propelled pedal boats and kayaks (single and double) available for rent. "Looking Glass" 50-foot glass-bottom boat tours.

They also offer combination cruise and mountain bike tours along the Railway Trail.

**Jessie James Cruises,** Albouy's Point on Front Street (Tel. 296-5801, Fax 296-7099, www.jessiejames.bm). Daily cruises depart 1:15 P.M., return 5:15 P.M., subject to demand and weather. Call ahead to reserve.

**Looking Glass Cruises,** Ferry Terminal (Tel. 296-5801, www.bermudashorts.bm/lookinglass). 2¼-hour tours depart from Ferry Terminal at 10:45 A.M. and 2:15 P.M. Ask for details about glass-bottom boat specials and historical and ecotours. Cruises take you to the calm and protected waters of the West End.

**Reef Explorer Safari,** Bermuda Island Cruises (Tel. 292-8652, www.bicbda.com). Glass-bottom boat cruises, Mon.-Sat. 10 A.M. and 1:30 P.M. Depart from Ferry Terminal. Two-hour cruise through the islands to the Sea Gardens. View the reefs and marine life—all explained throughout the cruise by the captain and crew, in a shallow-draft glass-bottom boat. Children receive fun activity books to help them learn more about the coral reef system, and a certificate signed by the captain.

**Island Calypso Party Cruise,** Bermuda Island Cruises (Tel. 292-8652, www.bermuda.com/bic). Departs Tues. and Thur. at 2 P.M. (three-hour tour) from Albouys Point (please arrive by 1:45 P.M.). Advance reservations requested. Afternoon of island fun and calypso music, cruising through the sound sipping an island drink. Stop off at a private island for swimming or just relax in a hammock under the palm trees. Snorkelling gear and kayaks at the island.

**Bermuda Water Tours,** Ferry Terminal (Tel. 236-1500, Fax 292-0801, info@bermudawatertours.com, www.bermudawatertours.com). Two-hour, glass-bottom, sightseeing boat cruises to the Sea Gardens.

**Allegro Charters,** Albouys Point (Tel. 295-4074, Fax 295-1314). Half-day or three-hour sail with Captain Richard through the islands of the Great Sound.

**Wildcat Adventure Tours** (Tel. 293-7433, mlawrence@logic.bm). Thrilling two-hour high-speed catamaran boat tour around the whole coastline.

## 6. Water Sports

### SNORKELLING

**Jessie James Cruises,** check-in 15 minutes before sailing at steps outside the Hamilton Ferry Terminal on Front Street (also Darrell's Wharf, Warwick) (Tel. 296-5801, Fax 296-7099, www.jessiejames.bm). For good-value snorkelling and fun beach cruises, snorkel three times at three different locations: (1) Beach and Island, (2) Historic Shipwrecks (subject to weather conditions), and (3) Coral Reef/Sea Garden.

**Hayward's Cruises,** Ferry Terminal, Hamilton (Tel. 236-9894). Departs seven days a week at 9:45 A.M. Morning snorkel cruise from the 54-foot motor cruiser *Explorer,* the camera boat used in filming *The Deep.* Ancient shipwrecks and the beautiful coral reef visible through *Explorer's* glass bottom. Trip includes snorkelling equipment, changing facilities, and freshwater showers on board (please supply own towels). Beer and soft drinks for sale, along with a complimentary rum swizzle on return trip.

**Bermuda Water Tours,** Ferry Terminal (Tel. 236-1500, Fax 292-0801, info@bermudawatertours.com, www.bermudawatertours.com). Sightseeing and snorkelling tour, including equipment.

### BOAT RENTAL

There's nothing like getting off the busy roads and onto the waterways, so when Hamilton's congestion gets too harrowing, try renting a small, easy-to-handle Boston Whaler from Rances Boat Yard, 46 Crow Lane at East Broadway (Tel. 292-1843). 13-foot Boston Whalers for rent, with capacity for four people.

## 7. Shopping

Bermuda traditionally has catered to the sophisticated buyer, although due to a recession this is gradually changing. To understand Bermuda's pricing structure you have to have some basic background in the economics of island living. Although there is no sales tax, almost everything is imported, and retailers have to pay steep overheads, customs and duty, and import charges and, due to the astronomical cost of living, meet high staff salaries. For the savvy shopper, however, it is possible to scoop up big-buck bargains—there are always sales on somewhere and if you look, you will find treasure troves hidden down side alleys.

Front Street, in Hamilton city, is famous for traditional top-notch shops and is the home of unique Bermudian upscale department stores such as **A. S. Coopers** (Tel. 295-3961), **H. A. & E. Smith's** (now owned by Trimingham's, Tel. 295-2288), and **Trimingham's** (Tel. 295-1183). **Gibbons Company** (entrances on both Reid Street and Church Street, Tel. 295-0022) is a less-expensive department store popular with Bermudians.

Front Street stores specialise in tax-free luxury items such as fine china and crystal, jewellery, and perfumes, with prices comparable to, or lower than, those in North America. Don't expect rows of cheap tourist trinkets; take time to soak in the old-fashioned quality of these fine stores.

## LUXURY IMPORTS

The following products are sold below U.S. retail prices at the exclusive stores on Front Street. Summer opening hours include some late-night shopping, usually when a cruise ship is in dock.

**Tableware and China:** Wedgwood, Royal Doulton China, Waterford Crystal, Atlantis Crystal Stemware & Giftware, Portmeirion, Royal Doulton Tableware, Minton Tableware, Villeroy & Boch Tableware, Royal Copenhagen, Royal Crown Derby, and other china for up to 30 percent savings.

**Jewellery and Perfume:** Rolex watches, Tiffany jewellery, and 18-carat-gold jewellery for up to 40 percent less than in the U.S. 20 percent savings on Tissot, Patek Philippe, Rolex, Gucci watches. Perfume at 15 to 50 percent below U.S. prices: Christian Dior, Yves St. Laurent, Chanel, Elizabeth Arden, and Givenchy.

## JEWELLERY STORES

**Vera P. Card,** Somers Building, 11 Front Street (Tel. 295-1729) and branches island-wide. Jewellers and gift store selling quality gifts that guarantee against U.S. prices for 90 days.

**E. R. Aubrey Jewellers,** 19 Front Street and 101 Front Street (Tel. 295-3826). Frequent sales (check out the local papers for coupons) and bulk buying make this jeweller worth searching out for all your jewellery needs.

**Crissons Jewellers,** Front Street, Reid Street, Queen Street, and branches island-wide (Tel. 295-2351, www.crisson.com). Good prices year round, especially on gold. This store sells interesting ladies' and men's Bermuda Triangle Watches.

Other jewellers in Hamilton: **Herrington Jewellers** in Washington Mall (Tel. 292-6527); **The Old Cellar,** Walker Arcade on Front Street (Tel. 295-4455); **Solomon's** on Front Street (Tel. 295-1003); **Sovereign Jewellers** on Reid Street (Tel. 292-7933); **Swiss Timing** on Front Street (Tel. 292-7933); and **Walker Christopher** on Front Street (Tel. 295-1466). Walker Christopher are manufacturers of jewellery, as are **The Gem Cellar Bermuda,** Walker Arcade (Tel. 292-3042). Walker Christopher also sell treasure coins recovered from ancient shipwrecks such as Spanish gold "doubloons" and silver "pieces of eight" set in gold jewellery.

## ENGLISH CLOTHES AND GIFTS

Visitors on the lookout for good-quality English products can find them available in the up-market stores in Hamilton and St. George's. Products include British-tailored wool jackets and cashmere sweaters. Liberty silk scarves can be found at 15 percent below U.S. prices.

**Trimingham** (Tel. 295-1183, www.triminghams.com) stores have a wide variety of English gifts, beautifully presented and packaged. There you can find china and crystal, preserves, teas, shortbread, and toffees, to name just a few items—all at competitive prices.

For high-quality English fare, try the food hall at **Marks and Spencer.** For Brits visiting Bermuda, Marks and Spencer has a Levi's store that sells jeans at much lower prices than those found in England. You can also go to the Levi's Shop on Front Street (Tel. 295-2928).

Another purveyor of British and Irish men's, ladies', and children's fashions is **Archie Brown & Son** (Tel. 295-2928) at 51 Front Street.

## FASHION STORES

The **English Sports Shop** (Tel. 295-2672). They sell dresses, children's wear, Bermuda shorts, blazers, sweaters, ties, and socks. The **Outlet Branch** of this store is next door to the Little Theatre on Queen Street (Tel. 295-2672) and has a wide variety of clothing—Bermuda fashions, evening wear, sweaters, and casual sportswear for the whole family. Also seasonal special discounts on selected merchandise, up to 50 percent off their regular store prices.

If you're looking for higher-priced fashions, try **Stefanel's** on Reid Street (Tel. 295-5698), **Cecile's** on Front Street West (Tel. 295-1311), and **Calypso** on Front Street (Tel. 295-2112). These upscale stores sell beautiful beachwear, accessories, sun dresses, sweaters, and pant suits. On the second floor of Calypso's, at The Studio, find permanent sale prices marked down 50 to 75 percent off shoes, pants, tops, and blazers.

**Sports 'R' Us,** 61 Church Street (Tel. 292-1891). Great selection of sportswear, including Nike and other brand names. Shorts, jackets, sweats, swimwear, exercise gear, and equipment.

Menswear can be found in **A. S. Coopers** department store (Tel. 295-3961, www.coopersbermuda.com)—plus at their men's store on Front Street as well as at **Trimingham's** (Tel. 295-1183). Men's modern boutique stores include **The Edge** (Tel. 295-4715) in Washington Mall. **Aston & Gunn** (Tel. 295-4866) sells exclusive brand-name silk ties, as well as upscale designer clothes such as Hugo Boss, and has great service to match.

Hip stores for teenagers and the young at heart: **Grant's Ladies Boutique,** Washington Lane (side of Washington Mall, Tel. 295-2711)—lots of reasonably priced fashions and accessories. DKNY and Calvin Kline wear can be found at **Gibbons Company** department store on Reid Street (Tel. 295-0022). The young love the cool hip-hop clothes at **Jazzy Boutique** in Washington Mall (Tel. 295-9258) and reasonably priced funky shoes at **Personality Footworks** (Tel. 292-9317). Personality is the last store situated on the outside level of Washington Mall. **Makin Waves** at 75 Front Street (Tel. 292-4609) is another popular store with young people and visitors. They sell lots of active sportswear, dresses, and tees.

## GIFT STORES

**Flying Colours,** 5 Queen Street (Tel. 295-0890). Chock-a-block with great souvenirs and clothes. Excellent array of tees—the more you purchase, the cheaper the price.

**Foreign Cargo,** 15 Burnaby Street (Tel. 296-3054). Tasteful gift ideas such as unusual candles, holders, plant stands, wine racks, and pottery.

**Smugglers Reef,** 29 Front Street (Tel. 295-8922). Very touristy store with lots of brightly coloured tees, shorts, and tropical clothes. Buy six shirts, get six free. They also have an extensive sunglasses centre, with Dior, Ray-Ban, Armani, Calvin Klein, and Gucci glasses, to name but a few choices.

**Onion Jack's,** 77 Front Street (Tel. 295-1263, www.onionjacks.com). Touristy store selling Onion Jack logo products—tees, gifts, etc., and hot sauce and specialty foods.

**The Irish Linen Shop,** 31 Front Street (Tel. 295-4089). You can find unusual hand-sewn gifts, and not just tablecloths either.

**Trustworthy Gift Shop,** 48 Front Street, Hamilton (Tel. 296-4164), and Globe Hotel (Bermuda National Trust Museum), St. George's (Tel. 297-1423). Open Mon.-Sat. 10 A.M.–4 P.M., Sun. from 1 P.M. in St. George's. The Trustworthy Gift Shop is a store owned and operated by The National Trust (www.bnt.bm), selling good-quality original handicrafts. Profits go to the preservation of Bermuda's historic buildings, artefacts, and open spaces.

## BOOKSTORES

**Twice-Told Tales,** 34 Parliament Street (Tel. 296-1995). Second-hand bookstore offering interesting selection of hardback and paperback used books. Prices range from $2 upwards. Owner, Ms. Souza-Fowkes, is on hand for advice and cappuccino, sometimes strumming her guitar or putting on background classical music. Internet surfing available.

**The Book Mart,** at the upper level of The Phoenix Centre, Reid Street (Tel. 295-3838, www.phoenixstores.bm), is Bermuda's largest bookstore, with seven-day opening hours.

**Washington Mall Magazines,** Washington Mall (Tel. 292-7420). Great for magazines, Bermuda books, and trade publications.

**Bermuda Book Store,** Queen Street (Tel. 295-3698). Conveniently located in the centre of Hamilton, close to Par-La-Ville Park, this store has been fully refitted since the unfortunate passing of its eccentric owner, Mr.

Zuill. There's a comfortable couch next to a window for reading. 30 percent of books sold here are Bermuda related, including this *Maverick Guide*.

**The Children's Bookshop,** 26 Bermudiana Road (Tel. 292-9078). Along with children's classics and modern books, they sell books for grown-ups too. There are a number of Bermuda books for children written by local authors, such as the Tiny Tree Frog series of books by Elizabeth Mulderig.

Bermuda has a number of Christian bookstores to choose from, such as **The Christian Bookstore and Gift Centre** on Burnaby Street (Tel. 292-3257) and the **Adventist Book Centre** on King Street (Tel. 292-4111), selling gifts, Bibles, music, and children's literature.

**True Reflections,** off Reid Street at 1 Chancery Lane (Tel. 295-9424), stocks Afrocentric titles for both adults and children by local, Caribbean, U.K., and U.S. authors. **The Metaphysical Bookstore,** 61 Reid Street (Tel. 295-5683), stocks healing, nature, and holistic medicine books.

## LATE-NIGHT SHOPPING

Most stores in Hamilton close at 5 P.M. For those emergencies when you absolutely need a convenience store, **Dismont Robinson,** Front Street (Tel. 292-4301), is open seven days 8 A.M.–10 P.M. This store sells food, general goods, beer, wines, and spirits. **Esso Automarket** on Richmond Road (Tel. 295-3776) is the only store in Bermuda open 24 hours a day—it sells foodstuffs, snacks, drinks, etc. A few stores are also open late nights during Harbour Nights on Wednesdays from April to October, and the weeks leading up to Christmas.

---

**Location of Public Washrooms in Hamilton**

There is a dearth of public washrooms in Hamilton (and the rest of the island). Most restaurants and eateries (not all) have them, and all the pubs and bars have them. Here is a list of a few others in Hamilton:

1. Side of Visitors' Bureau, adjacent to Bank of Bermuda (near Ferry Terminal).

2. Behind City Hall (close to Bus Terminal).

3. Victoria Park (behind City Hall).

4. Washington Mall, top level (key obtained from The Windsor Garden Restaurant or Phoenix Centre, upper level).

5. H. A. & E. Smith, Front Street (Ladies'—Second Floor, Men's—First Floor).

6. City Hall, Church Street (turn left after front entrance and up the stairs).

7. Trimingham's Department Store, Front Street (Third Floor).

# 8. Nightlife

Most of Bermuda's social scene and the favourite hot spots in nightlife entertainment are in Hamilton city. Alcoholic beverages are generally on the expensive side, so to save money, listed below are Happy Hours at some of Bermuda's friendly pubs. Always call first to confirm entertainment and opening/closing hours. Be warned, though; apart from the Bermuda Festival (see "Festivals, Ceremonies, and Major Events" in chapter 5, "Culture and Heritage"), there's not much to offer in the way of nightlife during the months of January and February.

During the summer months, you can always take a romantic evening cruise (see "Guided Tours and Cruises" section above).

There are a number of talented dance troupes on the island, such as United Dance Productions, In-Motion School of Dance, Jackson School of Performing Arts, and the National Dance Theatre. Watch out for advertisements of any of their special productions and recitals; they are well worth a visit.

Looking for local live entertainment? Scan the local papers for what's happening. You will find a variety of local talent doing the rounds in the pubs, clubs, and hotels. Choose from pop, rock, blues, jazz, and ballad singers. You may find them playing at the Jazz Festival in October or throughout the summer at Harbour Nights on Front Street. You may wish to listen (on CD) to Bermuda's own singer-songwriter, Heather Nova, whose 1998 album, *Siren,* was featured on the TV shows *Dawson's Creek* and *Felicity.* She also took part in the Lilith Fair women's tours with Sarah McLachlan.

Here is a list of some of Bermuda's best-known entertainers:

**Singers:** LeYoni Junor (sultry voiced), Gita Blakeney (Bermuda's Lady of Song), Gene Steede (Bermuda's Gentleman of Song), Delletta Gellespie (talented singer).

**Blues & Jazz:** Rob Berry & The Blooze Bandits, Jazz Band, Doc Simons, Denise Whitter, Chris Broadbent.

**Rock Bands:** 7th Heaven, The Kennel Boys.

**Top 40:** Xtasy.

**Calypso:** Grant Williams, Stan Seymour (Lord Necktie), Hubert Smith Sr., Tropical Heat.

**Musicians:** Shine Hayward (sax), Michael Fox (piano), Ed Fox (guitarist/singer), Vic Glazer (piano).

**Steel Bands:** Tropicana Steel Band (single act), Coca-Cola Steel Band.

**Reggae:** Jahstice.

**Mixture:** Rhythm (some jazz, some calypso).

## HARBOUR NIGHTS (MAY-OCTOBER)

In Hamilton on Wednesday nights, 5-10, Front Street is traffic free, with waterside vendors, local entertainers, artists, and monthly performances by the Bermuda Regiment Band. Many of the Front Street stores are open in the evening till 9; Bank of Bermuda is open till 7.

## FOLK SINGING

Informal sing-a-longs on first Saturday of every month, organised by the Bermuda Folk Club (Tel. 291-2070). Periodically, folk performances are held at the Old Colony Club (Tel. 293-9241).

## FREE LIVE ENTERTAINMENT IN THE PUBS

**Flanagan's Irish Pub & Restaurant,** 69 Front Street (Tel. 295-8299). Pub grub 11:30 A.M.–6 P.M., dinner 6-9:30. Live music every night during the summer. 45-seat sports bar with multichannel satellite TVs featuring all major sporting events; especially popular with North Americans and Brits.

**The Hog Penny,** Burnaby Street, off Front Street (Tel. 292-2534, www.hogpenny.com). Open seven nights until 1 A.M. Cosy English pub with live music entertainment nightly during the summer months and every Fri. and Sat. night during the winter. Serves English draught beer and ale.

**Hubies,** Angle Street (Tel. 293-9287). This popular local small bar has great jazz music on Fri. and Sat. nights between 8 and 10. Caters to the mature crowd.

**The Porch,** Front Street (Tel. 292-4737). Open Mon.-Sat. 11 A.M.–10:30 P.M., Sun. 5:30-11 P.M. Intimate pub and restaurant with inside and outside dining and live entertainment. Call ahead first to check.

**The Pickled Onion,** 53 Front Street (Tel. 295-2263). Open 11:30 A.M.–1 A.M., Happy Hour 5-7 P.M. Bar and restaurant with balcony seating. Live music nightly, 9:30 P.M.–1 A.M.

## CLUBS AND PUBS

**Blue Juice Disco Bar,** behind Tuscany Restaurant on Bermuda House Lane, just off Front Street (Tel. 292-4507). Open Mon.-Fri until 3 A.M. This disco and bar under the stars is named after the Blue Juice cocktail (blue curacao, vodka, lime, and Triple Sec). Video screens showing music videos are on display outside in the courtyard.

**Hilly's Jazz Club and Coffee Bar,** 123 Front Street (Tel. 295-1370, hillys-jazzclub@logic.bm). Previously Docksiders pub. Overlooking Hamilton Harbour, this club offers nightly live entertainment and full bar service. Cover charge Fri. and Sat. nights.

**Ozone** and **The Rock Room,** Emporium Building, 69 Front Street (Tel. 292-4978). Open nightly high season 10 P.M.–3 A.M. There are two sections to this club: one for disco, playing chart music, and the other for rock bands.

**The Palace,** The Stables Building, Spurling Hill (Tel. 296-6120, www.thepalacebermuda.com). Open daily noon-3 A.M. Free buffet Mon.-Fri. at 5 P.M. This is an adult sports bar with wall-to-wall, casino-gambling slot machines. Gambling is not allowed in prudish Bermuda, so I don't know how these guys sneaked in.

## HAPPY HOURS IN HAMILTON

Bermuda has several English-style pubs specialising in hearty meals and draught beers. Bermuda's drinks are generally expensive, especially compared to North American prices. Happy hour in a friendly pub is one way to spend part of an evening inexpensively, in a place where there is often free entertainment and finger food.

**Save lives: Please don't drink and drive.**

### The Hog Penny Restaurant & Pub
5 Burnaby Street
Tel. 292-2534
Happy Hour: Mon.-Fri. 5-7 P.M.
$4 draft beer, $3.50 bottled beer
Live entertainment at 9:30 P.M. No cover charge.

### Mariners' Club
Richmond Road
Tel. 295-5598
Happy Hour: Fri. 5 P.M.–1 A.M.
$3.50 beer, $3 highballs
Fri. night fish & chips $9.75

### Harbourfront Restaurant
Front Street (opposite Ferry Terminal)
Tel. 295-4207
Popular sushi bar happy hour: 5-7 P.M. (not Sun.)
$4.95 each order
Dishes: Sashimi, norimaki, temaki, and nigiri

### The Beach
103 Front Street
Tel. 292-0219
Happy Hour: 4-7 P.M. (Fri. to 8 P.M. )
$4.50 bottled beer and highballs

**M.R. Onions**
Par-La-Ville Road
Tel. 292-5012
Happy Hour: 5-7 P.M.
$3.75 beer and highballs
Finger food on Fri.

**Robin Hood Pub & Restaurant**
Richmond Road
Tel. 295-3314
Happy Hour: 4-8 P.M.
$3.45 bottled beer, $3.75 per pint draft beer
Very popular place with nine TVs for sports fans

**Flanagan's Irish Pub & Restaurant**
Emporium Building, Front Street
Tel. 295-8299
Happy Hour: 5-7 P.M.
$3.75 bottled beer, $4.50 per pint draft beer
Free food on Fri.

## THEATRES AND CONCERTS

**Harvard Hasty Pudding Club:** Due to an island connection within the Harvard Hasty Pudding Club, Bermuda has staged these musical satires every spring for the last 30 years and is the only place to do so outside of the U.S. The tradition of the Harvard Hasty Pudding Club dates back to 1795, when a group of Harvard undergraduates created a secret club (theatricals were not encouraged in those days). At their meetings they served hasty pudding, and consequently the club's name was acquired.

Tickets for Bermuda's show are available at the Visitors' Service Bureau on Front Street, Hamilton.

*Pudding Points:* Our colonial ancestors enjoyed hasty pudding in the morning for breakfast and after dinner for dessert. It's a simple cornmeal mush made with water or milk and sometimes sweetened with molasses, maple syrup, or honey. If it is not sweetened during cooking, a syrup or sweet sauce usually accompanies a hasty pudding. It's served hot, sometimes with milk or cream (information based on *The Food Lover's Companion,* second edition, by Sharon Tyler Herbst).

**Broadway In Bermuda:** Staged in the fall; lavish production organised by **Two Island Productions**—the two islands being Manhattan and

Bermuda. Broadway stars mix with local talent to stage a highly professional and entertaining musical evening at City Hall. Tickets are sold at Opus Encore, 12 Reid Street (Tel. 295-8073). If you are a Broadway fan, don't miss this show.

**Bermuda Musical & Dramatic Society (BMDS),** Dalesford Theatre, Dundonald Street (Tel. 292-0848, www.bmds.bm): Local actors from the BMDS regularly stage plays at this 120-seat theatre. Plays are generally very entertaining, with fine performances from dedicated amateur actors. Everything from Shakespeare to musicals to the Christmas pantomime staged at City Hall. Also, look out for a relatively new drama group, **Waterspout Theatre,** which produces contemporary-style plays at local venues.

The **Daylesford Singers** group, also a branch of BMDS, stages musical renditions periodically. BMDS assists other groups such as the Gilbert and Sullivan Society, the Menuhin Foundation, the Bermuda Ballet Association, and Two Island Productions.

**Gilbert and Sullivan Society:** High standard of flamboyant productions staged annually in October. Captivating cast of characters and colourful sets for these musical performances, which are not always by Gilbert and Sullivan. The Gilbert and Sullivan Society had the compliment of gaining the amateur rights from Cameron Mackintosh to stage the incredibly successful Broadway hit *Les Miserables*. It was a smash hit. Tickets for Gilbert and Sullivan shows are obtained from the Visitors' Service Bureau in Hamilton (Tel. 295-1480), a month before the production.

**Concerts in the Park:** Victoria Park (entrance on Washington Street or Cedar Avenue). Show: 5-9 P.M. Free, open-air musical concerts held in Victoria Park on Sundays once a month from April to October, with a Christmas concert in December. Showcase local and international talent, with everything from jazz to soul to Christmas carols. Children welcome. Bring blanket or towel to sit on.

## MOVIE THEATRES

**The Little Theatre,** 30 Queen Street (Tel. 292-2135). It's a good idea to purchase tickets at the box office prior to the performance, as this popular small theatre is quickly filled. Or you can call ahead and reserve your ticket by credit card. Box office open from 1:30 P.M.

**Liberty Theatre,** Union Street (Tel. 292-7296). Largest of the movie theatres, owned and operated by the Bermuda Trade Union.

For other movie theatres check out "The East End" and "The West End" chapters. For movie listings check local newspapers.

**Movies set in Bermuda:** *The Deep,* starring Robert Shaw, Jacqueline Bissett, and Nick Nolte; tales of shipwrecks, kidnapping, and voodoo. *That Touch of*

*Mink,* starring Doris Day and Cary Grant; Doris Day gets charmed into going to Bermuda with debonair bachelor Cary Grant (who wouldn't?). And see if you can catch Jimmy Stewart mention Bermuda the next time you watch Frank Capra's classic, *It's a Wonderful Life.*

## 9. Handy Phone Numbers

**Phone Cards:** Available throughout Bermuda at retail outlets, prepaid for long-distance convenience in denominations of $10, $25, or $50. When dialling some U.S. 1-800 toll-free numbers, you may be charged long-distance rates—if so, a recording will warn you and give you a chance to hang up.

**Airline Numbers While in Bermuda:**
Air Canada: Tel. 293-1777
American Airlines: Tel. 293-1420. AA Automated Flight Information: Tel. 1-880-223-5436 (have flight number ready)
British Airways: Tel. 1-800-AIRWAYS
Continental Airlines: Tel. 1-800-231-0856
Delta Airlines: Tel. 1-800-221-1212
USAirways: Tel. 293-3072
**Bermuda Chapter of the Society for the Advancement for the Handicapped:** Tel. (212) 447-7284
**Bermuda National Gallery:** Tel. 295-9428
**Bermuda National Trust:**
Historic Homes: Tel. 236-8306
Tours of Nature Reserves: Tel. 236-6483
**Bermuda Physically Handicapped Association:** Tel. 292-5025
**Chamber of Commerce:** Tel. 295-4201
**City Hall Box Office:** Tel. 292-2313
**Crime Stoppers** (confidential): Tel. 1-800-623-8477
**Department of Tourism** (Global House, 43 Church Street, Hamilton, Bermuda, HM 12): Tel. 292-0023, U.S.A. Tel. 1-800-223-6106, Canada Tel. 416-923-9600, U.K. Tel. 0171-771-7001
**Department of Tourism** brochures: U.S.A. Tel. 1-800-BERMUDA, Canada Tel. 416-923-9600, U.K. Tel. 0171-771-7001
**Drugstore** (Phoenix Drug Store): Tel. 295-3838
**Emergency** (Police, Fire, Ambulance): Tel. 911
**Hospital** (King Edward VII Memorial): Tel. 236-2345
**International Directory Enquiries:** Tel. 1 + (Overseas Area Code) + 555-1212, or call 00 for assistance (list of main U.S., U.K., and Canadian area codes in the Bermuda Telephone Directory)

**Local Directory Enquiries:** Tel. 411
**Library:** Tel. 295-2905
**Marine Forecast:** 977-2
**Post Office** (General): Tel. 297-7893
**Time and Temperature:** Tel. 909
**Transport:**
**Bus Enquiries:** Tel. 292-3854
**Ferry Terminal:** Tel. 295-4506
**Public Transportation Board:** Tel. 292-3851
**Scooter Rentals:** Tel. 295-0919
**Taxicabs:** Tel. 295-4141
**Wheelchair Taxi Services:** Tel. 235-2699 or Cell 234-7003
**U.S.A. Direct Service** (AT&T): Tel. 1-800-872-2881 (call box only)
**U.S. Consulate General:** Tel. 295-1342
**Visitors' Service Bureau** (Tourist Information), next to Ferry Terminal,
    Front Street: Tel. 295-1480
**Weather Forecast:** Tel. 977, Overseas: 1-800-297-7977, Tropical
    Storms/Hurricane Information: 977-3 or www.weather.bm

### SOAP SCOOP

No need to lose touch with your favourite soap operas. For updates while in Bermuda (local call rate), dial 976 plus the following numbers. For example, to hear what's happening on *All My Children,* dial 976-6000. You can have up to three selections on any *one* phone call by pressing 2 to interrupt and dial another recording.

**976 +**

| | |
|---|---|
| 6000 | *All My Children* |
| 6001 | *Another World* |
| 6002 | *As the World Turns* |
| 6003 | *The Bold and the Beautiful* |
| 6004 | *Days of Our Lives* |
| 6005 | *General Hospital* |
| 6007 | *The Guiding Light* |
| 6009 | *One Life to Live* |
| 6011 | *The Young and the Restless* |
| 6012 | Soap Scene (inside scoop on soap stars' private lives) |
| 6013 | Soap Trivia (quiz question on soaps) |

# 9

# The South Shore

Everyone wants to stay and play at the beach, so here is a whole chapter dedicated to the best coastal area in Bermuda—the South Shore. They call the South Shore the Gold Coast, but because of the coral colour of the sands, maybe it should be called the Pink Coast? Hey, it's just a thought.

The most famous beaches on the South Shore are Horseshoe Bay, Warwick Long Bay, and Elbow Beach; in between are charming little coves at the end of sandy trails. Out at sea, snorkellers and scuba divers may explore the reef necklace, but closer to shore, you will spot small round reefs commonly known as "boilers." Watch the sea foam up around them to see how they got their name.

If there is a small complaint by visitors regarding the South Shore, it is with regard to the lack of facilities and snack bars at many of the beaches. Horseshoe Bay does have a washroom/changing area, but other beaches are lacking. Take for instance Warwick Long Bay. It has an excellent children's playground but nowhere to pick up a snack or drink (although they do have a washroom). That means if you have travelled by bus, you may be stuck with little ones whining for refreshments. So be prepared and take a picnic with you, or at least cold beverages.

You'll find more information on Bermuda's famous pink beaches in the "South Shore Beaches" section below.

You'll also find the most romantic, seafront restaurants in Bermuda on the South Shore, especially at the hotels (see "Restaurants" below).

## 1. Transport

The buses that go to the South Shore are numbers 7 and 8. For Elbow Beach, you can get bus number 2 or 7 from Hamilton. Because of high waves and rocky coastlines, there are no public ferries to the South Shore, although if you are staying at the Fairmont Hamilton Princess Hotel, you can utilise their daily cruise.

## 2. Accommodations

### HIGHER-PRICED ACCOMMODATIONS

Note: To get deals on rooms at the large resort hotels in Bermuda, go to the "Package Deals" section in chapter 2, "Before You Leave Home."

**Fairmont Southampton Hotel,** South Shore, Southampton (P.O. Box HM 1379, Hamilton, HM FX, Tel. 238-8000, Fax 238-8968, Toll-free: U.S. 1-800-223-1818, Canada 1-800-268-7176, southampton@fairmont.com, www.fairmont.com).

This luxury hotel (formerly known as the Southampton Princess) is Bermuda's largest, with 600 rooms, its own 18-hole golf course, six restaurants, stores, cocktail lounges, tennis courts, dive school, beauty salon and full spa, fitness centre, and indoor and outdoor pools, to name but a few of its facilities. One of its main attractions is Dolphin Quest, a dolphin park housing nine playful dolphins in an enclosed pen, which the Fairmont Southampton runs from the Royal Naval Dockyard in the West End. Close encounters with these mammals are definitely of the memory-making kind.

From the hotel, a shuttle bus takes you to a lovely private beach club and seaside restaurant. As detailed in chapter 7, "The Business Traveller," the Princess also caters to business travellers, conventions, and groups.

**Standard double room rates:** $219 to $459 (depending on month), plus service charge and tax. Suites cost more.

**Elbow Beach Hotel,** South Shore, Paget (P.O. Box HM 455, Hamilton, HM BX, Tel. 236-3535, Fax 236-8043, Toll-free 1-800-344-3526, Reservations 1-800-223-7434, www.mandarinoriental.com/bermuda).

As you drive up the long palm-fringed road to this hotel, you realise you are going somewhere special. Maybe it's the 50 acres of landscaped gardens, or your first glimpse of the long stretch of perfect beach below. A AAA Four-Diamond Resort hotel, the Elbow has four restaurants, several stores, a beauty salon, exercise room with hot tub, five tennis courts with tennis shop, and pool with terrace bar service. On-site night-club, "The Deep," for over-25s. There are daily organised children's activities available during the summer.

**Double room rates:** $295 to $575 (depending on month and category of room), plus service charge and tax.

**Sonesta Beach Resort,** South Shore, Southampton (P.O. Box HM 1070, Hamilton, HM EX, Tel. 238-8122, Fax 238-8463, Toll-free U.S. 1-800-SONESTA, www.sonesta.com/bermuda). (Note: Due to damage sustained from Hurricane Fabian, this hotel will be closed for repairs until May 2004.)

Every visitor who passes Sonesta, whether on foot or by scooter, pauses to take in this large, white, crescent-shaped resort hotel situated on a sweeping peninsula surrounded by three beaches—one with waterfall—and flanked by an impressive-looking glass-dome-covered indoor pool. Sonesta certainly has the best first impression of any hotel on the South Shore. And when you see Honeymoon Point, where weddings take place, it makes you want to get married all over again, just to be in a more romantic location than the last time.

Choose from double rooms in the main hotel or in the separate waterfront "Bay View" complex with 26 minisuites. The beach circling the Bay Wing is for decorative purposes only, with sand about one inch deep. A convenient British double-decker shuttle bus transports guests around the resort and to the bus stop. Facilities include an on-site scooter-rental livery, shops, four restaurants, and one beach café, plus you can dine directly on the beach under a palm-frond canopy hung with net curtains for intimacy. There are six tennis courts and a pro shop set in a gorgeous location. Water sports include scuba diving, snorkelling, and fishing. Relax at the health spa (extra charge) with a massage or facial. Choice of either full meal plan, breakfast plans, or room only. There's a children's programme during the summer months.

**Double room rates:** $160 to $425 (depending on month and category of room), plus service charge and tax. 30 percent discount if you arrive on a Sunday or Monday. Other discounts include fourth and fifth nights free depending on month.

**The Reefs,** 56 South Road, Southampton (Tel. 238-0222, Fax 238-8372, Toll-free U.S. and Canada 1-800-742-2008, generalinfo@thereefs.bm, www.thereefs.com).

Owned by a former minister of tourism, The Reefs hotel has an excellent reputation. Located not far from Gibbs Hill Lighthouse and next door to Sonesta Beach Resort, The Reefs offers luxury and tranquillity. This hotel has a private beach and pool with choice of either rooms or cottages, all with ocean views. All accommodations are air-conditioned, but TVs are available only on request. Home of the popular tropical Coconuts Restaurant (see "Restaurants" section below).

**Double room rates:** $298 to $446 (depending on season and category of room), plus service charge and tax. Rate includes use of gym.

**Horizons & Cottages,** South Shore Road, Paget, PG 04 (Tel. 236-0048, Fax 236-1981, Toll-free reservations U.S. 1-800-468-0022, reservations@ horizons.bm, www.horizonscottages.com).

Horizons is a cottage colony about a five-minute walk to the South Shore beaches and across the road from the Coral Beach & Tennis Club. There are 12 double rooms with bath in the main house, or 13 cottages to choose from. Cottages have enchanting names like "Banana Tree" and "Skylark" and come equipped with air-conditioning, heating, and phone (TV and radios on request). There's a large pool and patio area and a nine-hole golf course, plus three tennis courts and a putting green. Exchange dining can be arranged between the Waterloo House hotel in Hamilton as well as the tennis, beach, and spa facilities at the Coral Beach Club nearby. Horizons is a member of Relais et Chateaux and the Horizons Limited Group of Hotels. *Gourmet* magazine gave Horizons top honours in their "Rooms at the Top" award, in their May 1999 issue.

**Double room rates:** $330 to $510 (depending on season and category of room), plus service charge and tax. Rate includes breakfast.

**Coral Beach & Tennis Club,** South Shore, Paget (P.O. Box HS 81, Harrington Sound, HS BX, Tel. 236-2233, Fax 236-1876).

This is a private tennis club overlooking a private section of Elbow Beach, with eight clay tennis courts and a resident tennis pro (the international Bermuda XL Tennis Open is held here every April). To stay here, you need to join the club, a task that requires no less than four letters of introduction from members, the board's final approval, and payment of annual fees!

The main house has several deluxe bed/sitting rooms and suites, some with sunken whirlpool tubs. The cottages on the property all come with a personal maid and are ideal honeymoon accommodations. Each cottage is individually laid out, some with private entrance to beach; one has its own freshwater pool. This is a rather formal resort where jacket and tie is expected for men at every dinner (black tie on Thursday and Friday optional) in the Clubhouse and weekly cocktail parties are part of the entertainment. Your maid can make breakfast if you stay in one of the cottages. Nanny service and babysitting are provided.

**Double cottage rates:** $380 to $704 year round (depending on cottage), plus service charge and tax.

## MEDIUM-PRICED ACCOMMODATIONS

**Coco Reef Resort** (formerly Stonington Beach Hotel), Stonington Beach, South Shore, Paget (P.O. Box HM 523, Hamilton, HM CX, Tel. 236-5416, Fax 236-0371, Toll-free U.S. and Canada 1-800-648-0799, stonington@northrock.bm, www.stoningtonbeach.com). (Note: At time of writing, this hotel is promised a $10 million renovation and refurbishment under its new owners. This will include five new deluxe suites, a beachside restaurant, and a bistro restaurant.)

Right next door to Elbow Beach Hotel, but nestled at the end of the bay, Coco Reef is in an ideal location for beach lovers, and all rooms have ocean view. Supervised college students from the Hospitality and Culinary Institute of Bermuda service this 64-room hotel (plus two cottages). Actually, this means that the standard of service is probably higher than lots of other places. All rooms have air-conditioning, heating, cable TV, radio, and phone. There is an inviting pool and two tennis courts. Facilities of the hotel include the use of the college campus for aerobics classes and gym equipment.

**Double room rates:** $263 to $448 (depending on season and category of room), plus tax. Rate includes service charge and breakfast. Golf and honeymoon packages available. (Note: Rates may differ after refurbishment.)

**Ariel Sands Beach Club,** 34 South Road, Devonshire (P.O. Box HM 334, Hamilton, HM BX, Tel. 236-1010, Toll-free: U.S. 1-800-468-6610, U.K. 0-800-917-0548, www.arielsands.com).

Ariel Sands has the distinction of being part owned by movie star Michael Douglas. Michael is part Bermudian on his mother's side and Douglas/Dill family reunions are spent in this recently refurbished exclusive cottage colony. There are 13 cottage units in addition to the mandatory main Club House. Set in peaceful surroundings and close to a lovely private beach, spa, exercise room, tennis courts, putting green, and seaside (alfresco) restaurant—Aqua. Rooms have porches and are fitted with private bathroom, air-conditioning, cable TV, and radios. Children are welcome (cribs available), although they are requested to dine at 6:30 P.M.

**Double room rates:** $210 to $375 (depending on month and category of room), plus service charge and tax. Rate includes breakfast.

**Grape Bay Cottages,** Grape Bay Beach, Paget (P.O. Box PG 137, Paget, PG BX, Tel. 236-1194, Fax 236-1194, Toll-free: U.S. 1-800-637-4116, Canada 1-800-267-7600).

These are two cottages in one of the loveliest settings in Bermuda, directly situated on Grape Bay, a secluded and unspoiled peaceful beach. Each cottage has two double bedrooms, one bath, living/dining room, kitchen, and verandah with sea view. They also have fireplaces for romantic fireside evenings during the cooler months. Dogs are permitted on advance request, although there is a fumigation charge on departure.

**Double cottage rates:** $210 to $315 (depending on season), plus service charge and tax.

**Surf Side Beach Club,** South Shore, Warwick (P.O. Box WK 101, Warwick, WK BX, Tel. 236-7100, Fax 236-9765, Toll-free U.S. 1-800-553-9990, www.bermudaresorthotels.com).

Small, hidden-away hotel with fully equipped, self-contained apartment units, all with magnificent views overlooking ocean and private beach (49 suites). Upper and lower units are snuggled into the cliff side—the highest unit is perched 130 feet above sea level. Meandering paths, bordered with flowering tropical bushes and plants, connect the units to the pool area and restaurant. Each unit has a porch, kitchen, microwave, air-conditioning, heating, cable TV, radio, and phone. This hotel has a large sun terrace with pool, bar, Jacuzzi, and sauna. Transport: bus stop at roadway entrance and on-site scooter rental. Alfresco restaurant, The Palms, serves breakfast, lunch, and dinner. Poolside buffets served once a week. There's a summertime coffee shop and bar on the pool terrace. Children welcome. Dogs permitted on advance request.

**Double room rates:** $130 to $300 (depending on season), plus service charge and tax.

**Deluxe suite rates:** $300 to $950 (depending on season and number of persons).

**The Breakers Beach Club** (formerly The Mermaid Beach Club), South Road, Warwick (P.O. Box WK 250, Warwick, WK BX, Tel. 236-5031, Fax 236-8784, Toll-free U.S. and Canada 1-800-441-7087).

This hotel consists of informal rooms and suites in a relaxed atmosphere, overlooking a pretty private beach. All rooms have air-conditioning, heating, radio, and phone. Most overlook the ocean from private balconies; some have kitchens (for an extra charge).

**Double room rates:** $130 to $296 (depending on month), plus service charge and tax. Children under three stay free. Suites for four people cost extra. Monthly rates available.

## BUDGET-PRICED ACCOMMODATIONS

Note: For a list of budget properties to rent, go to "Private House and Apartment Rentals" in chapter 2, "Before You Leave Home."

**Astwood Cove** (Housekeeping Apartments) (49 South Road, Warwick, WK 07, Tel. 236-0984, Fax 236-1164, Toll-free U.S. 1-800-441-7087, www.astwoodcove.com).

Opposite Astwood Park and beach; studio, standard, or superior air-conditioned suites and apartments with verandah or patio, clustered within a garden setting. Modern and bright with fully equipped kitchenettes. Facilities include large pool and sun terrace, sauna (extra charge), TV/common room, coin laundry, and free iron. Grocery deliveries are twice a day for your convenience. Astwood Cove has a long-standing, good reputation and is very well organised.

**Double room rates:** $110 to $190 (depending on month), plus service charge and tax. Honeymoon specials available.

**Paraquet Guest Apartments,** South Shore Road, Paget (P.O. Box PG 173, Paget, PG BX, Tel. 236-5842, Fax 236-1665, www.paraquetapartments.com).

Bright and clean air-conditioned accommodations within walking distance of beautiful Elbow Beach, close to bus service to Hamilton, and convenient to grocery store. No telephones in rooms but will deliver messages. Pedal bikes and scooters available for rent. There is a popular budget restaurant on site.

**Double room rates:** $132 to $187 (depending on season), plus tax. Rate includes maid service.

**Marley Beach Cottages,** South Road, Warwick (P.O. Box PG 278, Paget, PG BX, Tel. 236-1143, Fax 236-1984, Toll-free U.S. 1-800-637-4116, www.netlinkbermuda.com/marley).

Beautifully located on a cliff overlooking a secluded beach, cottage units and studio apartments all with private terrace, fully equipped kitchens, air-conditioning, heating, TV, radio, and phone. There is an on-site pool with whirlpool. Close to bus stop. Groceries delivered if required. Children by advance permission only.

**Double cottage rates:** $105 to $260 (depending on season), plus service charge and tax.

**Sandpiper Apartments,** South Road, Warwick (P.O. Box HM 685, Hamilton, HM CS, Tel. 236-7093, Fax 236-3898, sandpiper@logic.bm, www.bermuda.com/sandpiper).

Directly on busy South Road, five one-bedroom and nine studio, fully equipped modern apartments close to bus stop and not far from beaches. Each unit has kitchen, bedroom, living room, air-conditioning, heater, cable TV, radio, and phone. There is also an attractive pool and whirlpool. The management really look after their staff here and, in return, they give great service.

**Double apartment rates:** $100 to $130 (depending on season), plus service charge and tax.

**Clairfont Apartments,** Warwickshire Road, Warwick (P.O. Box WK 85, Warwick, WK BX, Tel. 238-0149).

Self-contained studio or one-bedroom apartments with kitchenettes and air-conditioning. Close to South Shore beaches. On-site pool.

**Year-round rates:** $100 to $120. Special monthly rates available between Nov. 1 and Feb. 28.

**Syl-Den Apartments,** 8 Warwickshire Road, Warwick, WK 02 (Tel. 238-1834).

Right next door to Clairfont Apartments (mentioned above) and close to South Shore beaches and Warwick Long Bay children's adventure playground. Apartments come with fully equipped kitchenettes and air-conditioning. Pool.

**Year-round rates:** $110, plus tax.

## 3. Restaurants

### HIGHER-PRICED RESTAURANTS

**Café Lido,** Elbow Beach Hotel, South Shore, Paget (Tel. 236-9884). Open for lunch and dinner. A place to go that shows off the natural beauty of the island, where the service is top-notch and the cuisine exceptional. In the summer, they pull back the sliding windows so you can enjoy the sound and breeze of the sea below. (Note: This restaurant was damaged during Hurricane Fabian, but, at time of writing, a commitment has been made to have it fully repaired.) Also, at this hotel you will find the Seahorse Grill, a fully refurbished restaurant that uses all fresh Bermuda produce.

**Newport Room,** Fairmont Southampton Hotel (Tel. 238-8000). Open for dinner from 7. Named after the Newport-Bermuda sailing race, this nautical-style upscale restaurant serves contemporary French cuisine. Service is to the highest standard: hovering waiters, Wedgwood china, and silver platters. At the same hotel is The Rib Room, an English steak and rib house, or try the **Whaler Inn,** overlooking the beach, for good seafood.

**Henry VIII Restaurant & Pub** (on the road opposite Sonesta Beach Resort), South Shore, Southampton (Tel. 238-1977 or 238-0908). Open for lunch and dinner, and Sunday brunch noon-2 P.M. Old English-style restaurant with nightly entertainment during the summer. The popular Sunday brunch is good value and includes two hot roasts, cold meats, fish, desserts, and complimentary glass of wine. Reservations recommended.

## MEDIUM-PRICED RESTAURANTS

**Coconuts at the Reefs,** Southampton (Tel. 238-0222). Open summer for lunch and dinner. Tropical thatched-roof restaurant with beach and sea views situated at The Reefs Hotel. Very romantic. The menu items are innovative and varied; for example, cockspur dry-aged filet of beef (glazed with dried cherries and goat cheese, served on sweet island yam and portwine jus). Also dreamy desserts such as banana-mousse-filled cinnamon crepes with butterscotch pistachios and a Blue Mountain coffee-chocolate sauce.

**Aqua Seaside Restaurant,** Ariel Sands Hotel, South Shore Road, Devonshire (Tel. 236-1010). Open daily. Romantic alfresco restaurant with dishes blending Italian, Mediterranean, Caribbean, Asian, and American themes.

**Seagrape,** Sonesta Beach Resort, Southampton (Tel. 238-8122). Open summer for lunch and dinner. It's difficult to know where to sit here: Either gaze at the cascading waterfall below, the pool on one side, or the palm-fringed beach on the other. Serves grill-fired dishes from the Pacific Rim. (Note: Due to damage sustained from Hurricane Fabian, this hotel will be closed for repairs until May 2004.)

**Mickey's Sand Bar,** Elbow Beach Hotel, Paget (Tel. 236-9884). Open June-Nov. Lunch deli until 4:30, dinner 6-midnight. This is Bermuda's only on-the-sand dining, serving frozen exotic drinks and cocktails. Light refreshments; self-serve deli. Casual dress allowed and definitely recommended. (Note: This restaurant was carried out to sea during the high winds of Hurricane Fabian; however, at time of writing, a commitment has been made to rebuild it.)

**Whaler Inn,** Fairmont Southampton Hotel, on the waterfront (Tel. 238-8000). Open May-Oct. noon-2:20 P.M., dinner from 6:30. This seafood restaurant has a reputation for serving freshly caught fish. Beautiful view of the ocean and beach below adds to the magic.

**Tio Pepe Restaurant** (on the road opposite Horseshoe Bay beach entrance), South Road, Southampton (Tel. 238-1897). Open daily for lunch and dinner, noon-10. Spanish and Italian cuisine including spaghetti Bolognese, fresh-made pizzas, pastas, and Petti di Pollo al Champagne (boneless chicken in light cream and champagne sauce). Just the ticket after a day's sunbathing on Horseshoe Beach on the South Shore. Outside dining for a romantically lit balcony, or inside for air-conditioned comfort.

**PawPaws Restaurant and Bar,** 87 South Road, Paget (Tel. 236-7459). Patio dining under big umbrellas makes this restaurant an inviting place to go after a day on the beach.

## BUDGET-PRICED EATERIES

**The Lighthouse Tea Rooms** (base of Gibbs Hill Lighthouse), Southampton (Tel. 238-8679). Open daily 9 A.M.–5 P.M. Afternoon tea from 2:30. Once the home of the lighthouse keeper, this Old World-charm tearoom is now run by the daughter of the very last lighthouse keeper and is open for breakfast, lunch, and afternoon teas. A plaque situated on the road below marks HRH Queen Elizabeth's favourite view of Bermuda. English fare served, such as ploughman's lunch (salad, cheeses, pickles, breads), specialty teas, pies, tarts and cream teas, English crumpets, and toasted tea cakes drizzled with butter. This tearoom is a perfect place to recuperate after a visit to the top of the lighthouse.

**Horseshoe Bay Beach Café,** South Shore, Southampton. Open daily 9 A.M.–6 P.M. Closed from the end Oct. till Mar. Alfresco fast-food café situated next to Bermuda's most famous beach. Burgers, fries, hot dogs, and ice cream. Busy, busy, busy.

**Paraquet Restaurant & Take Out,** South Shore Road, Paget (Tel. 236-9742). Open daily for breakfast and lunch. Connected to the Paraquet Guest Apartments. Dine on homemade Bermudian fare either at the crescent-shaped counter or in the dining area.

**Stonington Training College Campus,** Paget (Reservations: Hotel & Technical Department, 236-9000). Available during the students' college year: Oct.-Apr. (except midsemester breaks). A business lunch special is prepared and served by Bermudian students, which is a three-course meal for $15 per person! Don't miss a stroll on the beautiful Elbow Beach after your meal.

## 4. South Shore Beaches

Breathtaking. That's the only word to describe Bermuda's beaches. Whether it's wide stretches of pink sands on the South Shore or tiny inlets and protected fishing harbours dotted along the North Shore, Bermuda has everything to offer the sun worshipper and beachcomber. Unlike other tourist destinations, there are no high-rise buildings to spoil the view, and for those seeking tranquillity, it is easy to find a deserted beach.

### Bermuda Seas by Edith Farr Geer, 1894

I had not dreamt there could be such a blue—
Such blue! I caught my breath with ecstasy,
And felt my heart stop short; when into view
Over the shelving hill, there flashed the sea!

## WARWICK LONG BAY, WARWICK

This is Bermuda's longest stretch of beach, positioned at the bottom of small grass-topped sand dunes. Great spot for a jog or romantic stroll along the water's edge. Trails connect to other small coves. At the eastern entrance of Warwick Long Bay is an excellent children's play park, the perfect place for those little ones to run off steam. Nearest eatery is either Carolyn's lunch wagon (summer) or PawPaws Restaurant and Pastry Shop.

## HORSESHOE BAY, SOUTHAMPTON

Bermuda's most visited beach is popular with early-morning joggers, all-day sun worshippers, and evening strollers. Perhaps the most famous of all beaches in Bermuda and rated as one of the top 10 beaches in the world, Horseshoe Bay certainly lives up to its reputation. Full facilities: showers, washrooms, café, and chair rental. Lifeguard on duty during the summer. From the bus stop, it is about a 10-minute walk to the beach. During the summer, Mon.-Thur. 11 A.M.–6 P.M., a "Top of the Hill" shuttle bus service is on hand.

## ELBOW BEACH, PAGET

Expansive stretch of soft sand—so perfect for relaxing on, or for a romantic sunset stroll. Although Elbow Beach Hotel owns the eastern end of the beach, which is out of bounds to nonguests of the hotel, the remainder is accessible from the public entrance at the end of Tribe Road 4B, off South Shore Road, Paget.

## SOUTH SHORE INLETS

Apart from the larger beaches—Warwick, Horseshoe, Elbow—the South Shore has a number of tiny bays, often secluded, never disappointing, some with warm currents of shallow water teeming with marine life.

**Church Bay:** This cove is famous for snorkelling and viewing tropical parrotfish. Snorkelling equipment is for rent during the summer months.

**Chaplin Bay and Stonehole Bay:** Quiet, secluded little bays with azure waters.

**Jobson's Cove:** Much-photographed, tiny bay adjacent to Warwick Long Bay. During the high season, arrive here early in the day for a good spot on the beach.

**Astwood Cove:** Parklike setting; popular spot for wedding photos. There's a steep walk to two beaches with good snorkelling spots. Be careful about currents.

## 5. Sightseeing

**Whale Watching:** From the South Shore beaches and roadway, during the migratory month of April, you can occasionally have the unforgettable experience of viewing humpback whales playing in the ocean. For excursions to view the whales in their natural habitat, contact Fantasea Diving (Tel. 236-6339, www.fantasea.bm). Group and corporate rates are available if booked early enough.

**Gibbs Hill Lighthouse,** Southampton (Tel. 238-0524). Open daily 9 A.M.–5 P.M. Small admission charge. Because of the vast number of shipwrecks on the treacherous reefs off Bermuda, it was decided to construct a lighthouse to light the way for passing ships. On May 1, 1846, the good folks of Southampton Parish, in anticipation of the new lighthouse, put away all their whale-oil lamps and candles, mistakenly believing that the lighthouse would illuminate their homes.

The lighthouse rises 362 feet above sea level, and crafts 40 miles away can see the light. It is well worth a climb (185 steps) to the top for the sweeping views.

Tearooms are situated in the charming old lighthouse keeper's cottage (see "Budget-Priced Eateries" above).

## 6. Guided Tours and Cruises

**Dolphin Quest,** hosted by the Fairmont Southampton Hotel, South Shore (www.dolphinquest.org), now situated at the Royal Naval Dockyard (Tel. 234-4464, or you can book directly from Dolphin Quest in the U.S. at Tel. 540-687-8102). A chance to encounter dolphins up close and personal. As fully outlined in the section on bringing children to Bermuda (chapter 2), intimate dolphin encounters cost from $87.50 per person to $275 per person, depending on age and length of programme. The one-hour programme includes the entrance fee to the Maritime Museum, a beach towel, and a photograph. Swimsuits are required and water shoes are suggested.

## 7. Water Sports

**Nautilus Diving,** Fairmont Southampton Hotel, Southampton (Tel. 238-2332, Fax 234-5180) and Hamilton Princess Hotel, Hamilton (Tel. 295-9485, nautilus@logic.bm, www.bermuda.bm/nautilus). Introductory session, single-tank, or two-tank dives. Excellent scuba diving operation with caring PADI (Professional Association of Diving Instructors) certified trainers. For enthusiasts, try the four-day wreck-diving certificate programme.

**Fantasea Bermuda Ltd.,** Sonesta Beach Resort, Southampton (Tel. 236-1300, info@fantasea.bm, www.fantasea.bm). Diving and snorkel trips plus water-sports equipment rental including kayaks and pedal boats. Exciting underwater scooter tours are available here too.

**Blue Water Divers & Watersports,** Elbow Beach Hotel, Paget (Tel. 234-2909, www.divebermuda.com). Scuba diving, PADI instructors, boating, underwater scooter tours, and exploration of *Pollockshields* shipwreck site.

## 8. Shopping

Shopping on the South Shore is done mainly in the three large hotels: Sonesta Beach Resort, Fairmont Southampton Hotel, and Elbow Beach Hotel. There you'll find branches of Trimingham's, The English Sports Store, and Crissons Jewellers, to name but a few, and prices are the same as in the main stores.

**Rising Sun Shop,** Middle Road, Southampton, at the bottom of steps to Gibbs Hill Lighthouse (Tel. 238-2154). Well worth a visit for unique gifts not found anywhere else on the island.

## 9. Nightlife

**The Deep,** Café Lido Complex, Elbow Beach Sea Terrace, Elbow Beach Hotel, Paget (Tel. 238-9884). Open 10 P.M.–3 A.M. Admission is free for Lido Restaurant diners. Modern night-club on the beachfront at Elbow Beach Hotel with a strict dress code: casually elegant. No one under 25 admitted. There are three dance floors, a stage, private rooms, and mezzanine seating areas.

**Sonesta Beach Resort,** South Shore (Tel. 238-8122). Lots of entertainment during the summer months at this large resort. Call ahead to find out which nights. (Note: Due to damage sustained from Hurricane Fabian, this hotel will be closed for repairs until May 2004.)

**Henry VIII Restaurant and Bar,** South Shore (opposite Sonesta Beach Resort, Tel. 238-1977). Nightly entertainment 9:30 P.M.–1 A.M.

## 10. Handy Phone Numbers

**Crime Stoppers** (confidential): Tel. 1-800-623-8477
**Emergency** (Police, Fire, Ambulance): Tel. 911
**Fairmont Southampton Golf Course:** Tel. 238-0446

**Gibbs Hill Lighthouse:** Tel. 238-0524

**Hospital:** Tel. 236-2345

**Post Office** (Southampton): Tel. 238-0253

**Scooter Rental** (Eve's Cycle): Tel. 236-6247

**Supermarket** (Modern Mart near Paraquet Guest Apartments): Tel. 236-6161

**Taxi Tours** (G. Brown): Tel. 234-7377

**Visitors' Service Bureau** (Tourist Information), next to Ferry Terminal, Front Street: Tel. 295-1480

# 10

# The West End

For a small country, Bermuda has a great wealth of diversity. I once over-heard a visitor exclaiming her surprise at the vast variety packed into 21 square miles, the different atmosphere of each parish, and especially the difference between the West End and East End. There's a lot of friendly competition going on between Somerset in the west and St. George's in the east, particularly at Cup Match cricket time. All their lives, Bermudians are very loyal to the area they are born in, with much friendly banter as to which end is the best end.

From Southampton through Somerset Village and on to the Royal Naval Dockyard, with the Maritime Museum at its tip, there's plenty to dis-cover at Bermuda's West End: beaches, forts, nature reserves, trails, lots and lots of water sports, great walking, and great scenery.

## 1. Transport

Buses to the West End are numbers 7 and 8. Some only go as far as Barnes Corner (about halfway there), so if you're going to Somerset or Dockyard you need to make sure that it is going all the way. The nicest route to the West End from Hamilton is via the Somerset Ferry; it takes a bit longer but the experience is worth it. You can take your scooter on the ferry for the price of a passenger fare.

For cabs going to the West End, try **Sandys Taxi** on Hook & Ladder Lane (Tel. 234-2344). To save you money, they also have a minicab service. Also, **Gladstone Brown** provides air-conditioned taxi tours (Tel. 234-7377). For other taxi services, check Bermuda's Yellow Pages.

## 2. Accommodations

### HIGHER-PRICED ACCOMMODATIONS

Note: To get deals on rooms at the large resort hotels in Bermuda, go to the "Package Deals" section in chapter 2, "Before You Leave Home."

**Cambridge Beaches,** Mangrove Bay, 30 King's Point, Sandys, MA 02 (Tel. 234-0331, Fax 234-3352, Toll-free: U.S. 1-800-468-7300, Canada 1-800-463-5900, cambeach@logic.bm, www.cambridgebeaches.com).

Cambridge Beaches has one of the best reputations in Bermuda as a top-notch cottage colony and is one of the favourite haunts of celebrities such as Phil Collins and Donald Sutherland. From the air, the 25-acre site seems almost to be on its own island, being surrounded on three sides by five private beaches. It has everything to offer the water-sports enthusiast: private dock, sail- or motorboat rental, scuba, snorkelling, windsurfing, etc. A place to relax and be pampered in is their European Health Spa, with five spa treatment rooms, indoor pool, and exercise pool. Transportation options: private ferry to Hamilton, moped rental, and taxis.

**Double room rates:** $325 to $1,480 (depending on season and category of room), plus service charge and tax.

### MEDIUM-PRICED ACCOMMODATIONS

**Pompano Beach Club,** 36 Pompano Beach Road, Southampton, SB 03 (Tel. 234-0222, Fax 234-1694, Toll-free U.S. and Canada 1-800-343-4155, info@pompano.bm, www.pompano.bm).

This 56-room hotel including 21 oceanfront deluxe rooms with turquoise-sea views is a quiet, out-of-the-way place, adjacent to Port Royal Golf Course and overlooking the southwest shore. Rooms have spacious bathroom, private balcony, air-conditioning, heating, TV, radio, and phone. There is a heated pool, wading/children's pool, and Jacuzzis on a sun terrace overlooking the ocean. A water-sports centre in the summer offers windsurfing, sailing, kayaking, and snorkelling. Full breakfast and dinner in Cedar Room restaurant or continental breakfast served in room or cottage. Lunch on terrace; afternoon snacks at pool bar. Complimentary access to e-mails in the lobby area. Free shuttle to bus and ferry stop. All ages welcome.

**Double room rates:** $250 to $510 (depending on category of room), plus service charge and tax. Rate includes breakfast and dinner. Golf, scuba, and honeymoon packages available.

**Munro Beach Cottages,** Southampton (P.O. Box SN 99, Southampton, SN BX, Tel. 234-1175, Fax 234-3528, info@munrobeach.com, www.munrobeach.com).

Set amid five acres, fully equipped air-conditioned duplex cottages (some with connecting doors), all with bathroom and daily maid service. Cottages can accommodate up to four people and have fully equipped kitchens. Munro is off the beaten track, peaceful, and private, with an incredibly beautiful beach and crystal-clear water (it doesn't get any clearer than this), a few steps away from each cottage. Grocery delivery. Golfers' paradise—next door to Port Royal Golf Course. Close to floodlit tennis. About a 10-minute walk to main road and bus stop.

**Cottage rates:** $130 to $274 (depending on month), plus service charge and tax.

**Willowbank,** Ely's Harbour Sandys (P.O. Box MA 296, Sandys, MA BX, Tel. 234-1616, Toll-free: U.S. 1-800-752-8493, Canada 1-800-463-8444, reservations@willowbank.bm, www.willowbank.bm).

Willowbank is a Christian hotel with a devotional morning period each day for those wishing to attend. And what a perfect setting, too: sandy palm-fringed beach overlooking one of Bermuda's most tranquil harbours, not far from the peaceful grounds of 400-year-old Heydon Trust and chapel. This six-acre cottage colony consists of a main manor house, two private beaches, a fishing dock, two tennis courts, and a swimming pool. No charge for children's accommodation (charge for meals only). Children ages two-11, 50 percent off meal rate; children 12-16, full meal charge; children under two eat free of charge. Complimentary afternoon tea daily; breakfast and dinner served in the aptly named Loaves and Fishes dining room (men need to wear jacket and tie for dinner). Box lunches made on request.

**Double room rates:** $125 to $280, plus tax. No service charge. Rate includes breakfast and dinner.

## BUDGET-PRICED ACCOMMODATIONS

Note: For a list of budget properties to rent, go to "Private House and Apartment Rentals" in chapter 2, "Before You Leave Home."

**Garden House,** 4 Middle Road, Somerset Bridge, Sandys, SB 01 (Tel. 234-1435, Fax 234-3006).

Garden House is comprised of self-contained cottages set amongst three beautifully tranquil acres, leading down to an inlet at Somerset Bridge (said to be the smallest drawbridge in the world). The owner/manager goes the full distance in making her guests comfortable, even providing fruit from her many varieties of trees on the property. Garden House has all the charm of a Bermudian home in an extremely peaceful setting. The large cottage is very popular, with its four-poster bed, two en-suite baths, and private patio. Water-sport facilities are close by. Laundry facilities on hand. Smoking in grounds only. Pool.

**Double cottage rates:** Two-bedroom house for four: $235 to $265 (depending on use of air-conditioning); studio apartment: $110. All rates depending on month and category of room, plus service charge and tax.

**"Drybrow,"** 10 Bluebird Lane, Somerset (P.O. Box SB 224, Somerset Bridge, SB BX, Mrs. Karen Skiffington-Simpson, Tel. 234-0954, www.wall-bridge.com/karen).

A fully equipped housekeeping two-bedroom cottage with sea views, conveniently located at Somerset Bridge Ferry Stop and the scenic Railway Trail, especially popular with hikers and nature lovers. Informal home setting. Cottage comes equipped with microwave, barbecue, and TV. Long stays welcome. Guests must be dog-lovers.

**Double occupancy rates:** $800 per week inclusive of taxes.

**Greene's Guest House,** 71 Middle Road, Southampton (P.O. Box FN 395, Southampton, Tel. 238-0834 or 238-2532, Fax 238-8980).

Informal, family-run guesthouse overlooking the ocean at Jennings Bay. Rooms have private bath, cable TV, phone, and air-conditioning. There's a 40x24-foot pool and terrace on the property.

**Double room rates:** $100 (including full breakfast).

# 3. Restaurants

## HIGHER-PRICED RESTAURANTS

**Il Palio,** corner of Main Road and Hook & Ladder Lane, Somerset (Tel. 234-1049). Open Tues.-Sun. 6-10 P.M. This West End, fine-dining Italian restaurant features old-fashioned authentic cuisine from Tuscany, Italy. Il Palio also has a delicious, reasonably priced takeout menu.

## MEDIUM-PRICED RESTAURANTS

**Beethoven's,** Royal Naval Dockyard (Tel. 234-5009). Open Mon.-Wed. 9 A.M.–5 P.M. ; Thur.-Sat. to 9 P.M. Located at the Clocktower building in the Royal Naval Dockyard, this restaurant and bar caters to people looking for light and healthy food and provides excellent service in English, French, or German. Prepared from the grill, luncheon menu items include

Bermuda fish with mixed salad and mango ginger vinaigrette, or pesto chicken on organic greens with garlic dressing. Summer fare menu items: linguini with garlic olive oil and tomatoes, or wild mushroom and leek quiche with spinach salad and balsamic tomato vinaigrette. Some dinner entrées: Angus beef steak with Stilton and portwine sauce, or mahi-mahi with honey-roasted almonds and papaya.

**The Frog & Onion Pub and Restaurant,** Royal Naval Dockyard (Tel. 234-2900). Open daily 11:30 A.M.–1 A.M. Located in the historical Cooperage building of the Royal Naval Dockyard and featuring a huge 18th-century fireplace and massive floor candlesticks, the Frog & Onion has good English food and ale. The name of this pub originates from the fact that it is owned by a French man (the "frog") and a Bermudian (the "onion").

**Pirates Landing,** Royal Naval Dockyard, near ferry landing (Tel. 234-5151). Ahoy me maties, just the place to rest your cutlass and kick your boots off for a fine kettle of fish, and other hearty fare. Very friendly service.

**The Somerset Country Squire,** Mangrove Bay, Somerset (Tel. 234-0105). Open daily 10 A.M.–1 A.M. Make a wish with your loved one as you enter beneath the Bermuda Moon Gate of this traditional-style pub, and you will stay in love forever (or so legend goes). Situated in Somerset overlooking picturesque Mangrove Bay, the Country Squire combines casual indoor and outdoor dining. On the menu are spicy chicken wings, kebabs, ribs, and steaks.

**The Cedar Room,** Pompano Beach Club, next to Port Royal Golf Course, Oceanfront, Southampton (Tel. 234-0222). Open for lunch noon-2:30, dinner 7-9. Impressive views from this pleasant and refined oceanfront restaurant. Reasonably priced menu for lunch.

## BUDGET-PRICED EATERIES

**Mrs. Tea's Victorian Tea Room,** Southampton (look for the teapot sign next to Port Royal Esso gas station and the black tea kettle moulded onto the gate post, Tel. 234-1374). Open daily noon-5 P.M., closed Mon. Step back in time to a place not easily found these days and enjoy homemade fare at these pretty cottage tearooms. Sample the delights of a leisurely afternoon cream tea. (The cream goes on the scones [tea biscuits] not in the tea, as one Canadian friend thought.)

Mrs. Tea's consists of three theme rooms: Doll Room, Royal Family Room, and Christmas Festive Room. Each wood-floored room is chock-a-block with antiques, dolls, Victorian memorabilia, and every description of teapot.

**Alegria,** The Bermuda Golf Academy, 10 Industrial Park Road, Southampton (Tel. 238-8800, Takeout 238-8297). Open Mon.-Fri. 11 A.M.–10 P.M. Handy after either a Mini Golf Adventure game or a few shots on the driving range.

**Traditions,** 2 Middle Road, Southampton (Tel. 234-3770). Open Mon.-Sat. 7 A.M.–9 P.M., Sun. 8 A.M.–2 P.M. Situated en route to the Royal Naval Dockyard; local restaurant serving hearty homemade fare and marvellous milkshakes. Horse-hitching post at the side of building.

**The New Freeport Seafood Restaurant,** 1 Freeport Road, Dockyard (Tel. 234-1692). Open daily 9:30 A.M.–11 P.M. Situated at Royal Naval Dockyard's entrance; serves good wholesome food at reasonable prices. Seafood menu includes shrimp, scallops, and catch of the day. Lobster dinners available in season. Excellent children's menus, with entrée, fries, coleslaw, and soda. Nice service; popular with locals.

**Thel's Café,** 19 Somerset Road, Somerset (Tel. 234-1767). Open Mon.-Fri. and Sun. 6 A.M.–9 P.M., Sat. to 11 P.M. Another popular haunt of locals, open seven days a week for breakfast, lunch, and snacks. This café is friendly, clean, and simple.

**Misty's Take-Out,** Somerset Road, Somerset (Tel. 234-2449). Open Tues.-Sat. 11 A.M.–10 P.M., Sun. 7 A.M.–8 P.M. Small takeout food bar with freshly cooked and tasty fish sandwiches, fishcake on a bun, chicken wings, chicken nuggets, fries, and other fast foods. They also serve Sunday codfish breakfasts.

**Dean's Bakery,** Manchester Street, Somerset (Tel. 234-2918). Open Mon.-Sat. 6:30 A.M.–6 P.M. Local, family-run bakery and snack bar (eat in or takeout). Freshly made sandwiches, pastries, buns, chicken curry, and macaroni and cheese. Bermudian dishes available, such as cassava pie at Christmas and hot cross buns at Easter.

**Somerset Pharmacy Snack Bar,** Mangrove Bay, Somerset (Tel. 238-9419). Open Mon.-Sat. 8 A.M.–4 P.M. Tucked away at the back of the drugstore, with a couple of tables and a few stools at the snack bar; a good place to read the paper and grab a quick snack.

## 4. Sightseeing

**Royal Naval Dockyard:** At Bermuda's westernmost point lies the Royal Naval Dockyard. This historic fortress was built, stone placed upon stone, 200 years ago, by convicts and slaves from the British Isles who lived in atrocious floating prison hulks berthed in the harbour. In all, 9,000 men were shipped here, out of which 2,000 died in the process of Dockyard's construction; yellow fever was one of the several deadly diseases that killed them off.

Far removed from those cruel, dreary times, the Royal Naval Dockyard has been transformed into a waterfront complex, open seven days a week, with shops, art centre, craft store, cinema, water park, etc. The Bermuda Maritime Museum is housed here and boasts world-class exhibits (see below). Dockyard is a good excursion on a Sunday (after 11 A.M.), as Hamilton's shops and sights are mostly closed. For transport around Dockyard, try the nontrack train service (Tel. 236-5972), which runs primarily for the cruise-ship passengers but has some availability for other visitors.

As mentioned in "The Art Scene" section of chapter 5, "Culture and Heritage," **The Bermuda Arts Centre** (Tel. 234-2809) is housed at the Royal Naval Dockyard. Open daily 10 A.M.–5 P.M. For more art, there is usually an "Artist in Residence" based in a house at the entrance to the Victualling Yard.

At Dockyard you can also let the kids loose in the adventure playground adjacent to the museum. The jungle apparatus is shaped like a ship, and there's a fun water-play fountain to romp in on hot days.

**The Bermuda Maritime Museum,** The Keep, Royal Naval Dockyard, opposite Frog & Onion Pub (Tel. 234-1333). Open 9:30 A.M.–4:30 P.M. Closed Christmas Day. Admission: adults $7.50, children five-18 $3, children under five free, seniors $6. Family package: $15 for Mom/Dad and up to five children (if under 18 years).

Steeped in history, the Maritime Museum is a wonderful attraction for lovers of seafaring artefacts. Comprising six historical limestone buildings showcasing exhibits from Bermuda's maritime heritage: whaling, diving, fitted dinghies, and sloops. Stories of Spanish explorers and privateers and all manner of painstakingly gathered underwater finds, with examples of golden treasure culled from shipwrecks dotted around Bermuda's reef-riddled shores. History buffs should take a look at the exhibit "From the Era of Steamships to the Age of Cruise Ships." You can also visit the renovated 19th-century Commissioner's House—the first house in the world to have a complete prefabricated cast-iron structural frame, with an enormous initial builder's cost to prove it.

Around the museum's perimeter, explore ramparts with sweeping views of the West End of Bermuda. By the way, you can also see the dolphins from the Dolphin Quest programme, here at the museum.

**Mangrove Bay,** Somerset. Shallow bay fringed with palm trees in picturesque Somerset Village. Farther along at the wharf is a spot where the actress Jacqueline Bissett learned to ride a scooter for the famous movie *The Deep.*

**Somerset Long Bay,** Somerset, Sandys. Shallow bay and sandy stretch of beach set in a nature reserve.

**West Whale Bay,** Whale Bay Road (off Middle Road), Southampton. Small peaceful beach with rugged cliff walk, fort, and large grassy area ideal for picnicking. About a 10- to 15-minute walk from the bus stop.

**Scaur Hill Fort,** Somerset (Tel. 234-0908). Open 10 A.M.–4:30 P.M., with grounds open until sunset. Not far from Somerset Bridge (original bridge built in 1620 and said to be the world's tiniest drawbridge at just 22 inches wide at the mast opening) is Scaur Hill Fort. An interesting weather gauge, a sunken gun, and beautifully maintained grounds await you at this peaceful fortification. Worth the visit for some of the best views of Somerset and Ely's Harbour, especially at sunset.

**Heydon Trust,** Heydon Road, Somerset (opposite Willowbank Guest House). Open sunrise to sunset. Follow the winding pathway opposite Willowbank Guest House to discover the West End's best-kept secret, Heydon Trust. Here on the Trust property is a tiny, weather-worn, white-stone chapel that has remained mainly unchanged for hundreds of years. Once used as a tiny cottage dwelling, this has been a place of worship since the Second World War. Note the ancient raised water tank outside, and how the white-stepped roof has been worn smooth over the years. Inside the wood-beamed chapel, a plaque on the wall gives details of Heydon House, another property situated on the Trust:

> Heydon House was built by a Dr. Dalzell who served in Nelson's navy and later as a physician in the late 1700's, doing his rounds on horseback in a stovepipe hat with coat-tails flying and bottles sticking out of his pockets.

Strolling around the tranquil Trust lands, one can imagine Dr. Dalzell galloping off on his rounds to attend his ailing patients' conditions and complaints.

Opposite the chapel is a gnarled wooden cross with the clear blue sea as a spectacular backdrop, making this a splendid setting for prayer and contemplation.

Other features within the 43 acres of lush meadows are a scented rose garden planted in an old quarry and wooded trails leading to orange, lemon, and grapefruit trees.

**Lagoon Park,** Ireland Island, Sandys. Open daily. Situated on the western tip of Bermuda, where the winding road hugs the coastline: Wild wooded trails around the Lagoon and Royal Naval Cemetery.

**Hog Bay Park,** Somerset Road, Sandys Parish. Trail markers guide the way around this 38-acre natural parkland. Originally, this area was part of Richard Norwood's (Bermuda's first land surveyor) 1616 "overplus"—a parcel of land that was left over when Bermuda was first divided into tribes, later known as parishes.

Richard Norwood's daughter, Anne, was tried for witchcraft in 1651. She was found not guilty but "bound over to be of good behaviour," and then released for the sum of 200 pounds of tobacco! (Source: Terry

Tucker, *Bermuda and the Supernatural*.) See chapter 5, "Culture and Heritage," for more history on witches and warlocks in Bermuda.

**Springfield Plantation & Gilbert Nature Reserve,** National Trust Property, Somerset (opposite Marketplace Store). National Trust plantation home dating back to the 1600s, set in five acres of unspoiled woodlands and once the family home of the Hinsons and Gilberts (1671-1960s). The outbuildings were once used for slave quarters, and several digs, in cooperation with Colonial Williamsburg's Department of Archaeological Research, have uncovered over 80 bags of artefacts from colonial days.

Before the days of refrigeration, an outbuilding, designed with a high pyramid roof that was thought to catch the hot air, kept food cool. Called "butteries," they are dotted all around Bermuda, and Springfield has a beautiful example of an early one.

The house is used as a community centre, so only the reserve is open to the public.

**Mini Golf Adventure,** Industrial Park Road, off Middle Road, Southampton (Tel. 238-8800). Open daily 9 A.M.–10 P.M. An 18-hole miniature golf course, great fun for children and the whole family. Family restaurant on site.

## 5. Guided Tours and Cruises

**Bermuda Train Co. Ltd.** (historical train tours, May-Nov.), Dockyard (Tel. 236-5972, oleander@logic.bm). Dockyard historical 90-minute tours on the red-and-green Dockyard nontrack train—purchase tickets onboard. The Royal Naval Dockyard was built in the 1800s to defend British dominance of the seas and was dubbed the "Gibraltar of the West." Today you can still see this legacy left by the British Navy in carefully restored fortresses retaining Bermuda's historical heritage within the squares of stores and restaurants.

## 6. Water Sports

**Restless Native Tours** (hosts Kirk and Joan Ward, P.O. Box SB 83, Bermuda, SB BX, Tel. 234-8149, Fax 234-1033, restless@logic.bm). Informative, friendly, half-day catamaran, snorkelling, and sailing trips. The cost of $45 per person includes fruit punch and ice water, rum swizzles, and hot cookies baked onboard. Comfortable sailing with shaded lounge, spacious hammocks, and eco-oriented tours. Private charters available.

**Bermuda Snorkel Park,** Royal Naval Dockyard (Tel. 292-8652, bic@logic.bm). Operates Mon.-Sat. 10 A.M.–6 P.M., mid-Apr. to end of Oct.

Special group rates and discounts to the Maritime Museum. Protected marine park with well-marked snorkel trails. Floating rest stations and lifeguards on duty. Changing rooms available.

**Skyrider Parasailing,** Royal Naval Dockyard (Reservations: Tel. 234-3019, skyriderbda@northrock.bm). Available Mar.-Nov., weather permitting. Fly from the comfort of a two-man chair, without getting wet. Up to eight persons taken aboard, 10 minutes per person flying time (you certainly don't feel rushed). Parasailing is a great adventure and worth every penny.

**Blue Water Divers,** Robinson's Marina, Somerset Road, Somerset (Tel. 234-1034, bwdivers@logic.bm, www.divebermuda.com). Certification courses available. Year-round diving on 18 of Bermuda's wrecks: Morning two-tank dives for the experienced diver, shallow wreck and reef diving in the afternoon for fun easy diving. Also available are night dives, with video and camera rentals. Try the popular underwater scooter guided dive and explore caves and the wreck of the *Pollockshields*. They also offer snorkelling, personal watercraft, air beds, kayaks, aqua cycles, boogie boards, tubing, sailing, and electric-powered boats. Rates for scuba diving packages, equipment rentals, and certification course on request.

**Bermuda Water-ski Centre,** Somerset Bridge, Sandys (Tel. 234-3354, Cell 235-1012). Available May to end of Sept. Rates include water-skiing lesson, per group, up to five people. Qualified instructor for beginners or advanced skier. Also available with lessons: slalom, trick skiing, kneeboarding, and barefoot skiing.

**Windjammer Watersports,** locations: Cambridge Beaches, Mangrove Bay (Tel. 234-3082) and the Royal Naval Dockyard (Tel. 234-0250). 13-foot sailboats and 15-foot motorboat for hire. Also offers sailing and windsurfing lessons—one hour free sailing with every lesson. Also available: two-seater kayaks for one- or two-hour rentals.

**Boat Rental: Somerset Bridge Watersports** (Tel. 234-0914). Rent a small 13-foot Boston Whaler motorboat with 30-horsepower motor and all safety equipment, and gain instruction on where to go for most scenic routes, or just cruise around Ely's Harbour, one of the most picturesque inlets of Bermuda. Snorkel, fishing equipment, and coolers for rental.

**Jet Skiing: Somerset Bridge Water Sports** (Tel. 234-0914). One hour 15 minutes guided tour of the western end of Bermuda including the Sea Gardens and Dockyard. Single, double, or triple Jet Skis available.

**Dockyard Boat Rental,** Dockyard Marina, Dockyard (Tel. 234-0300). 16-foot Carolina skiff with steering wheel and Bimini top. Holds four people.

**Reef Fishing:** *Ellen B,* Michael Baxter (Tel. 234-2963 or Cell 234-9722). 32-foot boat for half-day tour. All tackle and bait provided. Other fishing expeditions available in the West End: **Russell Young Fishing & Taxidermy,** Somerset (Tel. 234-1832, Fax 234-2930); **Robinson's Charter Boat Agency,** Somerset Bridge (Tel. 234-1034). For a comprehensive listing of fishing charter boats, check the Bermuda Yellow Pages.

**Hartley's Undersea Adventures** (helmet diving), Watford Bridge, Somerset (Tel. 234-2861, hartley@logic.bm). Includes three hours on a glass-bottom boat. Underwater photographs optional but highly recommended. Leaves Watford Bridge, Sandys, at 11 A.M. and 1:30 P.M. A 25-minute walk at the bottom of the ocean wearing a specially designed helmet that keeps your head dry. An ecological adventure and education in the underwater world of tropical reef fish—fun for all the family. No skills required. Feed and play with tame fish while witnessing the living coral reef teeming with sea life. An unforgettable, unique experience that will make you really appreciate the marine environment.

## 7. Shopping

In the West End, you can shop at either Mangrove Bay in Somerset Village or the Royal Naval Dockyard at the very tip of Ireland Island. The sleepy village of Mangrove Bay has a branch of **Trimingham's** (Tel. 296-1291) as well as **W.J. Boyle & Son Shoe Shop** (Tel. 234-0530), **Somerset Pharmacy** (Tel. 238-9419), **The House of Style,** a great women's-wear store (Tel. 234-0744), a couple of banks, a post office, a couple of coffee shops, and a pub. That's about it, but it's nice walking around the village and bay with views of tiny beach-rimmed islands and the house of famous undersea explorer Teddy Tucker (isn't that a great name for an explorer?) across the water. Somerset folk are friendly, so don't forget to say, "Good morning."

On Middle Road, on the way to Dockyard, you shouldn't miss **Déjà Vu Antique & Flea Market** (Tel. 238-8525 or 236-4813). Open Tues.-Fri. 10:30 A.M.–5 P.M., Sat. from noon. Charming old curiosity shop full of collectibles, Bermuda knick-knacks, fascinating antique bottles, books, china—surprising finds at good prices. Linger a while. Cora Charles, the proprietor, is very helpful and friendly.

### DISCOVER DOCKYARD

A popular shopping spot with visitors is the Clocktower Centre and Victorian Arcade at the Royal Naval Dockyard—especially convenient for Sunday shopping after 11 A.M. Don't let the name Dockyard put you off; this is a truly tourist-oriented attraction, with its reclaimed nautical warehouses and landscaped gardens. Indeed, nearly every visitor to Bermuda spends at least some time here, either at the Maritime Museum, Craft Market, or Movie Theatre or sampling the delights of the Arts Centre. The Victorian covered cobbled arcades and the quiet roads make this a very unhurried and enjoyable excursion. The atmosphere is Dickensian, especially at Christmastime, when the halls are decked with festive decorations and the grounds are illuminated with lights.

**The Bermuda Craft Market** (Tel. 234-3208) is open daily 10 A.M.–5 P.M. There is a good chance to see local artists at work here. Vendors sell handmade quality gifts including candles, ceramics, Christmas ornaments, decorative paintings, dolls, gems, glass, jewellery, miniature furniture, needlework, quilts, wearable art, wickerwork, books, cards, and prints. The Craft Market should definitely be on your "must-do" shopping list.

## 8. Nightlife

Nothing much doing in the West End, I'm afraid. Dockyard has annual celebrations, such as Jazzfest in October and Festival of the August Moon (see "Festivals, Ceremonies, and Major Events" in chapter 5, "Culture and Heritage"). It's also a great place to catch the Regiment Band throughout the summer months (check the Tourist Information offices or local paper for dates). You can always take in a movie at the **Neptune Theatre** (Tel. 234-2923). Pubs in the West End are the **Frog & Onion,** Royal Naval Dockyard (Tel. 234-2900), **The Somerset Country Squire** (Tel. 234-0105), and the **Loyalty Inn Bar & Restaurant** (Tel. 234-4503 [bar] or 234-6092 [Greg's Steak House Restaurant]).

## 9. Handy Phone Numbers

**Crime Stoppers** (confidential): Tel. 1-800-623-8477
**Drugstore** (Caesars Pharmacy): Tel. 234-0851
**Emergency** (Police, Fire, Ambulance): Tel. 911
**Hair Salon** (Main Attractions): Tel. 234-3930
**Hospital** (King Edward VII Memorial): Tel. 236-2345
**Laundromat** (Duds & Suds): Tel. 234-2824
**Maritime Museum:** Tel. 234-1333
**Minibuses and Cabs** (Somerset): Tel. 234-2344
**Port Royal Golf Course:** Tel. 234-0974
**Scooter Rental** (Oleander Cycles): Tel. 234-0629
**Tourist Information,** Royal Naval Dockyard (close to Ferry Stop): Tel. 234-3824

# 11

# The East End

When Bermudians say, "Down de country," they mean the East End of Bermuda. This chapter covers the parishes of Smith's, Hamilton, St. George's, and St. David's Island. Mainly, though, this chapter features St. George's.

The old living-history town of St. George's, named after Sir George Somers, the admiral who accidentally landed in Bermuda during a hurricane in 1609, is the oldest colonial town in the Western Hemisphere. St. George's was the capital of Bermuda from 1612 to 1815, when the capital became Hamilton. This old settlement is now a UNESCO (United Nations, Scientific and Cultural Organization) World Heritage Site because of its global significance as a historical town.

History buffs really appreciate St. George's sense of history, narrow cobbled streets, and museums housed in unique National Trust properties. There are more original historical properties here than in the whole of colonial Williamsburg, Virginia. American history is inextricably linked with Bermuda; the nearest U.S. land is only 508 miles away, at Cape Hatteras. For instance, the historical links between America and Bermuda during the American Civil War (1861-65) are showcased in the "Rogues & Runners" Exhibit at the National Trust Museum (Globe Hotel).

Also of special interest is the twinning of England's picturesque Dorset town of Lyme Regis with St. George's in 1996. Lyme Regis is Sir George Somers' birthplace, and his old home, Berne Manor, is situated near there in Devon. Sir George's body was buried in Lyme Regis after his heart was buried in Somers Gardens, here in Bermuda, where a commemorative plaque marks the spot.

A Town Heritage Plan is in progress, designed to enhance St. George's historical treasures with informative plaques, cobbled walkways, old-fashioned lighting, and traffic-free, tree-shaded areas.

Spreading out from King's Square in the centre of the old town, go poking down obscure alleyways and meander along quaint little cobbled streets. Tucked away in the narrow side streets are many examples of early Bermudian cottages surrounded by walled, flower-filled gardens. And with lane names such as Featherbed Alley, Needle & Thread Alley, Privateer Lane, and Rum Alley, how can you not be intrigued and fascinated exploring the old town?

You will find St. George's to be a very inexpensive sightseeing town steeped in history. The major sights are within easy walking distance of each other, low priced to visit, and detailed in the sightseeing section of this chapter. There are lots of other historically interesting properties in St. George's that are best viewed on foot, such as Fanny Fox's cottage (Governor's Alley), Samaritan's Cottages (Water Street), or The Homestead (York Street), to name a few. Be curious, be nosy, and search them out.

## 1. Transport

The bus numbers to the East End are 1, 3, 10, or 11. You can board them at Hamilton bus terminal on Church Street.

To get to St. David's you need to take a bus to St. George's, and then transfer to St. David's on bus number 6.

During the summer there is a ferry to St. George's, from the Royal Naval Dockyard, at the western tip. This ferry service is proving to be very popular, especially as it drops visitors off right in the heart of the old town.

Once in St. George's you can catch a minicab at King's Square. For a nominal fee, this cab takes you to Fort St. Catherine and Tobacco Bay beach (both areas are great for snorkelling).

## 2. Accommodations

At time of writing, a Palmetto Bay hotel, located in Flatts Village and set in a picturesque fishing harbour in Hamilton Parish, is about to be rebuilt into an $18 million, 42-room hotel and health spa with townhouses and villas, for both tourists and business travellers. The new hotel is to be called **Palmetto Gardens** (www.bermudaresorthotels.com).

Also at time of writing, the new Castle Harbour hotel at Tucker's Point Club is being constructed. It is to be named **Tucker's Point Cottages & Greenbrier Spa** (Tel. 298-6915, www.tuckerspoint.com). Planned is a 61-room, cottage-colony-style resort with ultraluxury spa and state-of-the-art 6,361-yard golf course.

## HIGHER-PRICED ACCOMMODATIONS

Note: To get deals on rooms at the large resort hotels in Bermuda, go to the "Package Deals" section in chapter 2, "Before You Leave Home."

**Pink Beach Club,** South Road, Smith's Parish (P.O. Box HM 1017, Hamilton, HM DX, Tel. 293-1666, Toll-free U.S. and Canada 1-800-355-6161, www.pinkbeach.com).

An upscale cottage colony set in over 16 acres of landscaped grounds and overlooking, you guessed it, a pink beach (in fact, two pink beaches). Set in an amazingly gorgeous location and recipient of the 2002-3 Conde Nast Traveller Gold List Award, Pink Beach Club has been totally refurbished: 94 suites (74 brand new) with Italian tile floors and new furniture and fittings. There is also a new business centre for e-mail and other business services. Suites have air-conditioning, heating, phone, and TV for rent on request, but with such a gorgeous view, who wants to watch "the box," as they call it in England? Main clubhouse has a cocktail lounge and bar with TV and dining room. There are two California Hard-Tru tennis courts free of charge to guests, and golf can be arranged at the nearby Mid Ocean golf club. Rejuvenating in-room spa services are available on request. Breakfast can be served free of service charge in cottages or main dining room. Lunch is by the poolside terrace, or you can request box lunches. Dinner is served in the dining room or around the pool. Children are accepted.

**Double room rates:** $430 to $750 (depending on season and category of room), plus service charge and tax. Rate includes English breakfast, afternoon tea, and five-course dinner.

**St. George's Club,** Rose Hill, St. George's (P.O. Box GE 92, St. George's, GE BX, Tel. 297-1200, Fax 297-8003, www.stgeorgeclub.com).

Time-share, cottage-colony property on 17 acres in the historic town of St. George's. Close to 18-hole golf, with on-site tennis courts and swimming pools. Free ride to private beach club and two-minute walk to town centre for museums, stores, and restaurants.

**Double room rates:** $200 to $350 (depending on season), plus service charge and tax.

**Mid Ocean** (Private Golf Club), South Road, Tucker's Town, St. George's (P.O. Box HM 1728, Hamilton, HM GX, Tel. 293-0330, Fax 293-8837).

This is a private golf club in millionaire's Tucker's Town, and an introduction by a member is required. Comprises 20 bed/sitting units overlooking Castle Harbour with private bath, some with kitchenettes. There's a large private beach and coves, two tennis courts (small charge), clubhouse with dining facilities, and golf shop. Children under 10 years on request only.

**Double room rates:** $245 to $295 (depending on season), plus service charge and tax. Rate includes breakfast and afternoon tea.

## MEDIUM-PRICED ACCOMMODATIONS

**Grotto Bay Beach Hotel & Tennis Club,** 11 Blue Hole Hill, Hamilton Parish, CR 04 (Tel. 293-8333, Fax 293-2306, Toll-free: U.S. 1-800-582-3190, Canada 1-800-463-0851, Lsgrottobay@logic.bm, www.grottobay.com).

Informal hotel on 21 acres overlooking private beach, one mile from the airport. Rooms are situated in 11 separate buildings, each with balcony and views. Each unit comes with air-conditioning, heating, fridge, hair dryer, TV, radio, and phone. The main house has a dining room, two bars, gift shop, etc. There is a pool and pool bar, dock, one beach, and two small adjacent coves. Water sports can be arranged at the water-sports centre (Tel. 293-2915). Meals are served in either the dining room or poolside. The property is situated near underground caves that used to house a night-club but are now only for viewing. However, there is entertainment nightly and a weekly swizzle (rum cocktail) party. Children are welcome and there is a children's programme in the summer. Bus stop at hotel handy to St. George's. Grotto Bay Hotel is close to the Glass Blowing studio, the Swizzle Inn, Blue Hole Park, Perfume Factory, and Crystal Caves.

**Double room rates:** $135 to $230 (depending on season), plus service charge and tax. Rate includes daily afternoon tea.

**The Clear View Suites,** Sandy Lane, Hamilton Parish, CR 02 (Tel. 293-0484, Fax 293-0267, Toll-free U.S. 1-800-468-9600).

Directly overlooking the North Shore and on the way to Flatts Village for the Aquarium, Museum and Zoo, little pink cottages and suites, all with sweeping views of the bay. Each unit features air-conditioning, TV, radio, and phone and has patio or verandah. Some units have kitchenettes. There are two swimming pools, as well as access to a small private cove. Clear View is next door to Landfall Restaurant, which is open for breakfast, lunch, and dinner.

**Double room rates:** $170 to $214 (depending on season and category of room), plus service charge and tax.

## BUDGET-PRICED ACCOMMODATIONS

Note: For a list of budget properties to rent, go to "Private House and Apartment Rentals" in chapter 2, "Before You Leave Home."

**Taylor House** (Mr. Mark Rowe), Aunt Peggy's Lane, St. George's (Tel. 297-1161, mark@bermudagetaway.com, www.bermudagetaway.com).

Nestled in the heart of the old colonial town of St. George's, this adorable two-story (one-bedroom) townhouse was built circa 1690. Clean and brightly decorated with quaint features such as a Dutch door leading off to a cute Bermudian walled garden, this property is well equipped and maintained. Close to museums (perfect for history-lovers), stores, golf, restaurants, and buses. Separate bathroom and bedroom, fireplace, living room, air-conditioning, two cable TVs (one in the bedroom). Fully stocked kitchen/dining room with microwave, fridge, and stove. This accommodation is for two guests only.

**Double room rates:** $90 to $120 (depending on season and length of stay), inclusive of taxes.

**Brightside Guest Apartments,** Flatts Hill, Smith's (P.O. Box FL 319, Flatts Village, Smith's, Tel. 292-8410, Fax 295-6968).

Fully equipped housekeeping apartments with air-conditioning and verandahs overlooking picturesque Flatts Inlet, handy to Bermuda Aquarium, Museum and Zoo. There's a large pool and patio area. The two-level cottage is especially modern and spacious.

**Year-round unit rates:** Unit for two, $85 to $95; apartment for four, $160 to $170; cottages for four, $220 to $240 (additional person $20). All rates plus service charge and tax.

**Aunt Nea's Inn,** 1 Nea's Alley, St. George's (P.O. Box GE, St. George's, GE BX, Tel. 297-1630, Fax 297-1908, www.auntneas.com).

This informal lodging is full of old-island charm and is tucked away in the heart of historic St. George's, a wonderful location for history-lovers and convenient for exploring the alleyways and narrow side streets of the oldest working town in the Western Hemisphere. In 1804, right next door to the inn, lived Nea Tucker, who is written about by the famous Irish poet Tom Moore (1779-1852) and for whom the inn is named (see also Tom Moore's Tavern, below). Accommodations have air-conditioning, new furnishings, and four-poster beds (some rooms have Jacuzzis). There's also a common TV room. Paw Paws is the name of the honeymoon cottage on the grounds.

**Year-round rates:** $110 to $165, plus service charge and tax.

**Tarrafal Apartments** (Mr. Ed Kelly), 1 Tarrafal Drive, North Shore Road (P.O. Box 1555, Hamilton, HM FX, Tel. 293-2525, Fax 295-3559, ed-kelly@logic.bm, http://pwp.ibl.bm/~edkelly/guests01.htm).

Ed has two apartments, nicely decorated, with fully furnished kitchens and separate bathrooms. Cable TV ($5 extra per day), air-conditioning, and washer/dryer in each apartment. Bus stop close by, convenient to routes to Perfume Factory, Swizzle Inn, the old town of St. George's, and Shelly Bay beach. Ideal for couples or families with one child. Ed provides transport to and from the airport and to the beach.

**Year-round apartment rates:** $125 per night, inclusive of taxes. Honeymooners get their seventh night free. Enquire about free nights offered year round. $25 extra for one additional person.

## 3. Restaurants

### HIGHER-PRICED RESTAURANTS

**Tom Moore's Tavern,** Walsingham Lane, Hamilton Parish (Tel. 293-8020, www.tommoores.com). Open for dinner 7-10:30. Truly Bermuda's finest gourmet restaurant, having received the Five Star Diamond Award by the American Academy of Restaurant and Hospitality Science, Tom Moore's Tavern is *the* place to go if you like several waiters hovering over you, attending to your every need.

Set in a house that was constructed in 1652, and still maintained in the old style of stone walls, cedar beams, fireplaces, and antiques, this restaurant is in the Walsingham Nature Reserve, locally known as Tom Moore's Jungle. The house became a tavern over 100 years ago and is Bermuda's oldest restaurant.

Tom Moore was a famous Irish poet who, in 1804, came to Bermuda and had an amour with a local lady, Nea Tucker. The scandal was talked about for many years, especially as he wrote many poems about his dalliance. Tom Moore's portrait hangs in the hallway; his pensive gaze looks up and away to far-off times.

**Ode to Nea**
Written in Bermuda by Tom Moore

Nay, Tempt me not to love again,
There was a time when love was sweet;
Dear Nea! had I known thee then,
Our souls had not been slow to meet!
But oh! this weary heart hath run,
So many a time, the rounds of pain,
Not ev'n for thee, thou lovely one!
Would I endure such pangs again.

**Carriage House,** Water Street, St. George's (Tel. 297-1730). Built in the 1700s and in perfect character for this old town, the Carriage House serves lunch and dinner as well as a very British afternoon tea. Special early-bird four-course dinner Mon.-Sat. 5:30-6:45. The Carriage House has the reputation of serving perfect champagne Sunday brunches. (Note: The Carriage House sustained extensive damage during Hurricane Fabian but, at time of writing, was in the process of being repaired.)

## MEDIUM-PRICED RESTAURANTS

**San Giorgio Ristorante,** Water Street, St. George's (Tel. 297-1307). Open for lunch Mon.-Fri. noon-2:15, dinner Mon.-Sat. 6:30-10. Charming Italian eatery with inside or terrace dining. Either choose the café at the front of the building for pasta, wine, and pizza, or be seated in the dining room for beautifully prepared dishes such as tortellini, capellini, penne, lasagne, spaghetti, and pizza—all at good prices.

**Landfall Restaurant,** North Shore Road, Hamilton Parish (Tel. 293-1322). Open for breakfast, lunch, and dinner (call first to check hours). This unique restaurant is set in a beautiful old Bermudian cottage overlooking the craggy coastline of the North Shore. Menu items served: rack of lamb, steaks, fried chicken, beef fried rice, and many Bermudian dishes. Reasonable lunch menu and Sunday buffet served. Landfall has a very special atmosphere.

**Rustico Restaurant and Pizzeria,** 8 North Shore Road, Flatts Village (Tel. 295-5212). Open daily for lunch (except Mon.) 11:45-2:30, dinner nightly 6-10. Close to the Bermuda Aquarium and overlooking the water at picturesque Flatts Village, Rustico's is part Mediterranean, part North American, and part Bermudian, serving up such dishes as fishcakes, red bean soup, local lobster, salads topped with fresh local fish, asparagus, and avocado with yoghurt/orange/cognac dressing. There are plenty of pasta and pizza dishes on the menu, which is in keeping with the owners and chefs, who are Italian. Choose from patio with sea views or indoor dining.

**Black Horse Tavern,** St. David's (Tel. 293-9742). Open noon-10 P.M., closed Mon. Out-of-the-way tavern on water's edge, specialising in seafood dishes. Menu items include a seafood platter and a shark hash.

**Freddie's Restaurant,** King's Square, St. George's (Tel. 297-1717). Open daily 8 A.M.–11 P.M., dinner 5-11. Closed Christmas Day. Situated in the heart of St. George's, with balcony seating overlooking historic King's Square, a good place to be during historical ceremonies. Either choose the sports pub downstairs with six TVs, one a big screen, or eat at the seafood restaurant upstairs.

**White Horse Tavern,** King's Square, St. George's (Tel. 297-1838). Open daily 9 A.M.–1 A.M. Dockside dining overlooking St. George's harbour and the statue of Sir George Somers by sculptor Desmond Fountain. Choice of pub fare.

**Waterfront Bar and Restaurant** (formerly the Wharf Tavern), Somer's Wharf, St. George's (Tel. 297-1515). Because of its waterfront views this casual restaurant is the first port of call for many of St. George's visitors. Serves a mixture of Bermudian and American dishes.

**North Rock Brewing Company,** 10 South Road, Smith's Parish (Tel. 236-6633). Open Mon.-Fri. 10 A.M.–9:30 P.M. ; Sat.-Sun. 8 A.M.–9:30 P.M., lunch 11:30-3, dinner 6-10. Pub open till 1 A.M.

Bermuda's first microbrewpub and restaurant. Beer on tap, brewed on premises in large vats. English-pub décor—wood beams and brass rails—with inside or outside patio dining offering friendly service at friendly prices. Starters include deep-fried shrimp served with extratasty Cajun sauce, or munch on thick cheesy potato wedges with sour cream on the side. For the main course, try the North Rock steak sandwich, smothered in gravy and topped with sautéed onions on a French baguette, or Captain Morgan's Pocket, a fresh pita pocket stuffed with baby shrimp and fresh vegetables tossed in a lemon-yoghurt dressing.

## BUDGET-PRICED EATERIES

**Swizzle Inn,** Blue Hole Hill, Bailey's Bay, Hamilton Parish (Tel. 293-9300, www.swizzleinn.com). Open daily 11 A.M.–10:30 P.M., lunch noon-6, dinner 6-10:30. This popular inn is located just past the Perfumery, en route to the airport. Serves lunch and dinner on the upstairs or downstairs patios. Innovative, informal menu includes conch fritters, coconut shrimp, fish sandwiches, burgers, and homemade desserts such as Johnny-bread pudding with brandy sauce. Warning: Home of the Bermuda Rum Swizzle cocktail. These wonderful cocktails go down so smoothly their potency will take you by surprise.

**Pasta Pasta,** 14 York Street, St. George's (Tel. 297-2927). Open Mon.-Sat. 11:30 A.M.–10 P.M., Sun. from 5 P.M. Decorated in bright primary colours, this excellent Italian pasta bar has daily specials, a fresh salad bar, and great prices.

**Dennis's Hideaway,** Cashew City Road, St. David's (Tel. 297-0044). Open daily 10 A.M.–10 P.M. (hours may vary). Extremely informal, cheap, and cheerful eatery, full of character and famous for its shark hash. President Carter enjoyed a meal here once. Bring your own wine.

**Temptations Café & Bakery,** 31 York Street, next door to St. Peter's Church, St. George's (Tel. 297-1368). Open Mon.-Fri. 8:30 A.M.–7 P.M. (Tues. to 10 P.M. in cruise-ship season). Sample a slice of heaven at this café/bakery next door to historical St. Peter's Church. Serves delicious pies, cakes, and ice creams. Sit in or take out.

**Angeline's Coffee Shop,** York Street, St. George (Tel. 297-0959). Open Mon.-Fri. 7 A.M.–3 P.M., Sat. from 8 A.M., Sun. (codfish breakfast) 8 A.M.–noon. Located in the middle of the old town of St. George's, Angeline's is down-home Bermudian, with great fish chowders, fish sandwiches, pies, and homemade cakes.

**Reid's Restaurant,** Mullet Bay Road, St. George's (Tel. 297-1039). Open daily 7 A.M.–6 P.M. Local favourite, directly across from Mullet Bay children's park. Sells homemade fare such as curried beef, chicken and mussel pies, and fish dinners. Reid's Restaurant also leases the food concession at Clearwater Beach in St. David's.

**Speciality Inn,** Collectors Hill, Smith's Parish (Tel. 236-3133). Open Mon.-Sat. 6 A.M.–10 P.M. Open for breakfast, lunch, and dinner, serving pancakes, omelettes, fish dinners, homemade pizzas, and pizza pockets. Popular with locals; always seems crowded. Clint Eastwood, the famous spaghetti-western actor, dined here while on a golfing holiday in October of 1996. Clint requested an eatery that served "good home cooking," and so his taxi driver thought the Speciality would make his day. Clint had pasta primavera, mixed vegetables, and coffee, and his wife had egg muffins. And as the local paper reported, he paid with a fistful of dollars.

**Bailey's Ice Cream & Food D'Lites,** Hamilton Parish (Tel. 293-9333). Open Mon.-Sat. 11 A.M.–5:15 P.M., Sun. to 6 P.M. Closed Nov.-Mar. Seating inside or out. Located a few yards from the Swizzle Inn and handy after a visit to the Perfumery, this ice-cream parlour is an island favourite for homemade ice creams, sundaes, and light refreshments. The original owner, Frank Powers, learned how to make ice cream personally from Ben and Jerry at their Vermont headquarters, in exchange for a holiday in Bermuda, just before the pair hit the big time with their Ben & Jerry ice creams.

**Pizza House,** two locations in the East End area: Shelly Bay, Hamilton Parish (Tel. 293-8465) and 106 Southside, St. David's, next to the Cinema (Tel. 293-5700). The one at Southside has the only drive-in window in Bermuda. Serves homemade pizzas with 21 different toppings, burgers, subs, fried chicken, and fish.

# 4. Sightseeing

## YE OLDE TOWNE OF ST. GEORGE'S

For savings on admission into three of Bermuda's top museums, you may purchase a Combination Ticket for the Tucker House Museum, Verdmont

Museum, and the Rogues & Runners Exhibit (Globe Hotel), at the Bermuda National Trust Museum. Combo tickets can be purchased at any of the museums for $5.

**King's Square:** The hub of the town centre, where visitors can view replicas of the cedar stocks and pillory used to punish criminals in the 18th century, and where most people can't resist trying these out for themselves. During the summer on Mondays, Wednesdays, Thursdays, and Saturdays (winter on Wednesdays and Saturdays) starting at noon, experience entertaining historical reenactments with characters in period costume and the international-award-winning Town Crier, glorious in his colourful 17th-century outfit. A ducking stool, once used to punish nagging wives, is on hand, and volunteer female visitors are encouraged to try a ducking for the crowd's amusement.

Bristol University, England, in coordination with the Bermuda National Trust, sent a team of archaeologists to the King's Square area, to conduct excavations in order to find important evidence of early colonial life in the 1600s. Already they have discovered foundations of the first governor's house, built in 1612, along with artefacts of that time such as pottery.

**Bermuda National Trust Museum** at the Globe Hotel, corner of King's Square (Tel. 297-1423). Open Mon.-Sat. 10 A.M.–4 P.M. Admission: $3. Free to National Trust Members. The Globe Hotel was once the home of the second governor of Bermuda and was built in the 1690s. No longer a hotel, the Globe is now the Bermuda National Trust Museum, where a fascinating historical exhibit, entitled "Rogues & Runners," is centred on Bermuda's involvement in the American Civil War, and incorporates research carried out both in Bermuda and America. The museum displays a seal press with a copy of the great seal of the Confederate States that was used for official Confederate State documents. The original seal remains at the Museum of the Confederacy in Richmond. On the lower floor, showing daily, is a 13-minute video called "Bermuda: Centre of the Atlantic," recounting Bermuda's history. You also can buy this video for $14.95.

**Tucker House,** Water Street (Tel. 297-0545). Open Mon.-Sat. 10 A.M.–4 P.M. Admission: $3, $2 students. Free to National Trust Members. Limestone home built in 1711 for the Tucker family, whose ancestor, Daniel Tucker, was Bermuda's second governor. Other past inhabitants of the house include a Williamsburg judge and a U.S. treasurer. Antiques include original Tucker family silver and portraits. At basement level is an archaeological exhibit containing artefacts of the period found on site. The dig was cosponsored by the Colonial Williamsburg Foundation.

A freed American slave, Joseph Hayne Rainey, was a barber here and later returned to South Carolina after the U.S. Civil War to become the first black elected member of the U.S. House of Representatives.

**Historical Society Museum and Printery,** Duke of Kent Street (Tel. 297-0423). Open Mon.-Fri. 10 A.M.–4 P.M. Admission: $5 adults, $2 children under 12. Situated on the corner of Featherbed Alley and Duke of Kent Street, built around 1734, this fascinating house has four chimneys and five different roofs, easily viewed from the back garden. Green ferns growing between the stone slab steps leading to the house mark the passage of time. Inside the museum are antiques such as a pair of travelling pistols, a whale-oil lamp, and one of the first electric clocks ever made. Rescued from a shipwreck is a 200-year-old settle bed with a hinged "lee berth," which, for the non-navy among us, is a side-rail that rotates from one side to another to protect the sleeping sailor from falling out of his bunk on stormy nights.

In the kitchen is a fireplace with a kettle so heavy it needs a crane to hold it. Next to that is a bread oven where a fire heated the bricks inside; the embers were then removed and the hot bricks baked the bread. On the wooden table are ingenious early kitchen implements culled from the briny deep, such as a sea fan used for straining, and sea plants used for whisks (and unfortunately for beating children).

Portraits on the wall paint a tale of Bermuda's colourful people and past, such as the portrait of Nea Tucker, the governor's daughter, who was involved in a scandalous affair with Tom Moore, a famous Irish poet. Although Moore was run off the island, today there is a tavern named after him (see Tom Moore's Tavern, above).

**Featherbed Alley Print Shop** (Tel. 297-0009). Open Mon.-Sat. 10 A.M.–4 P.M. Admission included in Historical Society Museum entrance fee. A must-see activity while in St. George's. Charming curator in full 1700s costume explains the workings of the printing press used during the 1600s. Bermuda's first newspaper, which was called the *Bermuda Gazette,* was published on this press and was the forerunner of today's local paper, the *Royal Gazette.*

**The *Deliverance,*** Ordinance Island. Open daily 10 A.M.–4 P.M. Admission: $3 adults, $1 children under 12. Also central booking office for a number of water tours around St. George's, and visitor information site. Explore a full-scale replica of a 17th-century wooden ship built by the survivors of the shipwrecked *Sea Venture* in 1609 to carry them to the New World in Virginia. Notice how small the people must have been to fit into the bunks, and how cramped the living conditions were.

**State House** (end of King Street, before One Gun Alley). Open Wed. only, 10 A.M.–4 P.M. Bermuda's oldest limestone building, built by Gov. Nathaniel Butler around 1620. Bermuda's first government convened here. It was a tough life in those days—floggings were often carried out at the door. And one of the first Acts of Parliament was to send back to Britain anyone who was sick, old, or impotent! This building was used as a barracks for British troops during the American Revolution.

The State House is rented by a local Mason's lodge for the sum of one peppercorn per annum to the Accountant General, reenacted with much pageantry during the Peppercorn Ceremony each April (see "Festivals, Ceremonies, and Major Events" in chapter 5, "Culture and Heritage").

**Town Hall,** King's Square. Open summer, Mon.-Fri. 9 A.M.–4 P.M. Admission: Free. The old cedar-filled Town Hall in St. George's houses portraits of past mayors. An original flagstone from Berne Manor, Whitechurch Canonicorum, Devon, England, the ninth-century home of Sir George Somers, lies at the foot of the door. Sir George is the founding father of Bermuda and Lyme Regis, his birthplace in England, is twinned with the old town.

**St. Peter's Church.** Open daily 9:30 A.M.–5 P.M. St. Peter's Church is estimated to be the oldest Anglican church in the Western Hemisphere. Dating back to 1612, the current stone structure, rebuilt in 1712, is full of ancient treasures, cedar beams, wooden pews, and a 500-year-old font that predates Columbus. The unusual pulpit is on three decks. Look up to the tiny loft where servants used to sit and gaze down on the congregation. Surrounding the church is an ancient walled graveyard.

**Old Rectory,** Broad Alley (behind St. Peter's Churchyard). Open to the public Nov.-Mar., Wed. 1-5 P.M. Donations gratefully accepted. This attractive private residence was built in the 18th century by a pirate and was later the home of Rector Alexander Richardson, hence its name. Although today the Old Rectory has a typical Bermuda roof, evidence found in the eaves shows the house was probably once thatched.

**Somers Gardens,** corner of York Street and end of One Gun Alley. Opened in 1920 by the Duke of Windsor. Peaceful little gardens wherein lies buried the heart of Sir George Somers, symbolising his true home. His body rests in peace in Dorset, England.

**Bridge House Gallery** (off King's Square), Bridge Street, St. George's (Tel. 297-8211). Open daily 10 A.M.–5 P.M. National Trust property housing an art gallery, antiques, and gift store. This house was constructed prior to 1662 and in 1702 was sold for the sum of 110 pounds sterling. Bridge House is the oldest continuously occupied home in Bermuda. The gift store housed here sells Bermudian artwork, old bottles, banana-leaf dolls, memorabilia, cedar sculptures, books, and lots of treasures.

**Unfinished Church,** corner of Church Folly Lane and Government Hill Road. Open daily. Meant as a replacement in the 1870s for St. Peter's, this gothic-style church was never finished, as arguments among parishioners ended funding. Stabilisation work has been carried out by award-winning local stonemasons and an English mason whose résumé includes work on Buckingham Palace and Westminster Abbey.

**The Bermuda Heritage Museum,** Samaritan's Lodge, corner of York Street and Water Street (Tel. 297-4126). Open Tues.-Sat. 10 A.M.–3 P.M. Admission: $3. In celebration of black history, this long-awaited museum highlights achievements and struggles by Bermuda's black population, both during slavery and since its abolition.

## The Rest of the East End

### BEACHES

**Shelly Bay Park,** North Shore Road, Hamilton Parish. Open daily. Shelly Bay was named after Henry Shelly, a survivor of the 1609 *Sea Venture* wreck. About 20 minutes' ride from Hamilton by bus, Shelly Bay has 2.73 acres of beach with shallow water ideal for little ones. Stretching from the shore is a children's adventure playground and nature reserve.

**Tobacco Bay,** St. George's. Minibus to Tobacco Bay boarded from King's Square, St. George's. Tobacco Bay is the site of the famous Gun Powder escapade. A group of Bermudians in 1775 stole gunpowder for Americans to use *against* the British during the War of Independence, in return for much-needed grain. The governor slept soundly in his home nearby while the booty was rowed out in whaleboats to a waiting American ship anchored offshore.

Shallow water and full beachhouse facilities make this protected bay a favourite for children and snorkellers. Reasonably priced fast food on hand at concession stand. You can take advantage of snorkelling gear for a nominal fee. Tobacco Bay is half a mile away from Fort St. Catherine and St. Catherine's beach.

**Clearwater Beach and Turtle Beach,** St. David's. Out-of-the-way beaches (Clearwater being the longer one) and nature trails. Facilities include two playgrounds, public washrooms/changing rooms, and a picnic area equipped with barbecues, tables, and gazebo. On-site concession stand selling refreshments and fast food.

**John Smith's Bay,** South Road, Smith's Parish. Just when you thought you had seen all the beaches Bermuda has to offer, you turn on to South Road, where the shore pounds the coastline and the road curves into John Smith's Bay. Named after Capt. John Smith of Pocahontas fame, this perfect pink-tinged sandy beach is ideal for a picnic. Lunch wagon and lifeguard (summer only).

## OTHER SIGHTS

**Bermuda Aquarium, Museum and Zoo** (www.bamz.org), Flatts Village, Smith's (Tel. 293-2727). Open every day except Christmas Day, 9 A.M.–5 P.M. Admission: $8 adults, $4 children (under five free).

Opened in 1928 and home to many endangered species, this educational aquarium and zoo is set in an idyllic environment for a pleasant day out for all the family. Visit the hands-on learning centre for children ("Local Tails" room), or learn about Bermuda's marine life on a self-guided audio tour.

A must-see is the prizewinning North Rock Exhibit, comprising a 140,000-gallon viewing tank displaying Bermuda's water environment, with tropical fish, a separate North Lagoon display with marine predators, and a living reef feature. Part of the tank curves over viewers' heads, to give you the illusion of being submerged in the water.

The naturalistic "Australasia" wildlife exhibit, with animals from Australia, Malaysia, New Guinea, and Borneo, includes the tree kangaroo, wallaby, Komodo dragon, Asian fruit bats, mousedeer, and Asian otters. Some of the animals roam free and others are on display behind glass or in cages that reflect natural habitats and combine rocks, waterfalls, and native plants.

The Caribbean exhibit includes golden lion tamarins (squirrel-sized, fiery-orange primates) and a Cayman blue iguana as well as species of fish, birds, and reptiles. Discover how wind and water carried species over from the Caribbean regions.

Visitors can also view the Natural History Museum (explaining the natural formation of Bermuda) as well as turtles, flamingos, harbour seals, alligators, fish endemic to Bermuda's 50 miles of reefs, and a giant moray eel.

**Fort St. Catherine,** St. George's (Tel. 297-1920). Open daily 10 A.M.–4 P.M. Admission: $5 adults, $2 children under 12. (Minibus service from King's Square, St. George's.)

Mounted on a craggy hilltop, overlooking the Eastern Shore, is Fort St. Catherine. Built on the site of the original wooden fortification (initially constructed to protect Bermuda from Spanish invasion), it was later strengthened to protect Bermuda from a possible U.S. invasion. Luckily, neither invasion ever took place.

In 1609, the very first unplanned settlers were shipwrecked only ¾ of a mile from here. All passengers onboard were saved and lived to tell the tale, later inspiring the island's colonisation in 1612 (see history section in chapter 5, "Culture and Heritage").

Inside this completely restored bastion of protection, you will find cavernous ammunition tunnels, along with audio-visual presentations of the fort's history. Replicas of the English Royal Crown Jewels are also on display.

**The Bermuda Perfumery Gardens and Nature Trail** (www.bermuda-perfumery.com), 212 North Shore Road, Bailey's Bay, Hamilton Parish (Tel. 293-0627, Toll-free U.S. 1-800-293-8810). Open summer (Apr. 1-Oct. 31), Mon.-Sat. 9 A.M.–5 P.M., Sun. and holidays 10 A.M.–4 P.M. (Closed Sun. and holidays, Nov.-Mar.) Free entrance to perfumery, nature trails, and gardens.

Located in six acres of exotic tropical gardens with flower-hugging trails, this historical perfumery produces exclusive Bermuda fragrant perfumes (Easter Lily, Oleander, Jasmine, and Frangipani). Perfume is made in the 250-year-old Bermudian farmhouse, in operation for over 70 years. Perfume is on sale at the Calabash Gift Shop, located within the grounds of the Perfumery. There are ramps for the handicapped.

**Spittal Pond Nature Reserve,** South Shore Road, Smith's Parish. Open daily. On the Southern Shore of Smith's Parish, hugging the magnificent wild coastline, lies Bermuda's largest nature reserve. On stormy days, thunderous wild breakers crash against the rocks. Spittal Pond is home to approximately 25 species of waterfowl. Here you can find the so-called Spanish Rock, which is an inscription in the rocks 70 feet above sea level, consisting of a Portuguese cross and the date 1543. The inscription is believed to have been put there by early shipwrecked sailors (replica rock preserved at the Historical Society). Note: Wooded trails not suitable for strollers.

Just up the road from Spittal Pond, going east, is Harrington Hundreds Supermarket, where you will find mouthwatering freshly baked fruit pies from the deli as well as other takeout goodies.

**St. David's Lighthouse,** St. David's. Call 236-5902 for times of tours. Free admission. In the peaceful island of St. David's stands this small lighthouse built of Bermuda limestone. Built in 1879, standing 55 feet high and 280 feet above sea level, its beam can be seen for 23 miles.

**Walsingham Nature Reserve** (and Idwal Hughes Nature Reserve), Bailey's Bay, Hamilton Parish. Open daily. A prime Bermuda beauty spot, Walsingham Nature Reserve (locally known as Tom Moore's Jungle) is where you'll find Tom Moore's Tavern—an expensive fine-dining restaurant that dates back to 1652 (see eateries above).

There are many unique features to this nature reserve, home to much of Bermuda's endemic plant life, including Bermuda cedar and yellow wood. It is also the prime nesting spot for the night heron. Walking the trails here is the closest you're likely to get to the undeveloped Bermuda of several hundred years ago. Look out for oasis-like saltwater ponds and caverns.

**Blue Hole Park,** just past Grotto Bay Hotel and immediately before the Causeway to St. George's. Open daily. Pick up a map at the park's entrance and take Dolphin Drive Trail, once the home of a dolphin park, and keep going to Blue Grotto sunken cave. Along the way, you will come upon a bird-viewing pond, caves, a picnic area, and unexpected lagoons. Today, dolphins can be spotted at the Fairmont Southampton Dolphin Quest Park at the Royal Naval Dockyard (see "Bringing Children to Bermuda" in chapter 2, "Before You Leave Home").

**Bermuda Railway Museum,** 37 North Shore Road, Hamilton Parish (Tel. 293-1774). Open Mon.-Sat. 10 A.M.–4 P.M., weather permitting. Donations gratefully accepted. Located in an original railway station, this tiny museum is crammed full with artefacts of the Bermuda Railway that once tootled its way from Somerset to St. George's.

**Verdmont Historic House,** Collectors Hill, Smith's (Tel. 236-7369). Open Tues.-Sat. 10 A.M.–4 P.M. (hours may change in low season). Admission: $3, $2 students. Free to National Trust Members. Georgian-style, early 18th-century National Trust mansion, full of atmosphere and creaky wood floors, housing a large collection of valuable antique cedar furniture. Among the many fine pieces is a games table made with 84 different types of wood! A favourite room in the house is the children's nursery complete with antique toys and original framed embroidered samplers.

An innovative aspect of each bedroom is the closets, which are adjacent to the fireplace chimney in order to keep clothes aired and dry during the winter months. A walled kitchen garden growing herbs backs onto the old slave quarters, which are now occupied by tenants.

Verdmont is a particularly valuable acquisition of the National Trust, having remained virtually unchanged structurally for almost 300 years. The last occupier, who died in 1951, lived entirely without plumbing or electricity, and so the house was donated to the Trust completely intact as an original historical property.

**Carter House,** St. David's Road, Marginal Wharf, St. David's Island (Tel. 297-1642). Open Apr.-Oct. Tues.-Thurs. and Sat. 10 A.M.–4 P.M., Nov.-Mar. Sat. only. Small admission charge. The first stone house built in St. David's (probably around the mid-1600s), by the direct descendants of Christopher Carter (a survivor of the *Sea Venture* wreck). Tucked into a grassy slope, this picturesque cottage once overlooked Easter lily fields and an old family graveyard. Flanked by a huge chimney, the cottage has a sagging roof, original wood beams practically the shape of the tree they were hewn from, and shuttered windows placed directly under the house eaves. Typical of Bermudian architecture is the "welcoming-arms" staircase leading to the front door, so named because the curved shape of the walls flanking the stairs spans out at the entrance to resemble outstretched arms. In the basement is an amazing natural fireplace and scooped-out oven, with the charred remains of long-forgotten fires still evident. The museum features important aspects of the surrounding area: fishing, whaling, piloting, and lily growing.

**Devil's Hole Aquarium,** Harrington Sound, Smith's Parish (Tel. 293-2072). Open daily 10 A.M.–4 P.M., Tues. and Thur. evenings. Admission: $10 adults, $5 children and seniors (under five free). Kids and adults love this small grotto with a tiny underwater outlet where visitors feed colourful reef fish and turtles from a fishing line. An oasis of peace and quiet.

**Great Head Park,** St. David's Island. Open daily. 24 acres of park and cave-lined cliffs with panoramic views of St. George's, St. David's, and Castle Harbour. Good haunt for birdwatchers (longtails, great blue herons, finches, warblers, and kingfishers) and fishers. The trail leads to St. David's Battery—a derelict fort used during both World Wars. If you wander off the trail, beware of the poison ivy on the western section.

**Ferry Point Park,** St. George's. Open daily. Pleasant trail at the eastern end of the island. In the park find a Martello Tower, Lover's Lake, old cemetery, and two forts, plus a former horse-ferry landing. Trail also leads to the six-acre Nennemacher Nature Reserve, on the grounds of the Bermuda Biological Station.

## 5. Guided Tours and Cruises

**Historical Walking Tours:** On Wednesdays at 10 A.M., starting from King's Square in the old town of St. George's, you can join a walking historical tour. Due to the tiny narrow streets and alleyways, St. George's is best viewed on foot. It seems a shame to be stuck in a taxicab as it tries to wind its way around the one-way streets, and besides, how can you sense the historical atmosphere?

**Crystal Caves of Bermuda,** 8 Crystal Caves Road, Harrington Sound Road, Bailey's Bay, Hamilton Parish (Tel. 293-0640, crystalcaves@logic.bm, www.bermudacaves.com). Open daily 9:30 A.M.–4:30 P.M. Admission: $8 adults, $5 children five-11 $5 (under five free). In 1905, two boys made an exciting discovery while searching for a lost cricket ball. Somehow, the ball had dropped into the rocky crevices and the boys squeezed through, down 120 feet, into the wondrous underground world now known as Crystal Caves. The caves are not made of crystal; their name is derived from the incredibly clear water in the caves' lake. It took millions of years to evolve

Crystal Caves' formations and wonderful eerie labyrinths of stalactites and stalagmites. Today, there is a steep pathway with rails to dark passageways illuminated by electric lightways (there is quite a bit of climbing involved). Your knowledgeable guide explains the geology of Crystal Caves and, for added enjoyment, points out some amusing shapes the formations have created, such as the one that resembles the New York skyline.

Fantasy Cave can also be viewed here. It was reopened in 2001 and marine biologists have discovered 75 new species of minuscule marine life in the unspoilt pools surrounding the cave.

**Bermuda Aquarium, Museum and Zoo,** Flatts Village, Smith's (Tel. 293-2727, www.bamz.org). Daily personalised tours at 1:10 P.M. (Jan.-Mar., Tues., Sat., and Sun. only), where, on part of the tour, you can witness an entertaining underwater diver demonstrate the features of the reef. (See above in "Other Sights" for more information on the zoo.)

**Bermuda Biological Station,** Ferry Reach (Tel. 297-1880, www.bbsr.edu). Free tour Wed. 10 A.M. from the front desk. Nearly 100 years of research have taken place at the Biological Station on ocean currents, meteorology, global warming, ocean and human health, and ocean pollution. Because of its lack of industrial pollutants, Bermuda is ideally positioned for such research. A must-see place for those interested in the environment. (For other tours check out their Web site or call the number above.) For details of senior adventure vacations at the Biological Station, go to chapter 2, "Before You Leave Home."

**Argo Adventures,** St. George's (Tel. 297-1459, adventure@cwbda.bm). Central booking office for numerous boat rides, and water activities booked from the office of the *Deliverance* in King's Square, St. George's. High-speed ride, 1½-2 hours. Or take a slower 36-foot glass-bottom boat tour around the East End.

Exhilarating ride in the comfort of a 25-foot rigid-hull boat, around the eastern end of Bermuda and South Shore, touring the beautiful shoreline, coral reef, and billionaires' homes in Tucker's Town. Learn interesting snippets of Bermuda's rich history from your tour guide. The boat also passes Nonsuch Island, where an ecological programme is in place for the protection of endemic species and the conservation of Bermuda's indigenous plant and wild life.

**Coral Sea Cruises,** King's Square, St. George's (Tel. 235-2425, bevans@northrock.bm, www.charterbermuda.com). 60-foot glass-bottom cruiser tour. Commentary on reefs, fish, flora, fauna, and history. Snacks and refreshments on sale.

**Blue Water Safari,** Smith's (Tel. 236-5599, Cell 734-9098, info@bluewatersafari.com, www.bluewatersafari.com). The Water Safari Tour is 1½ hours in a state-of-the-art 25-foot Nautica Rigid inflatable boat, which has a 15-person capacity. The tour includes visiting a shipwreck, where you can feed fish, as well as sightseeing along the coastline. Or you can enjoy their *Aquarium Safari Tour,* which explores the local reefs and includes a visit to the Bermuda Aquarium, Museum and Zoo in the price. They also do romantic sunset cruises and private charters.

**Rising Son Cruises,** St. George's (Tel. 232-5789, beez@charterbermuda.com, www.charterbermuda.com). Daily catamaran trips departing from King's Square, St. George's. Sailing, swimming, and snorkelling trips. The three-hour trip culminates in a snorkel above the *Pelanion,* an Italian steamship sunk in 1939. They also have a beach cruise and a two-hour "Sunset Cocktail Sail."

## 6. Water Sports

**Scuba Look,** Grotto Bay Beach Hotel, Hamilton Parish (located five minutes from St. George's by cab, Tel. 293-7319 or 293-7338, Fax 295-2412, scubalook@logic.bm, www.scubalookbermuda.com). Dives: one-tank dive, two-tank dive, or night dive. All these dives charge extra for equipment. Two-tank boat dive scheduled every day with certified PADI instructors, dive guides, and licensed boat captains. Explores several shipwrecks from their 34-foot boat. Scuba Look is the only scuba diving centre located at Bermuda's East End.

**St. George's ParaSail and Water Sports,** Somers Wharf, St. George's (Reservations: 297-1542, Fax 297-1504). Harness style on single or tandem parasailing flight. Dry takeoff and landing. Open May-Nov., daily 9 A.M.–sunset.

**Bermuda Bell Diving,** Flatts Village (Tel. 292-4434, Fax 295-7235, belldive@logic.bm, www.belldive.bm). Experience undersea helmet diving and a chance to dive to the reef without even getting your hair wet (go to the Web site for a photo-gallery tour). No skill required. Dives offered Apr.-Nov.

**Island Water-Skiing,** Grotto Bay Beach Hotel, Hamilton Parish (Tel. 293-2915). ¼-hour, ½-hour, and one-hour trips. Open Apr.-Aug., weather permitting. Lessons included in price.

**Kayak Bermuda** (Tel. 50-KAYAK, kayakbda@northrock.bm, www.charterbermuda.com). Tour boat departs from King's Square, St. George's, and then it's a transfer to kayaks and onto shallow waters for some practise, followed by a paddle along island shorelines. Swimming and snorkelling finish off the tour (weather permitting).

**Blue Hole Water Sports,** Grotto Bay Beach Hotel, Hamilton Parish (Tel. 293-2915, bluehole@northrock.bm, www.blueholewater.bm). Motorboats, sailing, kayaking, windsurfing, snorkelling, and fun, electric Sun Kat two-man boats.

**St. George's Game Fishing** (Tel. 297-8093). There are several chartered fishing boats in St. George's (opposite statue of Sir George Somers): *Elaines Too,* Captain Fox (Tel. 297-1079), *Messaround,* Captain Kelly (Tel. 297-8093), Charisma Sailing Tours, Stuart Lambert (Tel. 297-2085), and *Troubadour,* Captain West (Tel. 293-0831). Check the Bermuda Yellow Pages for more fishing charters.

**Tobacco Bay Beach House,** St. George's (minibus from King's Square to Tobacco Bay). Shallow water and sheltered bay make this an ideal snorkelling spot, especially just beyond the rocks. All kinds of snorkelling gear available for rent at reasonable rates. Equipment for rent on a weekly or part-weekly basis also.

## 7. Shopping

**Market Nights:** For late-night shopping of Bermudian arts and crafts, as well as free entertainment, these special nights run from the middle of May to the beginning of October, every Tuesday 7-9. Go back in time while guides, local shopkeepers, restaurant staff, craft vendors, and actors in period costumes mingle with the crowd for this living-history event. Listen to period piped music and enjoy the free festivities, which are all part of the evening's entertainment in this 400-year-old town that was Bermuda's original capital.

**The Book Cellar** (Tel. 297-0448). A small, friendly bookstore with charm and character, situated in the basement of the Tucker House museum on Water Street. The Internet will never replace little bookstores like these.

**Swagger Out Gift Shop,** Swizzle Inn, Blue Hole Hill, Bailey's Bay, Hamilton Parish (Tel. 293-9300, www.swizzleinn.com). Specialising in Bermuda-made products. Sells the popular "Swizzle Inn—Swagger Out" T-shirt and cutting boards with the famous rum swizzle drink recipe printed on. So, why not swagger in on the way out to the airport?

**Glass Blowing Studio,** 16 Blue Hole Hill, Hamilton Parish (Tel. 293-2234, glassblower@cwbda.bm, www.glassblowing.bm). Shop open Mon.-Fri. 9 A.M.–6 P.M., Sat. to 5 P.M. Traditional glass-blowing demonstrations: $2 (none on Sun.). Each artist creates a unique piece from the raw silica mixture heated to over 2,300 degrees Fahrenheit. The result is all manner of decorative, hand-blown, coloured glassware on display: vases, fish sculptures, ornaments, etc.

## 8. Nightlife

**Waterfront Bar and Restaurant,** 14 Water Street, St. George's (Tel. 297-1515). Bar open 11:30 A.M.–1 A.M. Casual waterside dining on the wharf. Free live entertainment Wed.-Sat. in this pub on the harbour.

**Club Azure,** 511 Southside, St. David's (Tel. 297-3070). Large dance floor and stage, 54-foot-long bar, and separate games room.

**The New Clay House Inn,** 77 North Shore Road, Devonshire (Tel. 292-3193). Open Wed. for lively show with musical entertainment from the Coca-Cola Steel Band and the Fiery Limbo Dancers.

**White Horse Tavern,** King's Square, St. George's (Tel. 297-1838). Open daily 9 A.M.–1 A.M. Live entertainment usually on Wed. 9 P.M.–midnight: calypso, reggae, and rock. On-the-water dining at the Gombey Bar, Sun. 2-6 P.M., with live jazz.

**Grotto Bay Beach Hotel,** 11 Blue Hole Hill, Hamilton Parish (Tel. 293-8333, www.grottobay.com). During the summer months, nightly entertainment starts at 8 in the renovated pool area. The Bayside Bar & Grill also features two theme-night buffets, offering an island BBQ on Mon. and a fresh Seafood Buffet on Thur. (weather permitting).

**Swizzle Inn,** Blue Hole Hill, Bailey's Bay, en route to the airport (Tel. 293-9300, www.swizzleinn.com). Home of the rum swizzle cocktail. Dining area; munchies served all evening. Happy Hour Mon.-Fri. 5-7 P.M.

**Blackbeard's Hideout,** Achilles Beach, St. George's (Tel. 297-1200). Bar with R&B band and DJ nightly.

**Griffin's Bar and Grill,** St. George's Club (Tel. 297-1200). Dining and dancing certain days of the week. Call ahead to find out when.

**Southside Cinema,** St. David's (Tel. 297-2821). This movie theatre used to belong to the U.S. Navy when they had a base here.

## 9. Handy Phone Numbers

**Airport Transportation** (Bermuda Hosts): Tel. 293-1334

**Crime Stoppers** (confidential): Tel. 1-800-623-8477

**Drugstore** (Robertson's): Tel. 295-3838

**Elderhostel Programme,** at the Bermuda Biological Station: Tel. 297-1880

**Emergency** (Police, Fire, Ambulance): Tel. 911

**Hospital** (King Edward VII Memorial): Tel. 236-2345

**National Trust:** Tel. 236-8306

**St. George's Golf Club:** Tel. 297-8067

**St. George's Mini Bus** (pick up at King's Square for St. Catherine's Fort and Tobacco Bay): Tel. 297-8199/8492 (will do tours if enough people paying fare)

**Scooter Rental** (Dowling's): Tel. 297-1614

**Tourist Information:** Airport, Tel. 293-0030; 7 King's Square, St. George's, Tel. 297-1642

# 12

# The Rest of the Island

So, what's left after I've divided and dissected this island of Bermuda up into what I hope will be meaningful divisions to you, once you've arrived here? Not too much. Mainly it's the middle parishes—Paget, Pembroke, and Devonshire—and the parts of Warwick and Southampton not on the South Shore. There are plenty of accommodations to choose from, though—places like Salt Kettle Guest House on Harbour Road, which is one of the most heavenly places to stay, with heavenly room rates to match. There's also the only all-inclusive adults-only resort, the Harmony Club, a real money-saver that takes away the worry of wondering whether your holiday budget will stretch. In the "Sightseeing" section below, check out the Botanical Gardens in Paget, especially if you are a garden-lover. John Lennon had an interesting association here, which you'll read about later.

No matter how many maps you take with you, you probably will still get lost on your travels here, because there are not enough signposts. At any time of the day you will see tourists sitting on their scooters at one of the most important junctions on the island, Barnes Corner, on the road that leaves the South Shore and directs you either right to Hamilton or left to Somerset. But you see, most people are looking for Dockyard and have to stop and check their maps. One day, some bright spark at Works and Engineering will think to save all this confusion by adding the appendage needed: "Somerset *and* Dockyard This Way." And while they are at it, they may as well put up helpful directional signs all over the island. Don't panic, though; you can't be lost for long on 21 square miles.

To help you get your bearings: Bermuda is shaped like a fish hook, with one end being west, the other east, and in the middle Hamilton City and the middle parishes. There are four main through roads, self-explanatory by name: North Shore Road (hugs the North Shore and goes east to St. George's); South Shore Road (hugs the South Shore beaches); Middle Road (you guessed it, it's in the middle and leads to Somerset going west); and lastly, Harbour Road (hugs the harbour on the opposite shore to the South Shore and ends at Hamilton City). Happy travelling.

# 1. Transport

Buses to Paget: Numbers 2 and 7. Southampton: Number 8. Devonshire: Numbers 1 and 3. Warwick: Number 8. Pembroke: Number 4. Bus enquiries: Tel. 292-3854, www.bermudabuses.com.

Ferries go to Paget and Warwick. Ferry information: Tel. 295-4506, www.seaexpress.bm.

# 2. Accommodations

### HIGHER-PRICED ACCOMMODATIONS

Note: To get deals on rooms at the large resort hotels in Bermuda, go to the "Package Deals" section in chapter 2, "Before You Leave Home."

**Fourways Inn,** Middle Road, Paget (P.O. Box PG 294, Paget, PG BX, Tel. 236-6517, Fax 236-5528, Toll-free 1-800-962-7654, info@fourways.bm, www.fourwaysinn.com).

Fourways Inn (1727) was home for 200 years to the Harvey family of Harvey's Bristol Cream Sherry fame. The name of the inn derives from the four original entranceways it once had. This is a tranquil, first-class cottage colony with excellent gourmet restaurant, landscaped gardens, and freshwater heated swimming pool. Each cottage has kitchenette, minibar, air-conditioning, heating, cable TV, and phone. Tennis and golf are close by. Fourways Inn is a member of the Small Luxury Hotels of the World.

**Double room rates:** $130 to $595 (depending on season and type of cottage), plus service charge and tax. Rate includes continental breakfast.

### MEDIUM-PRICED ACCOMMODATIONS

**Royal Heights Guest House,** Lighthouse Hill, Southampton (P.O. Box SN 144, Southampton, SN BX, Tel. 238-0043, Fax 238-8445).

This spotlessly clean, modern, friendly guesthouse has panoramic views of Southampton and is close to famous Gibbs Hill Lighthouse and South Shore beaches. Pool. Rooms include private bath, private patio, TV, air conditioning, and continental breakfast.

**Double room rates:** $135 to $195 (depending on season), plus service charge and tax.

**Greenbank & Cottages,** 17 Salt Kettle Road, Paget (Tel. 236-3615, Fax 236-2427, grebank@logic.bm, www.bermudamall.com/greenbank).

Greenbank is located in peaceful Salt Kettle Harbour, surrounded by gardens with lovely views of the harbour and Great Sound and only one minute to ferry stop for Hamilton. The main house is 200 years old—its old cedar beams were used as ballast in the sailing ships that used to ply their trade between Bermuda and North America. All the cottages and apartments have air-conditioning, telephone, radio, private bath, fully equipped kitchenettes, and porch with view of the sea. There's also a private dock as well as floating dock for deepwater swimming. Breakfast is served to the two rooms that do not have kitchen facilities in the main house. Boat rentals close by.

**Double room rates:** $130 to $175, plus service charge and tax. Take off 25-50 percent for low season, depending on month.

**Granaway Guest House and Cottages,** Harbour Road, Warwick (P.O. Box WK 533, Warwick, Tel. 236-3747, Fax 236-3749, info@granaway.com, www.granaway.com).

Granaway is a typically beautiful Bermudian manor house, painted in soft pink with a sparkling-white roof, overlooking the sea and surrounded by a lush tropical garden with pristine pool. There are five guestrooms in the main house, each with bathroom. There's also a separate cottage, if you prefer, with private bathroom and kitchen.

**Double room rates:** $130 to $150, plus service charge and tax. Add $25 for an additional person. Cottage rate: $200 for two people.

**Harmony Club,** South Road, Paget (P.O. Box PG 299, Paget, PG BX, Tel. 236-3500, Fax 236-2624, U.S.A.: 1-866-STAY-BDA, www.bermudaresorthotels.com).

Bermuda's only all-inclusive hotel (excluding airfares), located two miles outside of Hamilton and roughly three minutes' ride from the South Shore beaches. Lovely garden setting with pool, tennis courts, sauna, and Jacuzzi. Solely for adults over 18. Package includes airport round-trip transfers, full American breakfast, light snacks available throughout the day, afternoon tea with pastry selection, daily cocktails and hors d'oeuvres, dinner, unlimited wine with meals, unlimited bar drinks, taxes, and gratuities. This hotel has 68 rooms and is furnished in the Queen Anne style.

Many of the rooms have wood or tile floors and are equipped with air-conditioning, heating, TV, radio, and phone. There's a daily shuttle service to Elbow Beach on the South Shore, one of Bermuda's finest.

**Package rates:** $330 to $431 (depending on season), inclusive of taxes. Rate includes all the above amenities.

## BUDGET-PRICED ACCOMMODATIONS

Note: For a list of budget properties to rent, go to "Private House and Apartment Rentals" in chapter 2, "Before You Leave Home."

**Vienna Guest Apartments,** 63 Cedar Hill Road, Warwick (Tel. 236-3300, Fax 236-6100, vienna@logic.bm, www.bermuda1.com).

Leo, the owner of these apartments, cannot do enough for his guests, and his going that extra mile makes Vienna a special place to stay. These spotless apartments are set in a quiet residential area, close to the ferry stop to Hamilton. Facilities: air-conditioning, TV, safe in closet, hair dryer, microwave, iron and board, barbecue, phone, and radio. Warwick Long Bay 10 minutes away. Families particularly welcome. Pristine pool and patio area. Excellent value for money and a real find.

**Double room rates:** $90 to $145 (depending on season), plus service charge and tax. Honeymoon specials and golf and diving packages available.

**Mazarine by the Sea,** 91 North Shore Road, Pembroke (P.O. Box HM 3153, Hamilton, HM NX, Tel. 292-1690, Fax 292-6891, mazarinebythesea@logic.bm).

Located right on the ocean (no beach), with deepwater swimming on Bermuda's North Shore, these adorable housekeeping units are only one mile from the city centre of Hamilton. Each cute unit comprises a bedroom, bathroom, kitchenette with microwave, and small patio overlooking gardens, pool, and sea. Rooms have phone, TV, and air-conditioning.

**Double room rates:** $85 to $120 (depending on season), plus service charge and tax. Honeymoon specials available.

**Valley Cottages & Apartments,** Valley Road, Paget (P.O. Box PG 214, Paget PG BX, Tel. 236-0628, Fax 236-3895, rsimons@northrock.bm, www.netlinkbermuda.com/valley).

Pretty pink cottages and self-contained studio apartments nestled together in attractive gardens. Each air-conditioned unit has kitchen, bathroom, living room, telephone, cable TV, and radio. Nearby to food market. Use of Harmony Club tennis courts and ferry to Hamilton. Closest beach is the magnificent Elbow Beach (free admission three-day tickets to private hotel beach, inclusive of chaise lounge and umbrella).

**Double room rates:** Studio apartment: $70 to $110. Cottage for two: $90 to $120. Cottage for four: $120 to $180. All depending on season, plus service charge and tax. Honeymoon specials and for stays longer than two weeks available.

**Midway Cottage,** 21 Keith Hall Road, Warwick, PG 01 (Tel. 236-3938, ramello@logic.bm).

Just off Harbour Road (one of Bermuda's prettiest winding main roads), hidden in a tranquil Bermudian garden, is Midway Cottage—a cottage setting so perfect it is hard to imagine. Single, tastefully furnished, and spotlessly clean studio comprises an open-plan living/kitchen/dining area. Large walk-in closet has well-stocked bookcase. Ceiling fan and air-conditioning for summer and gas-log fire for the off-season months. You can also choose from two other cottages—either the one bedroom or the two bedroom. The living area opens onto a trellised patio with cascading purple vines and overlooks cool green ponds with fountains stocked with fish and turtles. Guests can also pick from the many fruit trees around the garden or use the barbecue. Close to bus stops, groceries, two ferry stops, and scuba diving. Apartment is wonderful setting for couples, especially honeymooners, and cottages are good for families. Book well in advance as these accommodations are popular.

**Year-round apartment rate:** $90. One-bedroom cottage: $115. Two-bedroom cottage: $135 to $175 (depending on whether both bedrooms are used). Rates include taxes.

**Salt Kettle Guest House & Housekeeping Apartments,** Salt Kettle, Paget (Mrs. Hazel Lowe, Tel. 236-0407, Fax 236-8636).

Snuggled in Pruden's Bay, overlooking Hamilton Harbour and only a short two-minute walk to Hamilton ferry stop, Salt Kettle is a paradise found. You may find it difficult to book the self-contained units, as 95 percent of guests are repeat visitors. This is not surprising, as the ambience is very soothing and serene and the service is personal and helpful. Excellent value.

**Double room rates:** $90 to $110. Cottage with kitchen, bedroom, and sitting room: $100 to $130 (depending on season), plus service charge and tax. Rates include very hearty breakfast.

**Robin's Nest Guest Apartments,** 10 Vale Close, Pembroke, HM 04 (Tel and Fax 292-4347, robinsnest@cwbda.bm).

Located in a residential area, not far from the North Shore and Admiralty Park and close to Hamilton. Four spacious, well-maintained guest apartments, each with private entrance, in lush garden setting. Each apartment has fully stocked kitchen with microwave, fridge, and stove, as well as fans, air-conditioning, and cable TV. There's a beautiful pool and patio available to guests. Robin's Nest is ideal for couples. Nonsmoking except in surrounding gardens.

**Year-round rates:** Double $125, triple $175, quad $200, plus service charge and tax.

**Serendipity Apartments,** 6 Rural Drive, Paget, PG 06 (Judy and Albert Corday, Tel. 236-1192, Fax 232-0010, serendipitybda@hotmail.com).

Two fully equipped bed/sitting guest studio apartments located in a residential area, convenient to buses to Hamilton or South Shore and a 20-minute walk to Elbow Beach. One unit has a queen-size bed and sofa bed and the other has two twin beds. Each unit has bathroom, shower (no tub), TV (no cable), telephone, and air-conditioning (May-Nov.). Kitchens come fully stocked: microwave, stove, pots and pans, etc. Each unit has a private entrance and patio. Serendipity also has a pool and patio area, which guests can share with the family if they can swim. Smoking is not allowed in the apartments; guests must smoke outside only.

**Double apartment rate:** $80 to $90 (depending on month), inclusive of tax. Add $15 for an additional person.

# 3. Restaurants

## HIGHER-PRICED RESTAURANTS

**Fourways Inn,** Middle Road, Paget (Tel. 236-6517, info@fourways.bm, www.fourwaysinn.com). Open for dinner 6:30-9:45. One of the top gourmet restaurants in Bermuda, offering silver service and decorated in warm tones with soft lighting, cottage-style furniture, stone archways, and cedar beams. If you have time to spare, then the Sunday buffet, on the first Sunday of every month, is a treat for the senses. Extensive wine list. Jackets requested.

**Waterlot Inn,** Middle Road, Southampton (Tel. 238-2555, evenings: 239-6967). Open for dinner 6:30-10. Closed Jan.-Mar. Built in 1670 and famous not only for its harbour-side setting but also for its Mediterranean cuisine, the Waterlot Inn is part of the Fairmont Southampton Princess Hotel complex. For those who like the good life, cigars and port are served in the lounge.

## BUDGET-PRICED EATERIES

**Green Lantern,** Serpentine Road, Pembroke (Tel. 295-6995). Open Mon.-Sat. 9 A.M.–9 P.M. (Wed. to 3 P.M.). Closed holidays. A favourite with locals, this easygoing diner offers a variety of Bermudian and British dishes, including tasty curried meat and mussel pies.

**After Hours Restaurant,** 117 South Shore Road, Paget (Tel. 236-8563). Open Tues.-Sat. 7 P.M.–4 A.M. Late-night, very casual fast-food hangout whose specialty is chicken roti (curry in unleavened bread).

**King Edward VII Memorial Hospital Coffee Shop,** 7 Point Finger Road, Paget. Open daily 9 A.M.–3:45 P.M. Hopefully, you won't be in the hospital when you sample this excellent coffee shop run by volunteer "Pink Ladies." Wonderful service and down-home cooking. Save room for old-fashioned homemade desserts. Proceeds go to charity.

## 4. Sightseeing

**Botanical Gardens,** Berry Hill Road, Paget (Tel. 236-4201). Open daily sunrise-sunset. One of the great pleasures of Bermuda is the 100-year-old, 36 acres of exquisite gardens known as the Botanical Gardens. This impressive showcase of Bermuda's horticultural heritage has a rich variety of tropical flowers, trees, shrubs, and rolling lawns. Some of the trees are giant, such as the kapok tree, with its huge buttresses, and the banyan tree, with long aerial roots (a favourite with children). All can be viewed from winding pathways.

During John Lennon's summer visit to Bermuda with son Sean in 1980, he came across an orchid in the Botanical Gardens called "Double Fantasy." John took the name for his famous album, the last he recorded. And while he was at a local disco, Disco 40, someone asked John what he was doing these days, to which he replied, "I'm just sitting here watching the wheels go round," referring to the disco-wheel lights spinning on the wall of the club. He used that line as a double meaning in his song "Watching the Wheels."

**Palm Grove Garden,** South Road, Devonshire. Open Mon.-Thur. 9 A.M.–5 P.M. Manicured sweeping lawns and gardens on private estate, generously open to the public on certain days. Pond features a "water map" of Bermuda, subdivided into parishes by grassy banks.

**The Montpelier Arboretum,** Montpelier Road, Devonshire. Open daily. Spacious park setting with wide range of indigenous trees, tropical trees, and plants. A great place to throw a Frisbee.

**Devonshire Bay,** Devon Bay Road, Devonshire. Out-of-the-way little fishing harbour with a nice walk around a pocket-sized national park. Fresh fish sometimes for sale from local fishermen.

**Old Devonshire Church,** Middle Road, Devonshire (opposite Devonshire Marsh). Open daily. Restored national treasure. The original church was built in 1612 and later replaced in 1716; however, an explosion on Easter Sunday in 1970 destroyed it, necessitating a further restoration.

**Palmetto House,** North Shore Road, Devonshire, just past Palmetto Park (Tel. 295-9941). Open Thur. 10 A.M.–5 P.M. National Trust property built in the early 18th century and styled in the shape of a crucifix in order to ward off evil spirits. Three main rooms on display.

**Waterville Historical Home** (National Trust Headquarters), Pomander Road, Paget (Tel. 236-6483). Open Mon.-Fri. 9 A.M.–5 P.M. Waterville has many features, such as a beautiful old rose garden, and to the rear, ducks run wild on the property, jumping in and out of the harbour. You can view the National Trust's protected properties at their excellent Web site, www.bnt.bm.

**Paget Marsh Nature Reserve,** Middle Road, opposite Rural Hill Plaza, Paget (Tel. 236-6483). Open daily. This protected wooded area is an ideal way to gain a perspective of how Bermuda looked to early settlers prior to urbanisation. The marsh sports a boardwalk with bridges and habitat wilderness signs over its unspoiled 25 acres. The pond boardwalk protects the sensitive flora and fauna from damage. Access is at the junction of Middle Road and Lover's Lane.

## 5. Guided Tours and Cruises

**Botanical Gardens:** 1½-hour guided tours, weather permitting, at 10:30 A.M., starting from the car park outside the Visitors' Centre, Apr.-Oct., Mon., Wed., Fri.; Nov.-Mar., Tues. and Fri. In addition to the gardens, Camden, the stately official mansion of the premier, is open to the public Tues. and Fri. noon-2 P.M. (Tel. 236-5732).

**Salt Kettle Charters,** Salt Kettle, Paget (Tel. 236-4863, grebank@logic.bm, www.bermudamall.com/saltkettle). Open daily 9 A.M.–5 P.M. Cruises to reefs. Four hours on 55-foot loop; drinks and snacks on sale. Snorkelling gear and comprehensive instruction provided.

**Coral Sea Cruises,** Paget (Tel. 235-2425, bevans@northrock.bm, www.charterbermuda.com). Offers tours in 60-foot glass-bottom boat.

**Haywards Snorkelling & Glass Bottom Boat Cruises,** Paget (Tel. 236-9894, www.haywardscharters.com). 54-foot motor-cruiser and glass-bottom boat tours.

**Bermuda Barefoot Cruises,** Darrell's Wharf, Paget (Tel. 236-3498, barefoot@logic.bm, www.bermudabarefootcruises.com). 32-foot family cruiser, small enough to go to all the little bays and pass under bridges.

## 6. Water Sports

**Island Parasail,** Darrell's Wharf, Paget (Tel. 232-2871). Owner Phillip Anderson. Parasailing is a great way to view Bermuda, flying high above in the sky, in the peace and serenity.

**Eureka Fishing Ltd.,** 11 Abri Lane, Spanish Point, Pembroke, HM 02 (Tel. 296-5415, Boat 235-3836, Fax 295-3620, eureka@bermudashorts.bm, www.bermudashorts.bm/eureka). Fishing aboard 65-foot *Eureka*. Half-day fishing expeditions for families and full days for advanced anglers.

**Fantasea Diving & Snorkelling,** Darrell's Wharf, 1 Harbour Road, Paget (Tel. 236-6339, Fax 236-8926, info@fantasea.bm, www.fantasea.bm). Two-tank certified or noncertified dive. Accessible to all skill levels—recreational and advanced divers. Experienced dive guides and modern equipment on hand. Utilises the "Nitrox" system of scuba diving, allowing for longer and safer dives. Also hires out snorkelling gear. Other services offered: whale watching in April, snorkelling, water-skiing, and underwater camera rentals.

**Boat Rental: Rance's Boatyard,** Paget Parish (Tel. 292-1843). For rent, 13-foot Boston Whaler motorboats as well as 16-foot Cape Code Gemini sailboats.

# 7. Shopping

### BARGAINS AT YARD SALES AND THRIFT SHOPS

Some of the best bargains to be had in Bermuda are at house sales, especially "Leaving the Island" sales. Bermuda is a transient, affluent community, with overseas workers spending two to three years in Bermuda on work permits. Many times, expatriates have filled their houses with beautiful furniture, paintings, ornaments, clothes, toys, boat stuff, baby stuff, etc. Usually held on the weekends, "Leaving the Island" sales are advertised in the local papers and with signage along the roads. They are a great way to explore Bermuda's houses and back roads.

Smart shopping for the new millennium is found at second-hand stores. No longer is there any stigma associated with this type of bargain hunting; mixing and matching new with old is fun. The most famous thrift store in Bermuda is **The Barn** (Tel. 236-3155), located at 44 Devon Springs Road, Devonshire. (Directions: From Middle Road [between Esso Gas Station and Pet Care in Devonshire] turn onto Hermitage Road and make the first right, on Devon Springs Road. The Barn is around the corner on the right side after the Recycling Centre but before the main building of St. Brendon's Hospital.) Ideal for picking up suit jackets for required restaurants or winter sweaters for off-season evenings.

**"Back on the Rack"** (Tel. 236-1707) on South Road in Paget is a consignment store that sells designer wear at nondesigner prices. **Bears Repeating II** (Tel. 295-7477), 129 Front Street, Suite 9, Hamilton, is a quality baby and children's consignment store with an ingenious name.

## 8. Nightlife

**Bermuda Boot Scooters,** Country & Western line dancing, Prospect Police Recreation Club, 8 Headquarters Hill, Devonshire (Information: Joyce Hayden, Tel. 295-1890, bdabootscooters@hotmail.com). Every Mon. evening, 7:30-10, except public holidays, country dancing as well as rock, swing, and pop. Low admission price and inexpensive bar inside club.

**Slipaway's Lounge** (formerly the Anchorage Club), overlooking the North Shore bay, this smoke-free bar caters to the 25-and-over crowd.

## 9. Handy Phone Numbers

**Botanical Gardens Information Desk:** Tel. 236-5291
**Crime Stoppers (confidential):** Tel. 1-800-623-8477
**Emergency (Police, Fire, Ambulance):** Tel. 911
**Hospital (King Edward VII Memorial):** Tel. 236-2345
**Scooter Rental (Oleander Cycles):** Tel. 236-5235
**Visitors' Service Bureau** (Tourist Information), next to Ferry Terminal, Front Street: Tel. 295-1480

# Index

# Accommodations

# Eateries

# Places to Go & Things to Do on Sunday

*Unlike North America, much of Bermuda closes down on Sunday. So to help you plan your day, here is a list of things to do on the Sabbath.*

# Places to Eat, Open on a Sunday

*(Call first to check hours)*

Angeline's Coffee Shop (breakfast), 187

Aqua Seaside Restaurant (Ariel Sands Hotel), 161

Ascots, 127

Bailey's Ice Cream & Food D'Lites, 187

Barracuda Grill (dinner), 128

Black Horse Tavern, 185

Café Acoreano, 133

Café Lido (Elbow Beach Hotel) (dinner), 160

Carriage House, 185

Cedar Room, The (Pompano Beach Club), 171

Chopsticks, 132

Coconuts at the Reefs (Reefs Hotel), 161

Dennis's Hideaway, 186

D'Mikado Seafood House & Grill, 129

East Meets West, 136

Fine Dine-In (delivery service), 128

Flanagan's Irish Pub & Restaurant, 146

Four Star Pizza (takeout or delivery), 131

Fourways Inn, 206

Freddie's Restaurant, 185

Fresco's Restaurant & Wine Bar, 134

Frog & Onion Pub & Restaurant, The, 171

# What's Free in Bermuda